GLOBAL MOM

WHAT PEOPLE ARE SAYING . . .

"Here is a rich, frank, and funny book in which the essentials of family and friendship and community are combined with interesting travelogue and the best kind of spiritual writing. In short, this is a book about love."

—Kate Braestrup
New York Times best-selling author of *Here If You Need Me*

". . . a stunning picture of life . . ."

—*Deseret News*

"*Global Mom: A Memoir* is a brilliant hero's journey highlighting the challenges and triumphs of motherhood under unique cross-cultural circumstances. With honesty, sensitivity, and humor, Dalton-Bradford is a role model for all parents who will be relocating with children."

—Paula Caligiuri, PhD
Author *Cultural Agility: Building a Pipeline of Successful Global Professionals*

"The humor is self-deprecating; the pain—beyond compare. I found myself laughing out loud . . . and sobbing out loud, as well."

—*Association for Mormon Letters*

"After reading Melissa Dalton-Bradford's fascinating memoir of her adventures with her family I am left with many emotions—admiration, amazement, and, as a mom who has done her own fair share of moving her family around, deep empathy. This is one brave woman!"

—Sharon Galligar Chance
Author *The Cupcake Witch*, Garden of Book Reviews

"*Global Mom* provides an honest and poignant look at the unique challenges of raising a family across multiple cultures. It's a journey worth visiting for readers."

—Bicultural Mama (Blog)

"I laughed and cried so many times. . . . [The] account of life as a *Global Mom* and the . . . . immersion in the many cultures and languages are simply inspiring. I think [this] book should be required reading for all Americans working in global companies."

—Global Executive for a Fortune 50 Company

"*Global Mom* is a portrait of a family. At its heart is a story of unspeakable loss and grief, but also of hope and living onward. As a stylist, Dalton-Bradford ranks among the finest writers of literary nonfiction."

—Amazon reviewer

"*Global Mom: A Memoir* is the first writing I've encountered on this topic that took me beyond mere anecdotes, platitudes, and 'how-tos,' and transported me literarily. . . . Her prose is fresh, her style charming, her humor and wit delightful, and her ability to take her reader into deep waters and utterly meaningful substance left me feeling both nourished and hungry."

—Amazon reviewer

"Dalton-Bradford has crafted a book that—with consummate skill and unsurpassed insight—firmly grasps readers' hands (hearts, too) and takes them on a riveting, rocket-speed, country-spanning adventure unique in the contemporary memoir genre."

—Amazon reviewer

"*Global Mom* is not only a masterfully written memoir on creating a home in diverse landscapes, it is also a story with universal appeal— that of finding home and hope in the midst of love, loss, and change. Dalton-Bradford is both a master writer as well as an entertaining storyteller. . . . I love how Melissa Dalton-Bradford, in writing this book, has invited each of us—global or local—to her table where she feeds us and shares universal substance more dense than any hardwood."

—Amazon reviewer

"This exquisite memoir pulled me in from the very first page. It is profoundly entertaining and profoundly moving, the writing poetic, breathtakingly gorgeous, and utterly engrossing. . . . It's a beautiful and intimate portrayal of a close and loving family creating a home wherever they live in the world, and a brave, poignant, and honest depiction of loss, grief, and love that defies mortal bounds."

—Amazon reviewer

"Allow *Global Mom* to show you everything that is lovely, frightening, exhilarating, and humiliating about expat living and raising 'third culture' children. You'll smile knowingly, sigh longingly, laugh appreciatively, and cry sympathetically—your mouth will probably even water a bit."

—Amazon reviewer

"This is far more than a travelogue, as Bradford delves into the essence of parenting, global communities, and the transformative nature of grief. With poetic language and a richly detailed tapestry of experiences brought together into coherent chapter arcs, all colored by her faith and family, the reader joins their adventures and by the end feels like a personal friend, weeping and smiling together as part of this unfinished epic journey of life".

—Amazon reviewer

GLOBAL MOM

MELISSA DALTON-BRADFORD

Published by Familius LLC, www.familius.com
Familius books are available at special discounts for bulk purchases for sales promotions, family, or
corporate use. Special editions, including personalized covers, excerpts of existing books, or books with
corporate logos, can be created in large quantities for special needs. For more information, contact
Premium Sales at 801-552-7298 or email specialmarkets@familius.com

pISBN 978-1-938301-34-6
eISBN 978-1-938301-33-9

Library of Congress Catalog-in-Publication Data

2013933818

Physical book printed in the United States of America

Edited by Christopher Robbins and Maggie Wickes
Cover design by David Miles
Cover photo courtesy of Erin Brown
Book design by Dana Knudsen and David Miles
Chapter icons from Shutterstock.com

10 9 8 7 6 5 4

First Edition

For Luc William, Dalton Haakon, Claire, Randall James, and Parker Fairbourne— my Bradfords.

ACKNOWLEDGMENTS

As would be expected, a book called *Global Mom* has been a global under-taking requiring multiple moms, not just the one on the cover. Producing this manuscript has drawn on the gifts and graciousness of a worldwide circle of friends, some of whom I've already mentioned in these pages. Others, I wish to thank here.

Sharlee Mullins Glenn, mentor and wordsmith warrior, has been compassionate, visionary, persistent, and charitable. Her influence has sustained me and fueled not only this book, but also virtually all my writing. In my many moments of reticence, hers has been the firm hand on my shoulder pushing me onward. I thank her, ad infinitum.

Those affiliated with the women's literary journal *Segullah* aided in the development of my voice and the telling of this story. Angela S. Hallstrom, Michelle Lehnardt, Lisa Garfield, and Kathryn Lynard Soper offered in-valuable writerly feedback, hashing out and mulling through my prose, peeling it down to its core and then to its seeds. They brought me onboard their vessel as a poetry editor and also helped me cut my blogging teeth. Michelle filmed, edited, and produced the video trailer for this book's release.

Jacque A. White, Kristiina H. Sorensen, Bonnie Jean Beesley, Maja Busche Wensel, Sharon Leigh, and Elaine S. Dalton, my âmes-sœurs, or soul sisters, were at my side in pivotal life moments described in these pages. Astrid Tuminez, Mary Bingham Lee, Kimberly Carlile, and Sharon Eubank aided by reading early copy, to which they gave skillful editorial suggestions. Maggie Wickes and Amy Stewart, this book's official editors, picked through the manuscript like seasoned archaeologists pick through sand with a microscope and tweezers. Crystal Patriarche and Kim Cecere of BookSparks Public Relations put turbo boosters on my back and sent me sailing, book in my sweaty clutch.

Some of this book's "moms" have been men. Christopher Robbins, in-defatigable CEO of Familius, embodied the kind of wise guidance and accessibility most writers can only dream of finding in a publisher. While building a company, recovering from a severe ski accident concussion, and while living for months in a different time zone from his family, Christopher kept his sense of humor and never forfeited his cool, keen judgment. Above all, he honored my voice as it retold my family's story.

Christian Karlsson, the epitome of modesty and excellence, was my Norwegian correspondent. Jim Richards, Rick Walton, Jack Harrell, Kirk Lovell Shaw, and Tyler Chadwick each championed my writing and promoted it to others. Kirby Bivans, gentle sound master of La Forge studios in Versonnex, France, oversaw my recording of the audio version of this book. Robb White and Aaron Hubbard demonstrated the best of the human spirit in supporting our family throughout months and years of living with enormous loss.

My brother Aaron Dalton has been a valued constant in this peripatetic life we live, as well as my go-to guy for everything from pop culture to Proust quotes. He has not only read many of these chapters and offered sparkling insights, but has lived them right along with us. We are forever indebted.

My beloved parents, David J. and Donna G. Dalton, were my first, middle, and last readers. Some of my sweetest healing hours have been spent listening to them recite aloud to each other the first drafts of every single chapter. In more ways than I can describe, I owe them my life.

Finally: my Bradfords, without whom there is neither story to tell nor life to live. Claire Bradford, awe-inspiring daughter, gave her trademark sharp-eyed organizational help and cheered me sweetly on through every step of living and chronicling this life. Dalton Bradford—on-site tech support, camera crew, film editor, blog curator, current events commentator—gave his precocious and precious insights. Luc Bradford, our Luminous One, whose tech savvy at age ten outstripped mine at forty-something, got me quickly up to speed, and shared (too many) hours sitting at my elbow, both of us on our laptops. Parker Bradford, whose enormous and resounding mortal absence matches his echoing and infinite ongoingness. "Par Cœur" is the very heart of this book.

And Randall: my "part," not merely my partner. He has with constant and astounding generosity of spirit literally and figuratively given our family the world. While the demands of his profession might have made him seem absent in many of these pages, he is in fact the book's silent main character. His loving presence made this life and book possible, and makes any and all places for me home.

Prangins, Switzerland, June 2013

CONTENTS

LE CHEF, LE GARÇON, LE GUY, AND YOSEMITE SAM

H anging out the windows of our apartment that sits in an upper floor of a corner building one block south of the Seine are two men. In the narrow street below stand two more. All four are bellowing at each other. Part of me could join in, I guess, but I've decided to save my energy. I'll need it.

This morning I'm managing the shipwreck rescue of my life: there's this massive plank of timber bobbing like Moby Dick on dental floss outside my window, so many ropes taut and creaking, sweat drizzling in rivulets down my back, four Frenchmen sodden with perspiration in this summer's round-the-clock sauna, all of us hoping for a breeze to cool us off. Just a puff of air, I'm thinking, and that would do it. We could pull this leviathan through the double window and into the middle of our living room, the only spot where this piece will fit in our new place.

Our new place: A part of Paris called the *rive gauche* which refers to the left (or south) bank of the Seine which was once fishable water. But today? Today the catch we've pulled out of a moving truck isn't fish but pine, and a whale of a piece at that. It's our ten-foot long, three-foot wide, four-inch thick Norwegian table, our monument to five years spent living there in an island idyll.

We move nowhere without it. Not when we moved from that Norwegian island to the *Île de France* ("France's Island," the term used for the suburban periphery of Paris) and took up residence in Versailles, a comfortable jog from the château. And not now, either, when we've decided we're done with island hopping and are instead jumping feet first into blue blood. We've found an apartment in a skinny one-way parallel to the Rue de l'Université in the distressingly tony seventh *arrondissement* of a city, which is, at least for the coarseness of this moment, way too genteel.

Look lively, maties, I coax inwardly like the longshoreman I'm seeing I need to be in order to get my table up a couple of floors and through this window. *Quit your quarggeling and let's heave-ho.* No question I'm feeling more Norwegian than Parisian this morning, more hard-boiled than high-heeled, more rogue than vogue, sure of my sea legs and fit in a flash to shiver anyone's timbers. Parisian *delicatesse* I dropped a while ago when the movers nearly dropped the table the first time.

"You couldn't have left this thing in storage?" the guy with a red handlebar moustache, the one who reminds me of Yosemite Sam, says in French, heaving cables with raw, freckled hands. He's slimy with sweat, his bulbous belly spilling over the window ledge we're sharing. He's about five feet tall and five inches to my left. I can smell him well.

"Or back in Norway?" his colleague with the cigarette snorts with half a laugh. Then he sees I'm not so amused, so he busies himself by ripping down on a green rope coming from way above our heads, a rope that's threaded through the pulley contraption on the top of the building. He adjusts the blue blankets padding the windowsill. This guy (we'll call him Guy, pronounced *Ghee*) is surly, and growls at the oppressive August heat that's moved in over Paris like the bad breath of a forest fire. Which heat he combats, naturally, by smoking pack after pack.

The moving crew has assigned street watch to what must be their youngest crew member. This boy (we'll call him Garçon) stands on the cobblestones directly beneath where I'm keeping window watch. He's gangly, angular, with inky hair plastered to his forehead. His t-shirt is transparent with sweat, glued against ribs that roll and twitch as he moves like a backstage puppeteer coordinating strings. I've never seen such leglessness under jeans in my entire life. It's as if nothing but empty pants and a neon green fabric belt are holding up his torso. He whistles Bon Jovi's "Livin' on a Prayer," the irony of which softens the tension in my neck as I laugh. Once.

The *chef de l'équipe*, or crew leader, is pacing our narrow Rue du Colonel Combes in a black cap. He's bulky and smelling of bourbon already at

11:45 a.m., fine for *un vrai Bréton*, an authentic piece of Brittany, some-one from the westernmost region of France. But he's not from just any old place in Brittany, mind you. This gent reminds me he's from *Finistère*, and wags his scarred index finger, enunciating: "Feen-eees-taaaaaaiiiiiiirrrrr." He's proud, and should be, since that place is absolutely as far as things go, as its name says: End. Of. Earth.

And now he's acting like this is the end of the world, this table hoist. They've tried and tried, since 8:00 a.m. they've been trying. Up the nar-row stairway? No way, no matter how you angle it. With an automated *mont meubles* or furniture escalator? No. Far too big. Far too heavy.

"'Elicopter?" someone suggested, and everyone chuckled, except Le Chef, who waved off the idea, but only because the road's too narrow for landing anything wider than a kite.

"Madame," he had suggested after all this, eyes half-closed, looking crafty, "We might try . . . taking your table . . . apart . . . ?"

"Not on your life, monsieur," I had answered, craftier than he.

From my peripherals, I'm aware that my Parisian soon-to-be neigh-bors are gathering, eyeing the spectacle either from behind their lace curtains or from where they're standing, some of them now, on the sidewalk, wondering, as I am, how on earth this show will end. My orange shirt was a wardrobe choice that morning intended to exude resolve and energy. But it's not quite happening as I'd planned. I hadn't expected this Franco-Furniture war, hadn't foreseen having to negotiate quite like this between cultures, languages, genders, a suffocating heat-wave, and cables red, green, and yellow.

I press my palms to my temples. The noise of the men's barking gets the attention of the Portuguese *gardienne*, our building's landlady/watch-woman, who occupies a one room apartment off the entryway and has been demure till this moment. Wringing her hands in her faded green and pink floral apron, and shifting in her black orthopedic sandals from one arthritic foot to another, she suddenly steps forward—hobbles for-ward—and honks like a goose being throttled.

"This, *messieurs,* is a question of life and death!" she warns in French, with a pronounced Portuguese curliness. Her words ricochet down the street. The neighbors stare. Garçon drops the Bon Jovi. The guy we are calling Guy flips his cigarette from his bottom lip and it ends up on the sidewalk, spluttering next to some steaming-fresh dog droppings.

"The table survives, so do you!" she threatens. "Does not survive? *Alors* . . . I'll personally throw you into the Seine!" Her face is pulsing just enough to draw attention away from her hands, which are shaking.

I can tell even from up here. From where he's standing next to me, Yosemite mutters something about *"Les Norvégiens barbars."* But honestly, I'm neither *really* Norwegian nor *normally* barbaric. Normally I'm your friendliest American mother-of-four, who sings through her day, pumices her heels, and hides secret stashes of dark chocolate in places like . . . everywhere. A woman who uses an eyelash curler and a laptop every day of her life, so hardly barbarian, *merci beaucoup.*

But right here I'm channeling a few Vikings for effect. I slap my hands on my thighs, and swing my full attention to Yosemite, speaking slowly, plainly. "Well, *monsieur*, I can see it will take a *barbarian* and not a *Bréton* to save this table."

From the corner of his mouth without the cigarette, Guy mutters, "Ooooh, lah-lah-lah . . . "

And you know? It does the trick. With one eyebrow cocked, this man with facial hair straight from Looney Tunes emits a faint, soaring whistle, slaps his meaty hands together, rubs them vigorously, plants them on his thighs like a lumberjack all set for log-throwing, and says, *"Bon, alors, on y va!"* ("Alright then, let's go!") And in a heartbeat Yosemite becomes a gargoyle. A red-moustached, Merrie Melodies gargoyle. He's stretched out nearly flat over the empty air above the sidewalk, clawing the oxygen like he's playing an air harp, teeth bared, veins bursting as he expels the slow, raw yowl of an animated villain being impaled with a lamp post.

This little man and I pluck then yank the biggest cable, pulling it to us like we mean it. The plank groans. Then it leans forward. Leans back. Then leans toward us. Like it is shifting in bed. Our gardienne is down there trilling a dozen rapid-fire prayers. Garçon has folded nearly in half, a praying mantis with spindles bent over his head, and Chef has ripped off his black cap and is holding it to his heart, mouthing something to the clouds.

Guy looks on. Cigarette dangling in the right corner of his lips, his gaze opaque, he folds his arms across his chest. He turns his head once left, once right, in a grim, slow, *"Non."*

No thanks to him, we do manage to guide the table to its new home. And with one exhale, we plant it safely, right in the middle of the parquet floor.

We stand staring at it. Panting.

Then laughing.

Yosemite drags a cotton kerchief across his brow then mops his moustache. And tucking the wad into his left hip pocket, he extends his other hand, stroking the table's grain politely.

"Elle est belle, votre p'tite table norvégienne."
("She's beautiful, your little Norwegian table.")

And she is. But not beautiful in the way he thinks she is. Heaven knows there are fancier, pricier, more cosmetically remarkable tables, tables that are objects of art. You've seen them, maybe, the ones in high-end home décor magazines, the glossy ones that are made of such hard wood you can almost see your reflection in their oiled surfaces. And I've seen other ones, the regal specimens on display in European castles, the ones made of mahogany, walnut or ebony, the ones with deep crevasses formed over centuries of use. Wood so dense and resistant, if you were a gladiator, you could without a flinch thunk your spiked ball right onto them. Not as much as a scratch. Your knight-in-shining-armor spurs? Not even a pockmark.

That kind of beauty is for an other-worldly, fairy tale kind of table. Ours is a this-world, true-tale table. So while Yosemite pats her beveled edge, circling and appraising her, I only think of the true and invisible beauty worn deep in my simple table's grain.

And I let the man walk away tisking, whistling, shaking his head. Off to move easier pieces into this, our new home of the many homes yet to come.

1

TALES FROM THE FAMILY TABLE

I t wasn't easy explaining why we were moving to a glacier, especially right then when the New York City winter was beginning to sink in its fangs. There was always that teasing buzz that reddened my cheeks when I tried to qualify our move, particularly to theater friends.

"NOR-way? Like *tundra* Norway?" The producers of the big musical I was appearing in gaped. There were blank stares from other actors, raised brows from the music director: "Norway. Gotcha. Capital of Sweden, right?" The assorted smirks and sniggers: "Freeze-your-everlovin'-*earlobes*-off *Norway*?"

I triple-checked Oslo's coordinates just to get my bearings. Right there, yes folks, at sixty degrees latitude it sits, along the very same ice-gray line as Alaska, the Yukon, Siberia and a convivial speck in Canada's Northern Territories called "Eskimo Point."

No wonder I'd never thought much about Oslo, and hadn't given much thought to Scandinavia. But I had to start thinking, if even vaguely, about the details when, a few weeks earlier in October, things started really rumbling, and when I found myself in a theater production office in late November, negotiating my way out of my contract, evangelizing to the artistic director about a place I really had no clue about, except that my husband and I were taking our two children, his business career, and my barely-budding theater career there.

This October I'm telling you about takes place a bit before everyone and his hamster has a cell phone. The tech people have knocked on my dressing room door during intermission, motioning that there's a call for me on the backstage telephone. Randall's voice sounds like it's in Hoboken, not Oslo:

"Honey, I'm so sorry to call right now. But . . . things are pretty serious in today's interviews. I won't waste your time. Uh, so, remind me again, how does Norway sound to you?"

Cold, I think, and feel.

"You mean they're tendering an offer already? Like *now?*"

With my emerald green robe wrapped around me, I press my forehead against the wall, my hair in pin curls under a nylon that also holds in place the wire of the body microphone snaking up and over one ear like a beige garter snake sucking on my cheek. It will be covered in a platinum 1940s wig in a matter of minutes. Other cast members are scuttling by, focused on a space between their eyes and the floor running lines, or they're laughing, tugging shoulder pads and hemlines, patting each other's backs, humming their next number. A crew guy points at me and then his wristwatch, raising an eyebrow, wagging two fingers. Two minutes.

Would we be interested (I'm hearing these words), such a wonderful group to work with, ready to move, boss a great mentor, willing and available, beautiful office, this place is gorgeous, two or maybe longest three years? Spanning Scandinavia? Soon?

One minute. Finger hammering on wristwatch. Louder tisking. Time. Bad time. Bad timing.

I had thought something like this might hit us sooner or later. And let's face it, I hadn't, after all, put my pretty foot down forbidding Randall from going to a whole slew of preliminary interviews. On the contrary, I'd been crossing my fingers, hoping things would go wonderfully for him. A career and family opportunity like this one! It all would have been great. A once in a lifetime opportunity. Sooner or later.

But I'd been banking on the *later*, a year or two or three later. Maybe after I'd worked out the wrinkles in this crazy life, the life of a full-time mother and wife, an adjunct English faculty member, and an aspiring professional musical theater actress. Maybe after we'd found a place right in The City, I'd thought, or after we'd figured out how to split care for our two children with the demanding schedule of daily rehearsals, then tri-weekly matinées and nightly shows. After, I'd thought. After

Randall and I had mastered that complicated late afternoon handover on my way to the theater. Maybe later, like after I'd gotten that patchwork to a good place where I wasn't utterly exhausted during the hours I was with my children. (I came home from shows close to 1:00 a.m.; the children always got up and Randall headed out the door for work at 6:00 a.m.) Maybe later, after this show and another and another, later after I'd signed with one of the agents with whom I'd just lined up appointments.

So when he advises me, my Randall, there on the backstage phone just as the second act overture erupts in a brassy shout, that he's so sorry and he knows this is not what we'd expected but he has to give a yes or no in *a matter of hours,* I don't feel duped. I feel ambushed. Not to mention really close to missing my entrance. I feel pinched not punched, and not by my husband (I'd seen him off at the airport, after all, and had kissed him proudly, wishing him "All the luck in the world!"), but now I feel crammed up against a cinder block wall of choice I'd naively waltzed right into. And there from that corner I see I have no choice, given the timing, but to delicately decline the offer. And indelicately hang up on my husband.

But I don't.

Because right then there is this snowplow thing. Right when telephone and backstage tensions are most tense, when trumpets and trombones are exploding with the second act overture, when dressing room doors are swinging open and shut, shooting shafts of white my way like search lights, when a frantic crew guy is giving me the *Slit-Your-Throat!* signal, I slowly close my eyes. I bow my head. I rest my brow in that cinder block corner. And from that posture I tunnel inwardly to a quiet space in my mind, searching through my gray matter and the matter which matters more, my heart.

Randall waits on the line on the other end of the world. Then slowly, pushing through a blur like the view through your windshield during a whiteout on the Garden State Parkway, comes a calming sensation. It is the image of a big, humming, green John Deere snowplow. I can see its sun-yellow blade. It's cutting a channel right through the cold-wet weight of my mind. It scrapes right down to bedrock, clearing smooth the way ahead. So tactile is this utility tractor in my head, that I open my eyes expecting to see on the floor at my feet what is so evident on the floor of my brain. A way forward. Impossibly sheer walls of snow on either side. This clean, glistening sliced trail. Visible as that. Without lifting my eyelids, I see what we're supposed to do, what I am supposed to do.

A month later, I'm scouring New Jersey Burlington Coat Factory sale racks for winter outerwear for four: Mom, Dad, Parker, age four, and Claire, age two. Next thing, this terrific cast holds a big bon voyage party that makes me all smushy and doubtful for a few hours about the reliability of internal green power tractors as predictors for one's entire familial and professional future. Then I think of that pathway image, I sit on it for a while, rekindling the sensation I know I'd had, and remind myself that "foreign" isn't *really* so foreign.

We had in fact lived abroad, Randall and I, even extensively. Before we married, Randall and I had both lived and worked in Germany and Austria respectively. I'd studied in Salzburg and Vienna, and as a young couple we'd also returned together to work in Vienna. Before all that— before *us*, even—Randall's father had been a missionary in pre–World War II Germany, my father had been a missionary in post–World War II Germany and had then studied music in Vienna, had married my mother and moved to Munich where their music studies continued (his in violin, hers in voice) and where, after a rousing night at the opera, they had conceived me. My zygotic beginnings were, so to speak, "foreign." Twenty-seven years later, with our first child, newborn Parker, Randall and I had moved to Asia for his internship at a Hong Kong bank. Our one-day family, we'd planned from almost our very first kiss, we would raise internationally. The "how" was a mystery to us then. But we were kissing, so come on, details, details.

Cold and long dark winters, I'd heard that much. Übercool design, I'd heard, and those funky Northern Lights. And Ibsen. And Grieg. Aqua and A-Ha. And Lillehammer. And the Norwegians are all tall blondes with strong bone structure, I'd heard. So just like me! But they all skied. So *not* just like me. We'd done Hong Kong, Austria, Germany, and Norway was Germanic. The company was offering some support to save us from taking out a loan from the World Bank in order to survive as a young family in Oslo, one of the five most expensive cities on earth. We would learn Norwegian, which to us as former college instructors of German sounded like fun, the way hopscotch sounds fun, or making a model airplane sounds fun. What could be the challenge in packing up and moving there for a couple of years or so? My union membership in Actor's Equity would remain valid for three years while I took no work but focused completely on our children, assuming, as I did, that there surely wouldn't be any random professional theater productions rolling through Oslo with a part in English for a young mother of two. We'd take the two-to-three year Nordic package, bail from it at that point, and then get back to the center of things, to our previous trajectories. To our cheek-by-jowl, dry-wall Jersey town home development right off Route 1. Now tell me: what could be so complicated about that?

What awaited us in Norway was an eye-opening, life-altering, trajectory-yanking journey that was so thoroughly challenging and satisfying in every way I can't even fish out a word for it. It set our family on a course that, nearly two decades later, continues to define our places in and responses to living in this world. We couldn't have known this during that backstage phone call, but that single decision to leave our home country would be the decision to make our home in many countries.

The mechanics of leaving our home country to make another place our home begin (and this shouldn't surprise anyone) with feeling bile climb our throats. Vertigo. On some level we all fear the unknown, and we all fear being blown away, having our skirts blown skyward, having a blow to our pride, and somehow we know in our bones that however narrow and colorless that strip of comfort zone ledge might be that we're teetering on, leaving it, flinging ourselves off into a major geographic and cultural relocation, will expose us. It will expose our limitations, insecurities, weaknesses, and our baggy Superhero underwear.

But another part of us wants to take that step, to fall, as they say in Norwegian, "neck over head in love" with a new place, a new people, a new way of living in the world. Sometimes that move just begins in a cursory, sideways glance of curiosity about the place. We study the map. We watch the people, their way of moving and talking and gesturing in conversation and we take note of how they sing to their babies in the city park and how they greet old friends in the marketplace and how they drive their cars or their rickshaws or their camels and by now we're fascinated by observing how they hold their canteen or wine goblet or beer stein or how they hold their liquor at all. Before we know it, we're mirroring how they fold their origami or their crêpe Suzette or their slice of *pizza con funghi*, and next we're eating at their pace, slurping miso soup, spitting seeds over our shoulder, ripping the tip off the hot baguette, peeling our raw shrimp, and all of this with our eyes blindfolded and both hands tied behind our back.

In Norway, you do peel and eat raw shrimp, and you do it at a *langbord,* like our long farm table. It was our first and really our only major purchase when we moved there early in the winter of the Olympic Games of 1994. We were directed by friends to Peter, a craftsman who lived on our same island, a tall, scrubbed-clean, blonde specimen of gentle Nordic chiseledness who let us pick, from pictures, our own pine tree he would personally whack down and from which he would hand carve this long board of a table. In his workshop where he worked mostly alone and in silence, this Norwegian craftsman took our hand-selected pine, let it cure, carved it into this chunky plateau, then added (hand painted, in matte barn red) twelve pontifical-looking traditional Norwegian farm chairs. I am sitting in one now.

From this place the tale begins.

Next thing you know, that table from a quiet northern Norwegian forest and equally quiet workshop is surrounded with lots of noise. It's the noise of laughter and singing and the sound of utensils clanking and glasses clinking, and all of this is coming from new friends, some of whom are sitting at the adjoining fold-out tables crammed into corners of our biggest room. Everyone is speaking different languages. Most frequently, the conversations weave from one tongue to another, then return to one common tongue, swirl around there for a while gaining momentum, then drift into threads of different languages, different stories, different ways of gesticulating and coloring the conversation.

Just as often, there's food covering every inch of pine where there isn't white table linen (a gift from a new friend), pewter plates (a gift from another), or elbows. Faces are leaning toward the candlelight, toward each other. That was Oslo.

And that was Versailles.

And Paris.

And Munich.

And . . .

And that's just part of the tale, the glimmery, photo-op, made-for-movie, fairy-tale part that can be found in these pages. There are real people from across different cultures, people who helped us learn their languages, traditions, country's history, and views of everything from politics to religion to gender roles to school systems. Like the barn-red chairs, this family of friends wraps all the way around the table and around the world. They wrap around our family and our family's story. In point of fact, without them, there is no story to tell.

What lies at the heart of the tale of this table and is of greatest value, I believe, are not the dinner parties, no matter how scintillating, nor the into-the-wee-hours conversations, however colorful. At the very heart of this book is an enduring truth I've learned from so many years of living nomadically, of raising my family in the vortex of serial change. That truth is that just about everything, every last *thing*, every object is, ultimately, disposable. Things are, especially when you have to wrap and pack and load and unload and heft their weight time and time again, not only of comparatively little value, but they just plain make it tough to up and move quickly or gracefully. They're gravitational, pushing you deeper into this earth's crust, and when suspended against gravity, like our table, they cause neighborhood spectacles, make sailors sweat and swear, turn cartoon characters into gargoyles, and they bring out the beast in pleasant mothers who otherwise shave their shins, curl their eyelashes, and sample truffles in the bathroom.

Already you're catching me in one of my typically human contradictions. Why, if *things* like tables have "comparatively little value" (as I write), and if they are "ultimately disposable" (as I also write), why then such a brouhaha on a sunny Parisian morning? Why get the gardienne's apron in a bundle?

Because this table itself is needed to tell this or any of my most important stories. Like Julia Child said of her big Norwegian farm table, the one that the Smithsonian Institute has displayed with her complete home kitchen, our table is the heart of our home. Mrs. Child made no bones about it. If she was going to move from land to land—Norway, Germany, the East Coast of the US, twice in France (where her apartment in the Rue de l'Université was only a short walk from ours in Rue du Colonel Combes)—if she was going to be forever on the roam, then something, she insisted, had to remain stable.

This one table, *s'il vous plait,* may it stay?

Aside from my husband and our four children, who have always been my world amid this whirl, there are very few tangible *things* that have remained constant. Nearly all else at some point or another has had to be left behind. Houses, cars, sofas, pianos, beds, some few heirlooms, they have been left of sheer necessity: they didn't fit, they didn't match, they didn't survive or they didn't make it up the third floor stairway, down the cellar stairway or over the Atlantic.

My *people*, though, my most intimate, adored and invaluable people, they are my indisposables. Lose the rest of the stuff, go ahead, but do not lose my family. My family, *they* are what I knew would always remain. We did not have and never will have twenty or even ten accumulated years in a cul-de-sac, no decade or two of dreamy neighborhood cross-pollination that happens when a dozen or so families live hedge-to-hedge, enjoying parallel lives throughout everyone's pregnancy, preteen, and prom years, marinating in one another's lawn fertilizer and deck sealant, mixing barbecue sauces and swapping babysitters, swimming in one another's backyard pools, and sometimes even in one another's gene pools.

Well, one can't have it all, they say. The fenceless life and someone else's picket fence.

And they are so absolutely right. One can*not* have it all.

And so we choose. We choose to have each other.

Which brings me back to *friends.* Some of my friends are essential, the way air, earth, and the blue ocean are, the lifelong distance from whom exacts quite a cost. But today, thanks to rapidly advancing technology, you have an excellent chance of keeping in close touch with such friends. Still, the pattern I've experienced is that as soon as you start gathering new friends around that long table of yours, and as soon as you get the conversation rolling, the music pouring out of the corner with the piano, just when you get to the point where you're sharing forks with Sven or chopsticks with Su-Ling or childbirth stories with Svetlana, you have to break the news of your pending departure.

You have to do this to your children, too, who've also invested in their own friendships. The celebration around your table stalls in that difficult moment, the music recedes to a plunking tinkle, and you're back in that queer place where your muscles stiffen around your mouth, and you eke out a promise, as you've done how many times before, of remaining in touch. And possibly even visiting. *Next year,* you promise, smiling like you're waiting for your sixth grade school photo to be taken. After that, you express regret that you *didn't do more of this* or of that or of something else while you *still had the time together. Had we only known,* you usually have to say, *we'd be moving so far away.*

And so soon.

And so . . . soon you're unwrapping forks and chopsticks from that gray packing paper, the glasses from their bubbly plastic, and a crew is milling busily around you, chattering away in a language that for you in this moment is as good as Hmong played backwards and on high speed on a 1930s RCA Victor. It's a language for which you'd been forward-thinking enough to buy that slick pocket phrase book which is packed, as fate would have it, in the bottom of box #491.

So these crew members *merschgebirschgaborschk* their way through your narrow entry hall, waving a questioning hand here, depositing a bed but the wrong frame in the wrong room over there, and so you're belly-crawling through the soggy maze of your brain trying to find that doggoned cognate for "bed" and "frame" and "wrong," only to see out of the corner of your eye and through a ground floor window that the rest of said crew is now standing in the middle of the street surrounding your big table, your one and only indisposable *thing.* She's posed there, your table, in the open air quite bare and vulnerable and all defenseless in her raw pine, while the men are scratching their beards and beating back traffic, which is blocked because of the moving truck and immovable table, so the natives are honking crazily, the crew is swearing (at least you assume it is swearing, although it sounds just like *mershgebirschgaborschk* only with a certain corporeal emphasis), and the whole scene alerts the local police, who pull up, lights swirling and badges brandishing, all of which, of course, breaks the ice nicely.

Welcome to your new homeland.

So, you need your one and singular fix of comfort now and again. Our table has been just that, it has become almost like an essential friend, accompanying us for so long, witnessing so much of what this life has meant to our small unit. The morning after those parties I've described above, for instance (and you and I have to have a deal that you never tell my dinner guests about this), I changed my babies' diapers there. On its big surface I also massaged their little limbs with almond oil and essence of eucalyptus when they were congested and crampy. Here, I also massaged butter under the skins of turkeys and pheasants and between the blistered toes of little, sore soccer feet. It's along its dinged up but steady edge where our two youngest, Dalton and Luc, holding tight, learned to toddle. When older, they hid underneath it in ad hoc bed linen Bedouin tents. All four children have done more homework here than should be legal, with fountain pens in OCD graph squares typical of the French and German academic traditions. Dalton has practiced Chinese characters here, with a quill. The two eldest learned to speak Norwegian, all four French, Claire and her little brothers German, and a couple of us, Dalton and I, Mandarin while propping our heads in our hands, our elbows on this forgiving pine.

As a this-world, true-tale table, it has absorbed the marks of real life: drops of blood, vinaigrette, and tears, and has some small grooves from dropped (hurled) knives and Cocker Spaniel claws. These aren't complaints. I wouldn't want my table any different. If she were of a harder wood than pine, she might not have kept the scratches of our human traffic. I like soft wood like I like soft hearts; in them our life stories leave a deeper impression, scars of impact. I don't mind, in fact I prefer, the imperfections, the cracks and water rings, the nicks, bumps, and pen marks which, when I run my hand over them, are a living tale themselves, like the shush of hieroglyphics recounting something multi-layered, organic, compelling, undying.

This pine has been figuratively both behind the stories and in the middle of them, as well as literally underneath our stories from its very beginning, because throughout everything, I've recorded the story on top of this table. I've heaped up thousands of words: journal entries, stacks of mass-mailed or private letters, emails, song texts in many languages, pictures with intimate scribblings on their backs, newspaper clippings, school reports, letters from my children written in new and varied languages, my cherished pocket notebooks, annotated maps, and my favorite novels.

Working with them and still on this same table, I've written what's evolved into this volume, a memoir of a global family, of a global mother. In its pages, I begin to recount the geographies and landscapes both external and internal, the landscape of a family with its significant gains and its notable losses, its guffaws and faux pas, its "You-Will-Not-Believe-This-Ones," its new friends, its heartbreaking farewells.

So here it is, that story, written up and down the broad pine spine of this langbord. Here's where I invite you to sit and look out my back window, the Jura mountains of France on this side of the house, the Swiss Alps out the other, and I'll take you as far as my words can manage: to a few special spots far beyond these mountains, to places and people my family and I know well and love much.

"*Dis donc!* She is quite a table," a new Swiss friend said just this week as she walked into this part of the house with the large windows and the table. "*Elle est belle.* I'll bet she has quite a story," she said, tracing her fingers along the edge.

"She does," I said. "She has quite a story."

Pull up a chair right here, I almost said to my new friend.

I'll tell you the whole thing.

2

BARNEPARK

Every day when I drove up our hillside road with its view over the Oslo fjord, I passed a small sign hanging on a chain link fence: *BLAKSTAD BARNEPARK*. I knew *Blakstad* was the name of where we lived in a place called *Asker Kommune*, an area just a short drive west of Oslo. And it didn't take me long to figure out what *barnepark* meant.

Behind those fences were mounds of snow, and romping on those mounds of snow were children, or *barna*. They were, during those first few dark January days in my new home, the only humans I ever saw with any regularity. And they were parked there every day all day long, as far as I could tell, five days a week. Unlike what I remembered from my little brother's year in a kindergarten in Salzburg, Austria, which in my memory was a perpetual-springtime frolicking place with flitting butterflies and daisies, barnepark was a work camp packed with heavy snow and black ice. I couldn't find frolicking, flitting, or flowers. This barnepark thing was something else. And this something else chilled me to the bone.

In whiteouts or under steel gray skies, entire herds of red, blue, and green-clad kids were hurtling themselves at each other and down slopes, pinball machines without the machines, just bright balls ricocheting randomly. Or they would be standing squat in their tracks, arms slightly propped under all the wadding they were wearing. I was glued. Arctic-looking or not, that should be *our* kids, I thought. Our two barna needed to get their snow legs, their blood thickened, lots of icy air to energize and wear them out.

Above all, they needed to speak Norwegian, as did I. And immersion, even if it meant headfirst in the snow, was the only way. I knew this. But the very thought scared me stiffer than the below-freezing temperatures did.

My first journal entry in Norway:

> *Okay. I feel contained by this country, its language, its cold, its darkness. Maybe I've lost my sense of adventure. Or maybe I'm just tired. Is this denouement? Where's my motivation and momentum? Paradox. All this space, this time, this openness to explore and I'm stymied. I read a great description that seems to get to the point. The woman's remembering a major geographic/language change and says, "It was here that I fell out of the net of meaning into the weightlessness of chaos."[1] Yup.*

I hung there, too, but to me it felt more weighted than weightless chaos. Constant snowfall, constant dark, and the abrupt unplugging from the high voltage *ka-jang!* of professional live theater will do that to you. If I'm frank, the whole scenario—the thought of letting my little ones go off unprotected into the Hall of the Mountain King, having to slog through all the potential negotiations in Norwegian, walking out the door into the Nordic gale, pulling on thermals and a ski mask—it plain tired me out.

So of course I pulled out Barney. Yes, Barney, the purple dinosaur. Videos. They had been a good-bye gift from our town home community friends when we'd set sail for the north. Though I was no big Barney fan then, I was touched by our friends' thoughtfulness, and now, in hibernation mode, Barney tapes were looking mighty good indeed. Purple Barney over real barnepark. The piteousness wasn't lost on me. Still, I interspersed Barney tapes with the one half hour of what I learned was *Barne TV*, the thirty minutes of children's programming that showed every day from 5:30 to 6:00 p.m. from one end of Norway to another.

"Barne TV!" I would chirp, "Barne TV! Oooooo, let's cuddle up and watch it, sweeties! Sound fun?"

It was. Until eighteen seconds into it when Parker and Claire figured out that whatever I was calling barne was not *bar-nee*, but *bar-nah*, and had nothing purple, padded, or prehistoric about it. And it was thoroughly old world Norwegian. Gentle, slow-moving, sober-voiced, intimate and musical, a kind of programming that could have made Mr. Rogers look like Howard Stern. *Gen-tle*. Valium gentle.

Gentle wasn't going to cut it for these two products of the Jersey Turnpike. *Barne TV* only kept them in grip for a few minutes at a time. Their systems were still running on the entertainment equivalent of Fruit Gushers, Capri Suns, and Nerds: instantly explosive, punchy, a prickly kick to the system. Detox would take time.

Right now, though, the kids were already wandering to the window, looking out at our neighbor across the street.

"Why don't we go talk with her, Mom?" Parker asks, sipping a mug of cocoa while sitting cross-legged on the floor in his loge seat at our front ceiling-to-floor windows. Our neighbor, thirty-something, blonde pony-tail, in pink moon boots, is shoveling her snow. In a matching swimsuit.

"She looks so nice," my four-year-old son adds.

"So cold," I correct him.

"Nice," pipes up Claire, who is licking a ridge of cocoa foam from around her lips.

After an hour or so, our neighbor is worked up enough to have to cool down. I turn this into a cultural lesson. The kids and I study this native's customs from our front window. Now Exhibit A is putting the shovel in the snow bank. Now Exhibit A is walking up the driveway. And now Exhibit A is rolling in the slush hedges. Rolling and pouncing around.

I smooth the perma-bulge knees of my crusty gray sweats and tug straight the toe seam of my husband's stained athletic socks. I've worn nothing else but this for a good week.

"She's pretty," Claire sighs from where she's lying on her tummy on the floor next to me, chin cradled in her hands, head cocked lightly to one side. "Pretty pink boots."

"Uh-huh," I mumble, checking to make sure I'd correctly buttoned my (Randall's) earth-toned plaid flannel lumberjack shirt that morning.

"Can't we go play at her house?" Parker begs, now standing.

"Play with the pretty lady?" Claire beams, scrambling up to her knees, eyes popping.

This is a spot. Mrs. Pasty Domestic Globule—me—approach Ms. Snow Leopard? And with my couple of snort-and-grunt monosyllables? Delivered in tree-felling attire? Shoved into Paul Bunyan's Gortex boots?

And now my two plead with me, wearing me down. All they want—I know, I know, my socially starved darlings—is normal human con-tact. But all I want is to sleep the sleep of Rip Van Winkle and wake up feeling myself again, or, better, feeling like a self who can negotiate this new world. Then I'll definitely walk across the street, I tell myself. The newly-awakened me would, in polished Norwegian, find out what Exhibit A's name is. Borrow her shovel. Maybe even those boots. Maybe even the swimsuit.

"Not today, kids. It looks like she's all done, anyway. Whoops! Darn. Another time, okay?"

For an hour I leave them there, my young foreign voyeurs, steaming up the plate glass, while I lock myself in my room and a stuffed dinosaur sings "I love you, you love me, we're a happy family" on the other side of my door. I bleat into the mattress like Baby Bop without her blankey. Thank heavens my nonjudgmental journal listens, its unlined pages kind and open in their blank stare, accepting of my whole litany of true confessions:

> It's all I can do to keep getting up and dressed in the mornings. P and C don't notice my lethargy, and their hourly needs get me up, keep me vertical, keep me going. I'm doing an okay job of hiding my true feelings from them. But I can't hide them from myself. I feel three-fourths numb. It has something to do with hearth-tending, as I watch myself shrink to a fraction of my capacity, using over and over again one small muscle, to form an analogy, and not my whole body. One worn-out lever. It's probably as simple as missing my work, those friends, the buzz, so much fabulous singing. But it's more than that. I need a possibility for full-throated expression. Bless their hearts, they're kids. Their lives have been upended, too, and I have to be sensitive to how they're adapting . . . And the result of all this is that I feel a spreading dry basin in myself, a parched emptiness that makes it hard to offer much moisture to those who need it most. No moisture, except a few totally private tears.

I called Johanne, a local woman I'd met at church the week we arrived in Norway. She was from our local congregation in Sandvika. Like the dozens of people in that parish, she became part of a social experiment. Church had always been essential and even defining in every place we'd lived, but now church was an incubator, that one warm, bright, domed place where folks with know-how checked on us, their scrawny soggy chicklins, as we got on our shaky legs and gradually fluffed out our feathers. From day one, we'd told our congregation the same thing Randall had told all his work colleagues: *Ikke Engelsk, bare Norsk.*

What that means is, "No English, only Norwegian." Although we made a face like English was icky. And yes, Norwegian made us feel pretty bare.

Johanne was thoroughly Norwegian which meant she was thoroughly patient. She'd call me just about every day.

"*Heisann, Melissa. Dette er Johanne.*"

I'd hear that slow, calming voice of hers and would slink to the floor because I concentrated better on all haunches. The rest would be a dialogue, with me in painfully slow Norwegian.

"Hi, Johanne." Pause. Hand on forehead, searching, searching. "This is Melissa."

Pause.

"And how does it stand today?" Johanne's pleasant, warm-soup-on-a-blustery-day voice there in my ear, walking me through the basics.

"It stands well . . . Thanks shall you have, Johanne."

Pause. Then, yes! Another stock phrase:

"And you?! Does it stand well with you, Johanne?"

"Just fine, thanks. Children? Goes it well with them, too?"

And so on, for an hour, maybe, moving at glacier-pace, Johanne dragging my stiff self through the Norwegian steppes. As much as any other phrase we had to use with each other was "*Jeg forstår ikke.*" "I don't understand." If I had a Norwegian *krone* for every time I said, "I don't understand," I'd be richer than Norway.

Johanne is the one who, during one such phone call, revealed for me the world of barnepark. I learned that on one level barnepark is a state-run, primarily outdoor activity center available to all local residents for depositing their children for a morning, an afternoon, or a full day. On another level, barnepark is a practical and convenient place for children ages two to four to rough and tumble, tackle each other and the elements, and practice their social skills. On yet another level altogether and what I would find over the next many months, is that barnepark is *the* defining apparatus in Norwegian society.

I also learned that we'd missed the application deadline by about five years, so Johanne suggested I go immediately to our neighborhood *park* and beg for two *dagbarn plasser. Plasser* is "places," self-explanatory. The term *dagbarn* was one of the those typically economical Norwegian terms, and means, literally, day child. You could solicit the park for the part time day-by-day places that popped up now and again. Sometimes if you got in as a dagbarn, Johanne explained, you could finagle a permanent spot. "To become Norwegian faster," she said.

Another journal entry:

I'm thirty-one years old. Mother of two. Wife of one. Beyond that, the description tapers off. I've been in Norway for three weeks, which means I'm an American trying to come to terms with her foreignness. I do this by eradicating it. Language is key. I can't use my "newness" here much longer as an excuse for my inability to speak with confidence. From now on, these journal visits will be in Norwegian. Even my interior voice has to submit to the new language if I think I'm going to master it.

From the inside cover of my first Norwegian/English dictionary:

I have no time to float here in speechlessness. Must, MUST tackle Norwegian. Haiku is not my metaphor for living. Meantime, I have some chances to sing at church coming up. Something to wear pantyhose for. Cheap thrills. Have to shave my legs. I'll need a tractor mower.

What I knew was that Parker and Claire, at nearly five and exactly two-and-a-half years old, were prime candidates for gobbling up the language. They had no idea, but they were going to be fashioned into Norwegian-speaking Vikings, a bit of a stretch, maybe, but I was ready to at least try. Before petitioning the barnepark, as Johanne had suggested, I first set up a stealth surveillance post. Atop a hill and from behind a pine tree close to Blakstad barnepark, I hunched behind my steering wheel, warm in my down sleeping bag and earmuffs. Parker and Claire wore their hats and coats and were wrapped in a massive feather comforter while they read books to each other in the backseat so I could take notes on the social experiment playing itself out before me.

From this outpost, I spied a trio of red-suited adults (only later did I discover that they were women) standing sentinel amid fifteen to twenty or so small bodies that played in hip-high snow and chased snowflakes with their tongues. The women in red stood there, removed from the activity in the snow. Unless there was real trouble like the random child stuck feet up in the air, his torso in a snow bank, limbs flailing wildly for help, the women stood far away, stamping their boots every so often, clouds of breath rising from their faces. Occasionally, they would sip from thermoses or slap their mittened hands on their thighs. This same silent movie repeated itself all morning long, the sun never really rising very far into the sky, dusk a constant backdrop on those limpid midwinter days.

At midday, and with the ring of a handheld bell, all the children would gather into a small wooden barrack for an hour. After the hour, they emerged again. Repeat of the morning's silent movie. I would later learn that this was the pattern, day in and day out, sleet, snow, hail or high water, (all of which were norms for Norway) all year long, for three years of these children's lives.

And everyone in Norway did this. Everyone.

Just watching the ice slides made me choke on my swig of peppermint tea from my big red Land's End thermos. Some of those kids were whizzing so fast down slides packed so hard with gray ice, they looked like upholstered torpedoes shooting out of polished marble barrels.

One tiny figure in particular (to whom we still refer today as Hannah the Human Bullet) got my attention. She might have been three, but a small three. Her snowsuit was red as was her little knitted cap that looked just like a strawberry, green twig stem and all. From where I huddled in my unmarked car, I could just make out her mounds of cheeks, two buffed pinkish apples in a grocer's crate. She was either intrepid or on Fen-Phen. Circuit after circuit, she hiked the slick path to the top of a handmade precipice where she flopped herself prostrate, planted her mittens to get some traction, and like a teensy pebble out of a sling shot, exploded down the steep incline. Sometimes she landed on her belly. Sometimes on her back. Always, she caught some air. No one, least of all Hannah, seemed to flinch at the peril, the sure threat of injury, the astronomical potential for lawsuits. I, on the other hand, was left winded and jittery just keeping up with her above my dashboard.

Kids were roaming about, gluey noses scarlet with cold, all those clouds of breath hanging over their heads like empty thought bubbles in a comic strip. The tall red-suited adults only piped up every half hour or so at the most, while all the children kept doing normal kid-in-snow things like pelting each other with snowballs, grabbing the littler guy's shovel, constructing elaborate fort and tunnel systems.

When they were whonked over the noggin or got stuck in the frozen tire swing, no one came rushing with theatrical rescues and apologies for the misery of it all. No one came most of the time, in fact. Generally, a tall person's hooded head raised itself a bit, I would hear the faint holler, probably reciting a barnepark rule, and the child maneuvered itself to safety or self-consolation. Once or twice a big person split up a knotted wrangle of clawing cubs, barking in about four syllables something that shut down the scuffle like a lid over fire.

This? No, my children would never survive.

I had raised Parker and Claire—my treasures, my snoogly-wooglies—to be softies. Like me. This system, as I watched it with one hand slapped across my gaping mouth, would make them hardy, no question. But in the process it would give me a heart attack. Putting them here would be like tossing them into a doggoned menagerie, I shuddered, more of a farm, even, than any well-organized playpen. And what about their American preschool leg up? All that fine motor skill development? All that spatial training and computer literacy?

I second-guessed myself. I second-guessed barnepark. I was back to second-guessing Norway as a whole.

I also knelt at the side of our IKEA bed and prayed. Prayed in Norwegian, if you must know everything, because, 1) If I was writing in my journal in Norwegian, I wasn't going to be a slacker in prayer, 2) I'd heard God was a linguist, and 3) I was curious to see what language He'd answer in. *Ikke Engelsk? Bare Norsk?* I'll tell you what. Praying on my knees on that cold pine floor in my halting preschooler's Norwegian phrases was as bare—and true—as prayer had ever been for me. I bawled all the way through.

And holy Odin: God was thumbs up about barnepark.

After a couple of days of playing driver's seat anthropologist from an unmarked Saab and double-checking with the Powers That Be, I slipped into my best jeans which I tucked into my fancy red cowboy boots, a big hit with my New York City friends, making me immediately identifiable as The Girl From Utah. I pulled on a padded but flattering (and therefore actually not so padded and therefore totally useless) down parka, and checked my foreign newcomer smile in the mirror while drilling my Norwegian lines. I'd written them out phonetically while Johanne had coached me over the phone. With a prayer in my heart and one bundled child on each hand, I waddled gingerly all the way down the slope to the Blakstad barnepark barrack.

It might have occurred to you that the soles of cowboy boots are meant to slip easily in and out of stirrups, which is an advantage while roping calves in rodeos. But this never crossed my mind. And those slick soles were no good on a seventy-degree angle of black ice.

Slush-splattered, and limping lightly, with a bruise forming on my hip, I arrived with my two children. I'd timed our entrance for noon, knowing this was barnepark lunchtime, a prime opportunity to beg for *dagbarn plasser*. A few whacks on the wooden door and a very tall, attractive brunette woman wearing several layers of woolen sweaters under a lumpy red snowsuit unzipped to and gathered at her waist, opened the door to me. Her pronounced, flushed cheekbones pointed right to her broad, sympathetic smile. Behind her shoulder I caught sight of a spartan but cozy interior filled with a whole picnic table of ruddy-cheeked children, most of them tow-headed, leaning over small bundles of what must have been sack lunches. In silence they examined their strange, shivering visitors.

Two other blonde women, also in half-zippered red jumpsuits, appeared to be manning the lunch break. The interior looked so soothing after the piercing cold outside. Claire, shy and clingy in new situations, was gripping my brittle fingers so desperately I thought they'd break. And both children really needed a toilet. I was afraid. Afraid for them. Afraid for me. My feet were searing with pain. My rump was sodden and sore. I searched inwardly for my first line. This is where my years as an actress kicked in, shoving me through stage fright.

The woman waited, smiling.

I was frozen on all levels.

I licked my lips to defrost them, but they remained immobile. I took one step forward.

Out of a mouth that felt like two stacked Goodyear radials, I lifted the corners of my mouth to a rigid smile and forced out the following in a Vulcan's Norwegian:

"Good day. Sorry that I disturb. We are Americans. We inhabit house not far. We freeze. Have you dagbarn?"

Tall, gentle tante Britt, as I later learned was her name, responded in Norwegian-For-The-Learning-And-Hearing-Impaired, "*Komm in!*" motioning me at once into the barrack and into a wobbly but warm conversation. I might have said "*Jeg forstår ikke*" a record seventeen times. But this didn't seem to inhibit Britt. She just kept nudging my frozen-solidness forward.

All this was done while the two blondes, whom I was later to know as tante or aunt Eva and tante Anna, invited Parker and Claire over to sit on a bench and sing nursery songs with the others while I beat my hands back to life. They smiled, my two, a bit stiff with fear and separation angst and all-eyes-on-us self-consciousness. But that lasted less than three minutes.

My hands began to thaw. The palms started itching like crazy. I watched my two wriggle into a place between other children on the bench. Claire's cheeks a flaming shade of raspberry, Parker's bangs matted and angular after he tugged off his thin polyester American beanie.

A spot in my lower torso felt ignited, heat-filled, by the sight of my two crammed in between a girl, maybe four, and another, not much older. The first sat next to Claire and secretly put her hand on Claire's thigh, smiling, whispering something to Claire, which of course, she could not understand, but to which Claire nodded a bit sideways.

My eyes must have been defrosting, I knew this, because they were leaking down both my cheeks. But my fingers remained concrete. I never did get blood to them, in fact, but I nevertheless managed to sign, in runic alphabet, the paperwork that admitted our two as dagbarn the next morning.

3

SNOW ANGELS

One thing I had to do right away, Britt advised when I signed the children up for barnepark, was to outfit them in *ekte* (real) *vintertøy* (winter clothing).

To demonstrate what ekte meant, she pulled at her own three layers of hand knit sweaters, then showed a young boy's woolen leggings over full length thermal underwear, turned inside out the lined waterproof mittens, shook out a dense fleece head ornament, let me squeeze the substantial snow suit, and stomped on the ground to emphasize the sturdiness of her own, manly boots. To indicate what ekte was *not*, she glanced me up and down and let her stare bore into the pointed red toes of my fashionable rodeo attire.

That afternoon I found myself surrounded by wool and fleece at *Sportshuset*, The Sports House. A soft-spoken salesgirl, Synnøve, took my list in hand and expedited my mass purchase. We started close to the skin. There was specific underwear, tights, extra woolen calf-high stockings, hats and hat liners, turtlenecks, clips to affix hat liners and hats to turtlenecks, woolen pullovers, mittens that extend to the elbow, clips to attach mittens to outerwear, and, finally, the outerwear itself: the ubiquitous *parkdress*.

Synnøve and I took the children and dressed them in a whole truck-load of wool and insulation. I watched Synnøve's technique as if studying brain surgery: This goes in first. No, that pulls up there. No, that clips to this which you have to cram into that which, no . . . wait a sec . . . what's this rip cord for?

We were tugging and huffing; at one point I was straddling Parker, who lay wailing on the showroom floor, red-faced and hyperventilating. I kept panting, ekte, ekte, ekte. Synnøve had floppy, giggling Claire in a half-Nelson, shoving her dimpled body into tights that looked like so much sausage casing. After breaking a good sweat, we had Parker and Claire mummified. Rendered three times their normal circumference by inner wear, Parker and Claire were set for parkdress fitting.

The parkdress is the offspring, I had to conclude, of a NASA and NASCAR marriage. There is, as Synnøve lectured us, a specific type of weave in the synthetic fabric which allows for ventilation but which withstands the entrance of moisture or cold. Here, she pointed, was double lining and rubberized layers on the seat and knees, perfect for withstanding high speeds on glacial terrain. I looked at Claire and Parker: cocoons with feet, unable to bend a joint, let alone set land speed records. But I remembered Hannah the Human Bullet and listened to the expert.

After fork-lifting my two human tubers into their gear, we tried on Cheroxes, the only boots, Synnøve said knowingly, that won't freeze in sub-zero temperatures. That I was voluntarily buying clothes to enable my two darlings to hang out for hours in sub-zero temperatures felt dicey, even abusive. But five minutes and half our bank account later, I walked off with six heavy bags of ekte.

And only four months later I was back groveling at Synnøve's feet, another fat list in hand, in need of *ekte regntøy*—real rain clothing. This time, the leading manufacturer of outer clothing, Helly Hansen, had gone all Paris with its pink and periwinkle patterns, trademarks of their rubberized Spring Collection. Every barnepark I passed looked like a bedazzled Pride parade at the Arctic Circle.

What I should have done right then, but didn't think to do, unfortunately, was to buy every last bit of ekte in my size as well. From my journal:

> I spent over two hours shoveling snow in the middle of a major snowstorm this morning. While Parker and Claire stared on from the safe warmth of the house, their rosy faces pushed up against the window next to the front door, I snorted and huffed away like a rabid mastodon packed in neck-to-ankle Lycra. The craziest thing

about this is that everyone else on the street was doing the same thing, although perhaps not in Lycra. Not a one of us exchanged as much as a greeting, and in silent, sober duty we jammed our shovels, heaved the weight, and moved mountains. Half sissy, half Sisyphus, I clenched my jaw, doing my part to build neighborly solidarity.

As another meter of snow fell (and another two were forecast for that night), we scooped and piled, scooped and piled for a couple of hours at least. Our monuments grew much taller than the tallest man I could just barely get a peek at way at the bottom of our hill, digging and lobbing in the unbroken rhythm of jab-heave-heave-hurl, jab-heave-heave-hurl.

I'm not exactly sure what it is yet that I am learning in this new lifestyle. Maybe something to do with discovering the inherent significance buried in the mundane. I'll keep digging.

Sometime after that storm blew over, the sun shone brightly for an exceptional six days straight. This was just long enough to cause a crisis when the ice started to thaw. One Saturday morning, Randall and I found the entryway ceiling was streaming in about a dozen synchronized tributaries onto the floor. Seems we'd been distracted by snow removal from the shoulder down, and hadn't noted the glacier forming on the roof.

We should have known to climb on the roof and shovel off the weight, the tall guy from the bottom of the road announced dully as he took two long strides up the snow that was so high it met the bottom edge of the rafters, then over Randall's head and onto the roof. In a dozen or so mechanical swipes, he attacked the slushy beast with a pick and spade. A couple of muscular kicks with the toe of his hunting boot and my roof was dripless.

"Always clear the roof," he ordered in an accent I now recognized as from northern Norway, and he stabbed the shovel into the snow mound before leaning his bony elbow on the pick. "Next time, the whole roof could cave in and—" He made a fierce sound like a polar bear winning at Go Fish.

After every storm that followed I didn't wait for Randall to come home and help me with the shoveling. I was the first from my neighborhood to shimmy up the drainpipe: Shoveler on the Roof.

This was at about the same time Randall left for something euphemistically called a regional business retreat at the Olympic Games. He wanted me to come, too, but there was no housing left anywhere for a family of four, and I certainly didn't want to leave my two children behind (and where and with whom?), so I wished him a "totally wonderful and bonding time!" and told him to call often from Lillehammer. Which he did. He called me many times a day, in fact, feeding me with color commentary and cultural play-by-plays, always spilling over with details about this high-pitched initiation into the Norwegian spirit. At noon, he'd be yelling to me over the cheering spectators screaming on his right and his left; at midnight, he'd be whispering like a spy, reporting dispassionately below the gurgling drinking choruses on whoever was at that moment spread out cold under the table.

I took notes and pummeled him with questions prodding for more. And I hung, I'm embarrassed but not too proud to admit, on those calls of his. There seemed to be a big world out there. Out there where he was. Where I was not.

Not that I wasn't keeping very busy in my small world at home. I used that week to invite over a steady string of barnepark friends: Jesper, Eirik, Knut, Karolina, Per-Ole, Louisa. Bringing live Norwegian under our roof in a gallop was, as I'd hoped it would be, better than Berlitz. I played the half-mute, the kneeling hostess, the crawling mom who went everywhere the conversation went, watching the kids' lips, mouthing sounds with my brows furrowed, questioning them on every expression, repeating in a murmur every turn of phrase, writing things in my notebook. Most of the time, the kids smiled. Other times, they stopped and turned and spoke right to me. They'd stare at me as I knelt at their feet and with their noses crunched they'd say, "So . . . you're not one of us, are you? You're not Norwegian?"

"*Nei, egentlig ikke,*" ("No, actually not") I'd answer, trying not to show I was disappointed I'd been found out so soon. "But tell me, my friend," I continued, pulling in every last Norwegianism I could come up with, "How in all the world did you know I'm not Norwegian?" The flashy Jersey Girl clothes? The eye makeup? Two American children, perhaps?

"I knew because you speak a little bit weird, you know. A little strange. Funny." Karolina's eyes were a contact-lens shade of cornflower blue and each one as big as a hockey puck. Her voice was cautious, "Are you mentally ill?"

I actually didn't understand her last question right off, and I had to call over her friend Louisa for a little conference.

"Oh, yes," Louisa explained, smacking her own skull with a ball of wooly fist, "*Hjernet syk,* like if your brain is hurt." She placed a small, mittened hand on my forearm as if to steady me. Her eyes swam and blinked under snow white brows, "but Mamma says you're not dangerous."

That creatures who couldn't even pull on their own mittens could spew flawless Norwegian phrases strung neatly together as if they'd been drilling them day and night for years, those sing-songy loopty-loo sentences with immaculate word order and impeccable syntax and effortless intonation, with tightly held or loosely suspended vowels, with that perfect little so-subtle trill in the "r" and the delicately inserted "jo" and a gently hung "da?" at the end for folksy authenticity. . . . Ack! It made me *totally nuts.*

Actually, it made me cling to them. They had some magic about them, small good luck rabbit feet, all of them. So I kept on my knees. Because that's how they made me feel: ever their humble rabbit-foot-licker.

During a few unusually sunny hours in February, I had half the barnepark over for my homemade Olympics. I staged making snow angels with the kids, and demonstrated to the point of exhaustion correct technique and form. The sun was fading (it was a bit after 3:00 p.m., dusk in a Norwegian winter), which meant we'd soon be coming inside, and the very thought of undressing this whole fleet of soggy astronauts made my spine go floppy, and, as it turned out, my jaw go rigid. My whole backside was plastered with snow that fell off in big slabs when I lurched into the house to grab Randall's phone call.

"You wouldn't believe it, sweetheart," Randall laughed from the receiver, "but there are *trolls* everywhere here. Huge troll statues, little troll dolls, troll sweatshirts, troll oven mitts, troll bumper stickers. It's like some kind of troll convention. Wish you could've seen the poor guy in head-to-toe troll gear grilling meatballs. Incredible!"

I tried to conjure the picture. But there in front of me was Jesper, and this boy needed to go to the toilet, and for that he needed help to be undressed all the way down to layer four of seven, his woolen tights. Hard to execute, especially with a phone pinched between ear and shoulder. Randall kept feeding me images:

"And we just passed the biggest ice sculpture I've ever seen. Solid ice. Gorgeous. Mammoth. A Viking ship. Or a polar bear. Or something else, I think."

"Not a troll?" I asked, unzipping Jesper who now lay motionless on his back on my kitchen floor, and I was tugging at his rock solid Cherox snow boots so I could then pull off a couple of layers so he could now waddle, dripping a trail of snow through the whole house, to the bathroom.

"No, no. A moose, maybe? Anyway, I'm thinking winter's really not all that bad here, really, if you can do it like this every time: the press, the cameras, the celebrities, the perfect blue skies. I guess—"

I couldn't make out what he said for all the noise on his end. The phone line exploded in cheers.

"Where *are* you?" I asked him in my loud-but-certainly-not-the-slightest-bit-jealous voice, "What's all the yelling?"

I adjusted the phone in hand, mopping up Jesper's mush tracks with a rag under my foot, all the while keeping an eye on the scene of a whole bunch of trolls and angels including my own two, carving contorted body shapes deep into the white outside. And it's then I realize I'm making big swooping wing motions from my side of the window because these amateurs, they've obviously lost their cadence, like some lost flock of landlocked egrets fallen and flailing on this, a jumbo hunk of Styrofoam.

Randall was at the ice hockey rink where he was sitting only rows— "Only rows, honey!"—behind Hilary Clinton, who'd swung through Norway to support the US hockey team.

Up to that point, even if I was sweating bullets from all the work of managing my ad hoc Olympics, I was smiling. Smiling and nodding there on my end of the conversation. Flapping my wings like any good coach would from the sidelines. Huffing. Fluffing. But in that instant something stung. In my mind, the butting together of those two scenes—the truly Olympic, versus my backyard facsimiles—pinched a nerve.

And just then the hockey team made a goal. Pandemonium from Randall's end of the line, like a gigantic wave, smothered the silence on my end. And Jesper whispered from where he stood behind me in the kitchen doorway, "Parker's Mama?" I turned to meet his forlorn stare. His below-the-waist bareness and wide open eyes. They announced that he needed me.

Well, I'm not precisely what he needed. He needed toilet paper.

"Mel? Hon? Still there? Hey, if you can hear me, I got you a *great sweater* for Valentine's Day. Please tell the kids I'll bring them back real *troll hair.*"

Laughter. A roar for a missed goal, sounds like.

"Honey? . . . Mel . . . ?"

Some moments say more than one can grasp in the instant they strike. This was one of those moments. There I was in bigger-than-life Norway, the momentary focal point of the globe. Important people were discussing important things somewhere other than where I was; and even if the people and their conversations hadn't been terribly important, at least big people were together discussing *something*.

I realize too late that what set me up for this moment's nerve pinch was the letters from the day before—snail mail in those days before Facebook or even email—letters written and addressed by hand from Robin and Anne, actresses I'd worked with in my last show.

From Robin:

> *Hey, you! Wondering if you've frozen to death yet or could be talked into sneaking back to New York to finish the run. Everyone's starting to look for new roles about now. My cabaret act got a good write up in the* Times. *Jeri and Dori and John are all going on to other off-Broadway stuff, Roy's doing* Forever Plaid, *Tamara's been picked up by a major recording studio in Nashville. Someone else got a lead in the international tour of* Grease.*
>
> *You learning to ski now, or what, exactly?*

Writes Anne:

> *Just landed a national tour. Emily got a lead at the Roundabout and Bob, as you know, has opened as the lead in* Jekyl and Hyde. *Jean's up for a mini-series lead. Mark's up for a soap opera. Scott's doing voice-overs and a Disney soundtrack. But no one's done this disappearing act that you have, Melissa. We're watching the Olympics expecting a camera to show you somewhere. So, are you hiding, or what? Just do me a favor and don't forget where you're needed! We really miss you. Tons of love, darling!*

Standing in the kitchen with New York on my mind, Lillehammer in my ear, and a line of trolls at my window made me, I don't know, maybe the slightest bit Bruce Banner. Only a tad mouth-frothingly, schizophrenically Hulk. No, I wasn't popping the seams out of my ski pants or ripping the zipper out of my parka, but the earth beneath me seemed to be splitting, and I winced as I saw a scary fracture wrenching apart two geographies: Randall's World/Melissa's World. Parallel places but cloven. Not only did the world of theater and my whole identity that was tied up in that world feel as far away as the other shore of an ocean, but I had the feeling my husband's world, which to this point had overlapped rather neatly with mine, was now far, far apart from mine. Instead of being *there*, I was *here*. And all we had to link us was the fickle filter of a phone exchange.

The day before, I'd been grousing somewhat, pacing in circles inside my journal. This very feeling had been percolating close to my surface:

R. and I used to run side by side and cross the finish line in stride when we ran our 10k races. Always. But it looks as if "in stride" will take some time to figure out in this new life. Things feel wildly off-kilter. Off balance. Asymmetrical. We're having such totally different experiences. His days are structured, task-driven, cradled in a webwork of professional relationships, defined by a title, office, direct-reports. From day one he's had to function in Norwegian, which means there's little bandwidth left—or is that little need?— for questions about identity. It's intimidating for him, the expectations at work, and he says so every night as we "Ceiling Talk" in bed. But the same people making demands are the ones cheering him on. And he's energized by the need to rise to a high level of professional scrutiny. So, panel, do we see any problem with this? Should the wife be anything but happy for him? Incredibly proud? My guy isn't out of his element; he's actually finding his!

But my element? Hmmm. I'm in the role the expatriate world calls the "trailing spouse." So tell me, what Cro-Magnon fool came up with that cunning label? I try not to think it, let alone utter it. Reminds me of a squaw who has to walk ten paces behind her husband. Trailing? Try NOT.

"Thanks, sweetheart, for the sweater," I said. And I meant those words. *He is thoughtful, generous, attentive, has always trumped me on gift-giving. Look, he's even given us beautiful Norway.*

But this same guy hadn't heard my words over the hockey rink bedlam. A goal for the Finns. His voice punched with an "Agh!" then an "Ohhh!" then something that sounded like "Va noover hornkity ickmehooty klerp gong," a spotty Norwegian exchange with another male voice, one of his many ready-made friends from work. And then the big crash of men's laughter.

And with that, I handed a roll of toilet paper to Jesper.

"Mel? I can't hear you so well," Randall yelled, "So if you can make out what I'm saying, *Thanks, hon. I miss you so much here!*"

Click.

Jesper, with his strawberry blonde hair and meek glance, thanked me for the potty assistance, and I watched him clod out the door, watched him join all the children, watched the shadows falling while confetti snow began tumbling over the whole darkening horizon. I'd braved snow and dusk like this in the risky one-to-two hour haul from New Jersey to New York. Only a few weeks earlier, this had been the scene:

"She might have wet her pants just a second ago, darling, I'm so sorry!" I'm booming bullet points over the din of passing semis, doing that daily Chinese fire drill of passing our children and last minute instructions through car windows, hefting bodies and car seats and duffles of gear into Randall's idling Subaru in a parking lot south of Newark.

"Wipies outside pocket backpack! Hand sanitizer, inside pocket. Really, I am so sorry, honey! Really! Dinner set out on counter! You got her? Watch out, her head. Parker, can you be a fast climber for us all and get up into your booster seat for Daddy? Please?"

Thanks to a clot at a tollbooth I'm running late and, stepping on the gas, I glance into my rearview mirror, flicking my wrist in a goodbye wave as I screech out in a beeline heading north. My mind takes off in circles heading inward. Hope he drives slowly, reads to them tonight. Did I lay books on their beds? Alright concentrate. Did he check the car seat buckle? When's the last time we reviewed the Heimlich? That's it. Now, focus, focus. Buh-reeeathe.

Every night after the razzmatazz of a live performance, I make my return trek to New Jersey. I keep myself alert and hydrated by swigging tepid water from a plastic gallon jug like a hillbilly guzzles moonshine, jug propped on my elbow, head titled way back from behind the wheel. By the time I hit Route 1, it is always close to 1:00 a.m. and my adrenaline is on empty. So I save a certain ritual for the Exit 8 ramp: Keeping one eye on the road and another in the rearview mirror, I squint against the tug and slowly peel off my false eyelashes.

Here in a kitchen in a snug wooden house outside of Oslo I squint too, but against another vague tug that I sense while watching children through a window. I stare at the raw pine floor, where a puddle of snowmelt spreads in a dark pool around my boots. New York and Lillehammer feel a world away, impossibly removed from my world where tottering, snow-encased angel-trolls are now lined up outside along the floor-to-ceiling window smashing their pug noses and smearing slime on a frosty pane that barely muffles the odd music that's Norwegian. Then I don't hear the soundtrack of voices anymore. I'm fixed deeply on this row of children, their pillowy faces pressed to the transparency, mouths and nostrils shooting little gusts of spirit that cling to the glass. Like ragged circles of moist gauze. It's only then that I notice this most amazing thing: Parker and Claire, heads bobbing easily while their mouths speak Norwegian, tumbling and climbing with these others from whom they're indistinguishable, these small bodies weaving in and out of lights and shadows.

That Saturday would be Randall's last spent up at the Olympics. He returned with stories and sweaters, which I received (he told me this during Ceiling Talk that night) with fatigued enthusiasm. (Dang. I thought I'd practiced my lines better than that.) I was trying to adjust, I told him from my bed pillow, just trying to figure out how to do this new mute troll mother role I'd landed, and I didn't want to weigh him down, distract, or worry him. Besides, I said through a tight jaw, I was still recovering from the games I'd held, and was nursing a cramp in the lower back I'd gotten hoisting the last of all the children in and out of angel moulds, toilets, and layer upon layer of clothing. That's the reason for these dumb tears, I told him. A mild lumbar strain. That's the only reason.

The next day I don my brand new Lillehammer sweater, figuring that sitting in front of Barney videos would be more painful than braving a miserably cold day with my two at a place in town called Frogner Park. We drive right up to its wrought-iron gates in Kirkeveien and, for a modest fortune, park there. We struggle out of the heated interior of our family sedan, bundle, boot, and lug a couple of *rumpe brett* (literally "bum boards") through the entrance. Except for that lumbar kink that makes me walk like Quasimodo on his way to rehab, I had all engines revved to be in top mothering form. I can pour myself into this moment, I think, drink in the spartan beauty of the winter setting and have fun with these two adorable barna of mine.

Child latched to each hand, I see straight through those big gates and up through the central colonnade of trees to one of the most stunning revelations of my life: the Vigeland sculptures. We trudge over speed bumps of snow dodging three human blades, the cross country skiers I'd been told to watch for. These rangy figures are cutting deep symmetrical grooves that crisscross the vast park grounds, making a latticework of the snowfield. Either that, or the Norse gods have tossed a handful of silver pick-up sticks onto a fitted white bed sheet.

We first cross a wide bridge lined with bronze statues of dancing and wrestling humans on either side, then notice a discreet pathway feeding down to the left of the head of the bridge to an islet, a lip enclosed in low hedges. Here's the sculpture nursery, where all the statues are crawling babies, pudgy toddlers, small bodies playing with their toes, a perfectly curled fetus balancing on its head. Dragging our sleds along a washboard of ice, we approach a large fountain around which bronze men and women spin and reel, arms entwined or swinging free, legs leaping or folded, perpetual motion rendered static in metal. The fountain stands at the base of broad stairs that mount to the heart of the collection, the obelisk. Still holding their hands, I search for the clumps of meaty twigs that are my own children's fingers inside their gloves and clasp them firmly in triplicate—squeeze-squeeze-squeeze—our code for "I Love You." From the right and from the left, come back three soft squeezes each. Love in stereo.

We hike up the stairs, we three lovers.

In front of us is this soaring column of squirming bodies trapped in granite. I begin weaving, my children on each side of me, between the clusters of human forms that are situated in tiers of three on the steps ascending to the stage where the column stands. The kids want to climb on top of all twenty-four of them. There are the girls, standing in a knot with heads together and arms wrapped around shoulders; then the child riding bareback on the mother who plays on her knees; the babies, the parents comforting their small children, the couples holding tight, the old man cradling the old woman in his arms and all stages of progression, all the shapes and stages of life in between. It took the sculptor Gustav Vigeland forty years, half his life, to complete this, his magnum opus. I am completely into this place.

But Parker and Claire are mostly into the snow, and they begin catapulting off snow banks and sliding down icy slopes. "En, to, tre!" (one, two, three) Parker calls down from the top steps of the monolith terrace. His volume has a way of splitting the sea so passers-by know: I'm comin' down. And I'm comin' down fast.

"En, to, tre-e-e-e-e!!" he barks the threat again. And with that, he torpedoes head first down the slickest, steepest hill of them all, the slope at the foot of which Claire is standing, watching with wonder as the little puffs of frozen air float up out of her mouth. I see it coming. But I'm slowed by back pain and can't move fast enough to flop myself across the line of approach as an interception. And in one smack, Parker bashes into Claire at shin level and knocks her into the air. Clean into it. She flies. And flies. She falls. She lands with a crack flat on her belly. And her face.

Parker's still traveling. Like a guided missile, he meets head-on with a wall of snow. Now Claire's screaming, stopping Dobermans in their tracks, sending winter ravens cawing into the sky as if they'd been electrocuted on the branches of trees. I race on ice to my children, Quasimodo on Quaaludes, slipping, grunting, floundering, moaning, losing traction at every step, and calling in gulps of stinging-cold air, *"I'm here! Mama's here!!"* I dive to my knees, pulling Claire into my arms where I cradle her close to my chest. A badly slit lip and ice abrasions on her forehead, but otherwise no bumps on the skull, which I finger through her sweaty blonde hair. Teeth? All there. Tongue? Not severed. No glassiness in her stare. She's not lost anything but bladder control, which I can tell by texture and smell on my thigh where I'm holding her so she can be close to my heart.

Parker is just clamoring to his feet, his face a paper maché mask of snow with a seeping ring of red around his nose. Beautiful, nearly, against all that white. He's laughing, kind of, but only for the instant before he meets my cutting stare, before he sees blood on Claire, which makes him reach up instinctively to touch a glove to his warm nose.

Blood.

Operatic duet of grand howling and curdled gagging that paints scarlet the pale and disapproving skies that now sink lower and lower over Frogner Park.

I lean into this Wailing Wall of the Wounded taking both children in my arms, and I sway, sway slowly in silence, eyes closed, mouthing a string of curses and prayers, while the children shout accusations at each other like two gorillas in heat. I hold my eyes tightly shut. To not see. To not be seen. There in my sightless invisibility, I think I feel the shadows of onlookers weighing on my back judging the three of us: Woman Exorcising Tots with Demons.

This unholy pietà rocks and rocks back and forth and I hum and hum, trying to cover not just the noise of my children's fear and anger, but the inner noise of my own. And we just stay like that for a long time until the sun disappears fully behind the cold edge of the world.

"En, to, tre," I groan, lifting my two to their feet. A handful of snow and I've rubbed off most of the blood. A couple of firm brushes, and the ice is off our knees. I readjust mittens, pull woolen caps over matted hair, circle my shoulders, and suck in enough cold air to give me the confidence to turn around and graciously wave off the stares of what I'm convinced are dozens of people judging this scene of family bliss. Ah, those judges I fear. Those jeering, stony judges.

Stony indeed.

I turn to realize that only Vigeland's monoliths hover over me, and concede that they're too preoccupied with their own place in the cycle of life to take notice of our bloody huddle. Next to them, in the last fading spotlight of sun amid the expanse of gray, is a Bassett hound alone, sitting, watching. I meet his eyes, which stare through me as he tilts his head. Inquisitiveness? Or indifference?

We would come back to Frogner Park many, many times over the years. It was just what I'd been told it was in fall, spring, and high summer when rollerbladers replaced cross-country skiers and when the bronze sculptures and humans were hard to tell apart.

But to this day, those monoliths always evoke, before any and all other seasons, the dead of winter, that first winter of our new lives together. When stones and flesh taught me something eternal. Those lessons remain preserved—frozen—in that bitter cold memory when the three of us showed up to discover some artist's attempt at the cycle of life, and discovered, instead, each other.

4

JEG ER NORSK

I t might be the chilliest 17th of May I've ever known in my life, but heat's rising. We're all gathered in the center of Oslo at the top of Karl Johans street in an open commons at the foot of Slottsvei, the road that comes down from the royal palace. There's a scowling sky that might unload rain any moment, and the wind keeps licking over what looks like a sea of flags. That's a lot of licking. There are a lot of flags. I'd say there are more flags than people, even, since everyone seems to be holding, waving or wearing at least one.

"We" could mean all four-point-something-million Norwegians— at least it seems the whole country is here today—but here, "we" is our family plus Aaron, my visiting brother, and our friends the Karls-sons and the Bakkens. We're their guests at what is, right along with Christmas or the Holmenkollen Ski Jumping Championships, the peak event of the year. It's Norway's Constitution Day, when the country cele-brates its final cut from a tangled history of imposed rule by Sweden. The long path toward the victory of self-determination began when Norway drafted its first Constitution in 1814 and claimed autonomy, then skipped back under Swedish rule, until finally declaring itself independent on May 17, 1905.

I've got an idea of what national holidays like this are about, at least those I've witnessed close up in Austria, Germany, and the States. So when Bente Karlsson tips me off early in the week that this is very *høytidelig*, meaning we should all dress in our finest attire (the Karlssons and Bakkens will be in national costume), I'm baffled.

Høytidelig, before I look it up, means, literally, "high time-ly." But a "high time" to the American in me means firecrackers, high school bands and marching squads, stilt walkers, clowns scooping manure, and bloated cartoon characters blimping in the air above Main Street, noise makers, megaphones, floats with beauty queens who dispense taffy. A bazooka-and-hullabaloo sort of "high time."

How we're all going to sit in plastic lawn chairs in the gutters and manage our Coleman ice chest lunch on a blanket while dressed in our Sunday best has got me curious. Randall's going to look silly waving sparklers in a tie. I'll have a hard time diving for taffy in heels.

Bente and her Swedish sister-in-law, Pia, have to gently school me here about what a high time means in Norway. Bente was lucky; she knew the codes from birth. Pia, married to Bente's brother, Børre, was less lucky because she was a latecomer. She was adopted into Norwegianness at around twenty, but made up for her lateness by being a quick study. Now, twenty years later, she is totally indistinguishable (in accent and loyalties) from her whole Norwegian family.

Bente's husband, Jan Åke, is also a Swede, meaning he and Pia could have formed a little resistance had they been rabble-rousers. But they didn't. Even when not around the rest of the family they spoke Norwegian to one another. Something about Norway worked like a spell.

"No, Melissa, we won't need Coleman ice chests," says Bente.

"And," adds Pia, "there won't be clowns or cheerleaders."

"Or blimps," Jan Åke shrugs.

What? No stretch convertible limo dressed as a paper maché alligator? (I know, I know. I couldn't picture a parade without one any more than you can.)

"What there will be," Bente tells me, "is *barna*."

"The children wave to King Harald and Queen Sonja," Pia says softly.

"And the King and Queen will wave back to them," Bente pantomimes waving. And seems to be teary-eyed.

I start to get the point, take my friends at their word, and dressed myself, my husband, and two children accordingly. Shoes and handbag matched. Ties cinched. Hair licked in place. We are set for a high time.

Down in Oslo's city center, the procession begins, and if we crane our necks just enough, all of us in our party can see the beginnings of the *barnatog*, or children's parade which, like a colorful tide, is pushing its way from the bottom of Karl Johans street up past us and toward the palace where the royal family waits to wave. Considering the throngs, we're pretty well positioned. All of us, that is, but our own children, who seem to be missing whatever magical Norwegian gene keeps a best-dressed preschooler solemn while standing for two and a half hours in a frigid public square waiting to catch a glimpse of even one of several hundred flag-waving, well-wishing, elementary-school-aged children. Thirty minutes into this, and already it's becoming clear that whatever it takes to really appreciate the moment, Parker doesn't have it, so Randall practically has to sit on our boy to keep him from hucking dusty gravel at every national costume in sight.

The name for the sumptuous hand-embroidered heavy wool (and very expensive) national costumes is *bunad*, and on this 17th of May there are many, many bunads to huck gravel at. Aaron—you would love my baby brother—is twenty-something, single, camera-wielding, and has long since disappeared into the blonde bunad forest. We won't see him again until later after he's taken two-hundred pictures and four pages of names and phone numbers.

Then we hear music—singing—nothing piercing or piped-in or thundering from truck-top loudspeakers; just the mellow stream of children's voices sailing atop the sea of small bodies and banners that is slowly coming our way. The sound is artless, unaccompanied, uncomplicated and pristine. It hushes the talking among us, freezes Parker mid-huck. It's some sort of Happy Camper song, and Tobias and Joachim Karlsson, handsome teenagers in traditional costume, seem to know it like most everyone surrounding me. They're half-grinning, nodding, and humming. Pia and Børre are lipping the text with their girls, Ninnie and Rikke, recalling what is, I'm wagering, a barnepark standard.

The first wave of singing children gushes past me, their eyes alternately furtive, worn-out, enthusiastic or mischievous, and the women in my group let out a collective coo. So much tousled white hair, so many missing teeth, such innocence and simplicity merged into one bright stroke of color. Something happens to my impatience. I stop toeing gravel and find myself softened and stirred at once; one great big shivering smoothie.

The Karlssons' oldest son, Christian, is standing next to me. Towering, actually. He's a well-limbed tree, a sparkling sample, if there ever was one, of Norwegian young manhood, Aaron's age but he seems at least a foot taller (and Aaron's tall himself). Christian can remember the time he got to *gå på tog* (walk in the parade) and *hilse på Kongen* (greet the king), and gets that faraway, kind of homesick look in his eyes.

All these people around me, I'm realizing, had done it, in fact; herded up Karl Johans street with their school class, bearing flags, singing school songs from some common Norwegian Folk Melodies binder. Everyone has to do it once, I'm told. It's a rite of passage.

Beginning toward the bottom of the river of children rises a modest rustling of applause, the sound of a sudden surge of water coursing over rocks. "*Russ,*" Christian says to me, not taking his eyes off the scene as if he's a storm watcher and is whispering a tornado warning. I get up on my tippy-toes so I can see two big patches of red and blue like vibrating, opposing soccer teams, coming at us.

Russ is an untranslatable term really, but is roughly the Norwegian equivalent of "high school senior." These graduating classes spend the whole last month of high school dressed in either a red or blue jumpsuit, the color signaling their projected direction of further study: liberal arts (red) or technical/trade school (blue).

Like competing squadrons of mechanics, they then drive around in big buses they've bought collectively, painted, and plastered with graffiti. Starting in May you see these buses littered all over the landscape like escapees from a KOA campground. The kids form kibbutzim around these parked carcasses: it's where they live, get drunk, get stoned, get wild, get crazy. The Partridge Family meets Woodstock.

At first glance, the Russ *tog* is an absolute head-banging opposite of everything dainty the children were: they're rowdy and obnoxious; they're barking Metallica lyrics and shoving each other into bushes, and some kids who come closest to us smell of booze though it's not even noon yet.

Then there are those goofy jumpsuits. I can't get my brain around them, and my mind wanders off into all sorts of dim deviations about jumpsuit origins, jumpsuit design, jumpsuit factories, and shipping orders, and overstock. Then suddenly a girl with brown braids and blue polka dots painted all over her red jumpsuit and face is launched from someone's shoulders and lands, arms flailing, around Randall's neck. A real, speckled bombshell. We exchange glances, my destabilized husband and I, and, laughing hard, help her stagger back into the red and blue current, the blue polka dots growing purple on her flushed cheeks.

Børre steps in to explain away his country's bad manners: this is all within the understood limits of Russ decorum, he says. The kids know how far they can go, Christian says. They're under so much pressure to conform all year long, Pia says, that now they know they can let loose. There are limits, Jan Åke nods. Always limits, Bente double nods.

These big kids aren't so different from the little ones, I think. Each tog offers a context, which empowers its participants to do things they probably never would do were they alone. Children, surrounded by like children, buried in the security of a group, can yodel in front of thousands while marching right up a main thoroughfare to greet a king and queen. Russ, surrounded by like Russ, buried in the uniformity of a group (and beneath the anonymity provided by ill-fitting Jiffy Lube duds) can catapult themselves into crowds and carouse 'til the cows come home. All without consequence. They can do it, in fact, with the whole country's— not to mention the king's and queen's—blessing.

Maybe I need to give you a closer translation for the word tog. A tog is both a "train" and a "parade," the dictionary will tell you. "Train" gets you close: it's a moving, linked vehicle that progresses on parallel tracks. Although composed of pieces, it forms a unit and that whole unit travels in absolute unison. A Norwegian tog is not really a "parade" in the American sense but is, I decide, a "procession." A procession's about community over the individual: the engine, cars, caboose, and tracks make a train. We move together. We sing together. We wear train conductor outfits together. Individual children are no longer Mette, Sven, Kari, Astrid, or Geir. They're something else, a fused something else, and one of their songs exclaims it: "*Vi er norske barn!*" ("We are Norwegian children!") The teens, too, are no longer Tarjei, Silje, Louisa or Anne-Marit. They're a bigger thing, a big amalgamated identity, as one of *their* chants exclaims: "*Vi er norske Russ!*"

At no point do I hear, "We Are the Champions."

Why? Because a procession makes you think horizontally, sideways, always keeping things level and watching out for your neighbor, we do not compete or race—we will all arrive at the royal palace as one. There are no honking jalopies and unicycle flame throwers, no entertainment in that sense to distract us from the essential. The mood here is subdued, the sound level is restrained, Russ included.

A procession is *høytidelig*—solemn—and a procession is Norwegian. And Norwegians love a procession.

Unlike a procession, in a parade the individual *I* comes before the communal *We*. You advertise disparate and distinct entities. In an American parade you *parade* things; you advertise. Period. Your normal Fourth of July parade is a three-hour string of competing floats, competing bands, competing beauty queens, competing convertibles, all bearing banners for the likes of State Farm Insurance, the Shriner's Charity Car Wash, or Porky's All-You-Can-Eat-Rib-and-Spud-Split-Your-Gut Buffet. It's a distinct entity upon distinct entity panorama tied together by an emcee and a few renegade jugglers.

A parade advertises not only its individual parts, but its cause (on the Fourth of July its ostensible cause is Liberty), and that with clamoring, sometimes ear-splitting, commotion. Think of Katie Couric's prolonged hoarseness after shouting into her mic over the din of the Macy's Thanksgiving Day Parade. But our pilgrim fathers were solemn guys, I thought.

So what? So an American parade is loud. We Americans would like to think it's loud because it's proud. It's vociferous, boisterous, explosive like fireworks. It's supposed to get you up and outta your lawn chair. It's designed to make you think vertically, head-and-shoulders-above-the-rest. Up! Sky's-the-Limit! Its flow is punctuated by the sharp blasts of trumpets, their bells pointed to the clouds. Its beat is aggressive, combative even, with snare drums rattling your nerves and big bass drums heading up the rear, quaking the ground and shaking your Coleman ice chest. It's a spectacle, entertainment, sometimes breathtakingly tacky, sometimes—think of a Sousa march detonated by a polished marching band—spine-chillingly stirring.

A high time.

A parade is American.

And Americans love a parade.

Our speckled Russ friend has just regained her footing when a voice over a loudspeaker announces flatly that we will all now sing our national *Hymne.* Russ and barna and every single body across the stretch of my vision stops dead in their tracks. And I hear the song for the first time, soft orchestral score broadcast over the heads of thousands of common singers whose voices weave in and out of tree branches:

Ja, vi elsker dette landet,
Som det stiger frem,
Furet, værbitt over vannet
Med de tusen hjem . . .

Yes, we love with fond devotion
This, our land that looms
Rugged, storm-scarred o'er the ocean,
With her thousand homes.

I understand at least that much of the text, and can't help but draw a comparison between it and "The Star-Spangled Banner," a very different poem entirely. The first is a hymn to the land itself—the soil, the mountains, the pines, the water—to the country's violent beauty, wounded physicality, to its protective powers and to the powers that have protected it. It looks horizontally, drawing together community.

The second is an anthem constructed around a military scene and the image of the flag held high. It looks vertically, over the ramparts where there are rockets and bombs bursting in air, and over the towering steep where it waves in triumph *over* the land of the free and the brave.

Whatever the comparisons and contrasts are, the moment is a Kodak one. Christian's baritone is barely discernible, but I'm taking his lead. We sing two verses while everyone stays perfectly still. I can pick out individual children's, teenagers' and adults' voices, and I feel I'm standing not only in sudden harmony, but in a sacred moment. I turn when the song ends to see Christian, and he shakes his head once, takes a deep breath, and closes those eyes to whisper, "*Jeg . . . er . . . Norsk.*"

I am Norwegian.

What it means to be *Norsk* fills up more than a few dinner conversations over the five years we live in Norway. But on that first 17th of May we get a good overview in one evening eating outside on the Bakken's terrace. Between Børre's grilled ribs and salmon steaks, Pia's mustard herring, Bente's new potatoes, our first taste of *lefsa*, a special bread, all washed down with nonstop sparkling cider, we start to peel back the layers of Norway's very special breed of patriotism.

To understand being Norwegian, Bente begins, you must first understand *Janteloven*. Ha, but I'd already learned about that word from Idar, a common friend of ours from church who happened to be a linguist. I told the whole 17th of May table this same story I'd told Idar. It happened at barnepark: Tante Britt approached me one afternoon when I arrived to pick up Parker and Claire at the Blakstad fence. Her eyes lowered, Britt told me there was a problem.

"*Et problem? Hva er det?*" What was the problem, I needed to know.

"*Problemet er med matpakken.*" Britt was telling me the problem was the sack lunches I'd been packing. She was still smiling, but was also a bit uneasy, I saw this.

"*Med matpakkene?*" Their sack lunches? I'd taken careful note what the other children were bringing: sliced whole grain bread with one chunk of cheese or some liverwurst or both; a thermos with a drink. I'd copied the exact menu for my two.

Well, okay. Almost. There *were* those raisins. I'd brought a supply of mini boxes from the States. You know, the friendly little red box with the smiling brunette in a white bonnet on the front?

Britt lowered her eyes and stretched out her hand, empty raisin box in the curve of her palm.

"*Dette er problemet.*"

This was the problem? I stared at the slightly smashed box.

"*Det er ikke lov,*" Britt whispered.

This is not allowed? What, was Parker using them as B-Bs during song time? Or had Claire been stuffing them up her nose? Or up Thea's?

Softly but with undeniable gravitas, Britt explained that none of the other park children had such exotic additions to their lunches. So my children could no longer bring them. "If everyone can't have them, no one can have them," she explained. "You wouldn't want your children distinguishing themselves like this, of course."

Of course.

Det er ikke lov, I'd heard every day, it seemed. But the phrase Britt used for "distinguish themselves"—*skille seg ut*—I didn't understand. Still, when I heard it, I nodded and tisked audibly at myself. *Skille seg ut,* as Britt said it, sounded scandalous, nasty. No, heaven forbid, I most certainly did not want *that* for my children.

So it was to our linguist friend, Idar, that I had turned. He explained the whole context behind the raisin ban and anything else that might not be allowed because it might distinguish one person from another. *Janteloven.* Idar cocked his head, let out a big sigh, swinging his head languidly from left to right. And then he went on to tell me that Janteloven (literally; the laws of Jante) is a creed governing a fictional village (Jante) created by Danish/Norwegian author Aksel Sandemose in his novel, *En flygtning krysder sit spor* (*A Refugee Crosses His Tracks*). In this work, the author satirizes the Scandinavian effort to reinforce egalitarianism by squelching ambition and discouraging originality.

The ten laws of Jante are as follows:

- Don't think that *you* are special.
- Don't think that you are of the same standing as *us*.
- Don't think that you are smarter than *us*.
- Don't fancy yourself as being better than *us*.
- Don't think that you know more than *us*.
- Don't think that you are more important than *us*.

- Don't think that *you* are good at anything.

- Don't laugh at *us*.

- Don't think that anyone cares about *you*.

- Don't think that you can teach *us* anything.[1]

In light of these laws and in retrospect, I now understand that I got away with being outspoken, driven, and maybe a bit quirky (red Dolly Parton boots) only because I was an outsider, an American. The rules of Jante didn't *really* apply to me. Or at least, they did not apply to me as seriously, say, as they did to my children, who were testing limits with their snack food. Pushing the raisin box.

Janteloven: my Norwegian friends had mixed feelings about it. Kjersti, a young Norwegian student, had cautioned us early on about responding correctly to the typical greeting, "*Hvordan går det?*" (How are you?) Kjersti lowered her voice to emphasize that it was socially unacceptable to say anything but "just fine." Anything else would be excessive and would border on self-importance. It was not suitable, not Norwegian, to be anything more than just fine. Sure, you can answer that you're bad or awful, but not great or terrific. Because neither you nor your day, mind you, can be going any better than your neighbor's.

Some friends loved to tell me how, when there was a temporary stretch of oil rationing, their King Olav rode the public streetcars just like everyone else did. Skis in hand, poles slung over his shoulder, His Royal Highness was the model of Janteloven equality.

A local minister who invited me to solo at an event in his church took me down after the concert into the *sakristie*, or casket room. Every last casket he showed me—dozens of them lined up in the room—was a simple pine box. No elaborate sarcophagi, no mahogany coffins lined in red velvet, no hand-carved walnut *objets d'art* with ornate gold plated hinges and brass locks and wiring for an internal stereo system. Every last one was the selfsame pine box. Every Norwegian went into the earth in the identical box. King Olav, even, the streetcar king himself, would be buried just as the streetcar ticket checker himself, in one of those boxes one day.

"And his headstone?" I asked.

"Same size as everyone else's," said the minister. "The state has set strict guidelines regarding height limit, and there are equally strict rules for inscriptions, font, decoration." I got excited, if you can imagine the scene, looking at a row of nearly identical grave markers lined up like dominoes against the back wall. The minister might have thought I was irreverent, but then he'd probably never seen Napoleon's, Mao's, or Lenin's tombs. He merely smacked his lips, wrinkled his brow, and smiled the worn out smile of someone who's watched plenty of these boxes go underground.

In death, as in life, in Norway there would be no tall-poppy *or* tall-headstone syndrome.

A highly trained doctor of science at Randall's work was formally forbidden, after a vote taken among the secretaries, to use her "Dr." title when signing letters. "What happens with me, then," the ringleader secretary asked, "who doesn't have such a fine title?"

Børge Ousland, polar explorer, who'd trained for years by dragging stacks of winter radials tied to his waist in and out of fjords in various degrees of frozenness in order to complete the two-month-long, first-ever solo crossing of the Antarctic, and whom Randall was able to meet and interview on the topic of individual motivation—even he called that stupendous feat a "good challenge" but nothing to "act proud about."

Another friend, Rut, taught me there were addendums to the ten laws of Jante. We knew already that you should never brag or express confidence or be enthusiastic about yourself. But you should never brag about having a good job. Or a strong horse. You should not mention the brand of your car. Your tractor. The location of your house. If it has a deck, view to the water, plumbing. You should not publicly praise your husband. You must not strive. You are not "gifted." You are not entitled to any exceptions for any reason due to talent, birthright or ambition. Keep your head low. Keep your personal goals knee-high where all of us can reach them, just like you. Do not distinguish yourself. Think small.

And oooo, you shall never, ever, *ever* brag about your children. Call them whatever you want, but it must be average or worse.

By about now, I'm almost certain there are some Norwegians reading who'll take umbrage with what I'm saying. Some will claim I'm exaggerating, or more likely, that I'm equating being laid back (as Norway generally is) with being suppressed in some fundamental way (which of course not all of Norway is) or that these people are somehow proud of their humility (which, actually, many Norwegians, laughing at the topic and themselves, say is sometimes true). But two things are true beyond question. First, you get five minutes into a chat with a Norwegian and, bingo!, Janteloven pops up. Everyone has their stories. And believe me, some are at least as interesting as mine. Second, times are rapidly changing in Norway, as everywhere. Last time I visited, there were small red boxes of raisins available in every grocery store.

I went on to learn more about the practical application of Janteloven. It helped me understand why my neighbor's seven-year-old daughter had been forbidden by the principal to ride her bike to school even though it was a four-minute ride on a marked path directly from her back door. Was there really a safety issue in question? No. It was because not *all* of the school children are able to ride bikes at the age of seven. And if all can't bike, yet she does, they would feel underprivileged. The girl should not incite feelings of inferiority in others.

Of course, the school policy allows for all children, beginning at age ten, to ride bikes to school. But don't be surprised, if you bike before that age, to find your bike chain confiscated by undercover vigilante Janteloven enforcers.

I started seeing evidence of Janteloven everywhere. When my friend complained about the Norwegian singer, Sissel Kyrkjebø, having been "good until she began to think she was somebody," this was evidence of Janteloven. When Sissel chose to crop her waist-length, blonde hair into an ingénue pixie-cut and color it chocolate brown, the whole country seemed offended. Was she trying to distinguish herself? Was she getting just a wee bit uppity? Maybe someone needed to rein her in, needed to hold her down. Sissel, the story continues, withstood these sideway glances of suspicion, married a Dane, kept her hair cropped, and has enjoyed a steady, healthy rise in popularity singing a wide repertoire in which traditional folk tunes and old, Lutheran hymns figure heavily.

But you'd have to see her perform to comprehend the effect: she is utterly unassuming, unglamorized, understated. And captivatingly beautiful, both musically and physically. Maybe the public has tried to look past her "look," giving her compensation points for sticking mostly with their country's traditional music and not philandering too much with flashy sorts.

It says something that, when she was selected to sing the mystical, humming underscore of the opening credits of James Cameron's *Titanic*, the Norwegian press pounced on the thing like it was a huge break—not for Sissel's career, but for Norway's visibility. Papers were quick to say that Sissel was "proud to be able to represent her country in this manner."

There was, as I'd noticed that first winter in Norway, one special twist to Janteloven. I witnessed this at the Olympic Games. Even before the broadcasting of the games began, Norway's own press had the entire country set up to not expect much from these games. The Norwegian officials, analysts and commentators prepared their country for a passable, but not extraordinary, kind of show. "The most ordinary Olympic

Games ever!" the campaign seemed to go. We're a little country, the media soberly reminded everyone. Lillehammer is a little town. Will you look at us? We have little experience in big happenings. We're simple folk. Small fries. Pitiful, meek trolls, all.

Who can help but compare the manner of the athletes like Italian downhill racer Alberto Tomba (also known as "Tomba la Bomba"), the swarthy and showy Casanova of the Slopes who takes the silver medal in slalom, with Norwegian gold medalist in the super-G, Kjetil André Aamodt? Muscle-flexing, skirt-chasing, media-hungry Tomba seems to have a whole, manicured speech in his back pocket, fingertip-kissing finalé and all. There's no question in anyone's mind (including Tomba's) that this Adonis is God's gift to the slopes. Amid shrieking worthy of a rock star, he swaggers off my TV screen.

Then the camera pans to Aamodt. He's looking more like he just sauntered in from clearing an entire forest than from waxing his brows. He's comfortably disheveled, half-smiling, and clearly camera-shy.

"So how does it feel, Ka-jettel, to be one of *the* most decorated Alpine skiers in history?! Tell us how that must *feel!*" The American reporter leans into the question.

Aamodt scratches his jaw and ducks his head.

"C'mon and tell us, Shettel!" another reporter yells. "What do you have to say about your amaaazing job here, huh?!!"

There's a brief pause.

Aamodt hums. He haws. Then he clears his throat, head still ducking and says something to the effect of:

"Well, I think I could've done a bit better, maybe, but I guess I did my best and, well, I was just glad to be able to do something like this for my country."

Supporters standing behind him, some teammates, howl "*Alt for Norge!*" ("Everything for Norway!")

Aamodt ducks his head again, waiting for the camera to go away.

Now, when Norwegian public voices come to wish athletes the best of luck (because they'll sure need it, the tone implies), the athletes themselves bow their heads, already contrite, promising to, oh-ho-hum, give it their best shot. Never do I hear the slightest hint of confidence, even passionate determination.

And while I wait for it, I never once hear a single participant admit to actually wanting—imagine this—*to win.*

Winning for oneself? That kind of contraband, like a box of raisins, never creeps in.

Although lo and behold. Norway goes on to rake in a record-breaking twenty-six medals overall.

That's what you get from telling your kids to mind their raisins and their Janteloven.

ENDNOTES

1. Sandemose, Aksel. *En flyktning krysser sitt spor (A Refugee Crosses His Tracks).* Oslo, Norway: Den norske bokklubben, 1972.

5

NEI!

You know, Melissa—it *is* Melissa, right?—I've *done* my two years here." The woman chewed on her words and picked the speck of lint off the arm of her gray Chicago Bulls sweatshirt while escorting me through her house. It was situated on the top of a snowy precipice so that when I glanced out the huge plate glass windows I saw slopes of inky pines, jutting fists of granite and beyond that a silver fjord meeting the horizon like the cleavage of a book, that perfectly still line where two pages meet.

"Hey, I've paid my dues here, I told Barry," her accent was Midwestern, her volume reached in all directions, "and now it's high time I get back to the real world. I'll tell you something since you're new here: The only way to survive Norway? Get *outta* Norway."

She escorted me through her home decorated with tourist treasures: Black Forest cuckoo clock from Freiburg; dainty tourist spoon collection from Italy; Club Med photo collages from Spain, Greece, the Adriatic; miniature alpine horn from the Swiss Alps (she tooted it for me: a kazoo); glass curio cupboard with plastic dolls clad in synthetic frills "indigenous to all the major European countries," she underscored, adding as an aside, "These babes cost me a freakin' *fortune!*"

She'd traveled two to three weeks out of four, she said, using Norway as a necessary offloading port, sticking around just long enough to keep her farm of ferns watered.

"Forget *this* language!" she said. "Spanish. Now *that's* the future."

Actually, by this time I was trying to inch my way back out her front door, back to her *Welcome!* mat, back into the comforting winter chill. But first I asked her something.

"So, have you been able to make any friends?"

She looked at me like I'd just told her I wasn't much of a Bulls fan. Or spoon fan. Or plastic indigenous dolly fan.

"These Norwegians? You know *these people*. Frosty. Frozen solid, more like. Couldn't get a decent 'Hello' out of one of 'em with a blowtorch. It's like digging out of an avalanche with a crowbar. No chance."

She couldn't have known it, but that woman whom I saw only once, the one whose house was a monument to *not* living in Norway, made me, as much as anything else, *want* to live there. Should I have told her that I had already made many Norwegian friends, and had done so without a blowtorch or crowbar—in fact, without as much as a cigarette lighter?

In my increasing encounters with my neighbors—folks named Sten (stone) and Bjørn (bear)—I began to see proof of something an anthropologist might call *the topographical imperative*. By that, I mean the broad and deep imprint that the elements that make up Norway had on the people of Norway. What I'm talking about is the effects of centuries upon centuries of people pick-axing out an existence on this impenetrable landmass plastered on the top of icedom. Hidden from one another by snowy steppes, ice fields, fjords, and formidable granite mountain ranges throughout long, dark stretches of the year, these people developed a manner, one that newcomers (especially amber-waves-of-grain Americans) might incorrectly call cold, brusque, unwelcoming.

In truth, the manner, other than frostiness, is more a mix of modesty, caution, introversion, and submission to the elements. The centuries of living private lives plus the weightiness of a muted landscape plus the plain hard work needed to just make it out your door in a storm makes Norwegians who they are. You can see the effects in their walk. Measured. Contained. There is a softness in greetings. A practical toughness. Little tolerance for anything as flamboyant or conspicuous as the color pink.

Or red cowboy boots.

Or fishnet stockings.

Unless they're dragging behind your boat and hold the day's catch.

Barnepark was the incubator for all things Børge Ousland-ish. Polar exploration. Solo survival. Winter-radial-tires-harnessed-to-your-park-dress training. That's Norsk. And that begins in barnepark.

Barnepark's purpose, among a few other things, is to whimper-proof the whole population. Because when weather is as fierce as it is in Norway, when the climate is unpredictable or dramatic, there's no room for melodrama. In the heart of an arctic squall or a hammering late-April downpour that has lasted two days straight and promises to go on until Thursday of next week or even next month, there's no patience for whiners. The climate doesn't let up for breakdowns, and it has zero tolerance for snoogly-wooglies. It is training ground for Vikings like Ousland, who know as well as anyone that function (and a polar bear spear and polypropylene thermals) way out-trump form.

An excerpt from my journal:

> Only noon and I've already been stuck twice in the ice thanks to characteristically Norwegian heavy snowfall followed by freezing rain and thanks to the lumbering, back-wheel-drive "safest-vehicle-on-the-road" Swedish wagon of ours that can scarcely creep over a seam in the freeway, let alone our hilly environs. Hello, February. I have slush splattered up to my belt buckle. February. I have grit in my ear canals and frostbite on my eyebrows. February. Now is an unusually blechhhy time of year if you're to focus on the weather, and if you're hoping for beauty in the landscape, you'll want to do a U turn right back into winter. The tons of gravel strewn over four months of icy snow are now grimy gray ice piles along the roadsides. Trees, now free from the weight of several inches of damp snow, are all but bent in half, their limbs frantic ice claws cracked at every joint. Limbo season, we call it, with neither the serene, soft grandeur of white-on-white winter nor the gloriously persistent daylight of spring and summer. Aeeeech, I need to stop complaining. I'll take it over February on the Jersey Turnpike any day.

When I cursed a cloudburst that soaked my fashionable and skimpy jacket and made a sloshing mud pit of the parking area, a pit I now had to mince through and which, yick, got my color-coordinated booties all blechy-yicky, a mild-mannered (and J. Crew model-type) father shared with me a major clue to the universe. He was tugging something over his drenched head that looked like a Navy Seal tarpaulin pop-up tent with armholes and a zipper when he whispered to me one of the key couplets that defines Norway: "*Ikke dårlig vær, bare dårlig klær.*"

No bad weather, only bad clothing.

A couplet, that's right. No more than ten syllables. Done with it. Speech over. The language—like the clothing, like the cuisine, like barnepark, like the philosophy for living—has little need for embellishment. There's no patience for too many adjectives. No mind for prissiness or for any griping about how the wooly mammoth hair leggings itch and, well, be honest: do they make me look chunky? How the rawhide back satchel has no adjustable straps and, *what*? No inner zipper pockets for lip gloss? And how about that twenty kilo horned helmet thingie? Would you just take a look? It totally ruins your blow-dry. And the cut—have you even tried this monster on?—it clearly doesn't make the most of your bone structure. And besides, the molten brass tone is definitely meant for someone with spring coloring, not your summer.

I was always reminded that these were the same folks who, centuries earlier, were not just Vikings pillaging the countryside, but were also simple spit-and-grit farmers who tended their narrow patches of earth sticking out along the steep walls of the west coast's sheer-walled Geiranger fjord. Historians tell us that these farmers used to tie one end of a long rope around their toddlers' waists, and the other end to a boulder. Then the parents could work freely all day, creeping far away from outcropping to outcropping, tilling their scraps of soil knowing that, if their little Viggo happened to make a false step, at least they'd just dangle there until Mama and Papa came home later that day, the lone, hoarse cry of "Mama? Papa?" echoing down the fjord.

A firmly attached rope. A slightly detached parent. You gotta do what you gotta do, and faced with ekeing out your bushel of rutabagas so your whole family survives the bitter winter, sentiment might need to fall by the wayside, if not down the face of the fjord.

Even if it did have a view over Oslofjord, Blakstad barnepark wasn't as perilous a place as that. And in no time at all, it became our creed. Every morning after Dad pulled out for work, Mom began the aerobic exercise of dressing Claire and Parker for cultural and climatological immersion. We'd be greeted midmorning by Britt and her assistants at the entrance of the chain link fence that encircled the park itself. There in the snow (or later, in mud; then later, in dirt), with little more than their own bodies and minds to work with, they spent hours of social integration, language acquisition, team building, fine and gross motor skill development, and spatial patterning.

Imagine what an adjustment it must have been for our Norwegian friends who moved with their small children to Brussels mid-rain season.

There, they showed up the first day to the Belgian equivalent for barne-park, their own children outfitted in indestructible rugged outerwear, only to see the chain of local parents lifting their Pierres and Angeliques and Marie-Claudes and Maximillians from the back of the Peugot and carrying them—tip-toeing over the mud puddles, holding huge umbrellas over their heads (but mostly over their children's heads)—into the building. Why step so gingerly? Because the children were dressed in fashionable bisque linen and white cotton. Their hair had been coiffed. Their shoes had been polished. Their anklets had lace trim.

I, on the other hand, learned quickly to do what I observed other practical parents do at barnepark. When I pulled up to gather Parker and Claire from the end of their play, I always did so armed with garbage sacks. By that, I mean that when it was messy (which Norway was eight or nine months of the year), I took big black industrial garbage sacks with me in the back of the car. When I picked up my children, I took them to the back of the car, stripped them down to their underclothing, and crammed the outwear into the bag. When, on occasion, the snow or mud was too messy to even deal with, I worked out a system for drop-ping the kids themselves into the garbage bag—the bags reached to their necks—then buckling them in for the ride home. Once home, I carried them inside and stood them, sack and all, in the utility shower where they then peeled the sack down to their boots and I hosed them down, head to boot.

At the end of seven months of barnepark, Parker's energy reserves seemed to have been well tapped, and the elements appeared to have humbled him into submission. Claire, formerly retreating and de-pendent, had become less so. And both had become fluent speakers of Norwegian. They became, to as full an extent as is possible with a moth-er who sings Gershwin while snow-shoeing on her rooftop, Norsk. And both had become complicit ice maniacs with Hannah.

But for me? What did I learn? From my post next to that chain link fence, I made more important cultural observations. Day in and out, I watched while parents tugged their little Jens or Marit out of the Volvo, tromped said child over to the gate, and handed the child over unceremoniously to the waiting woman's sturdy handling. There was, I noticed at drop-off and pick-up, something like ruggedness in the parents, a lack of theatricality I'd perfected when it came to interaction with children. There was no hysteria, no exaggeration of the pain of separating from Mama or of leaving little dumpling in the snow. Just good-bye. Break a leg—er, uh, don't, if you can help it.

Right at the hinge of that gate, I learned what to my untrained ear seemed to be the most frequently-used Norwegian word. The blunt, single-syllable snap of, *"Nei!"* (underscored with the firm, single stamp of a foot). Tante Britt barked it at the children, who obeyed. The parents barked it at their children, who obeyed. The children barked it at each other, who often yelped "Nei!" back. In grocery stores, in school rooms, at church gatherings and in doctor's office waiting rooms, rang "Nei!"

It sounded definitive.

"Nei!" is a battle cry of conservatism, of setting limits, which, all my new friends told me, was the first Norwegian rule of childrearing. *"Barna må kjenne grenser."* Children must have limits. My Americanness startled at the idea of setting limits and telling my children no, especially if I meant it. Indulgence was a swift American current, a hard one to get out of, and I'd never been a sterling model of withholding myself from my children or denying them their demands. So now the scoop, was I supposed to tell my children "Nei"? That they only got thirty minutes of TV a day? That the TV should never be turned on when the sun is shining? Sunshine was precious, I was told by my friends, so we shouldn't waste it in front of a screen. And candy, if you were thinking of having any with your TV, could be eaten only on Saturdays? (That's why we have a name for it, Lena and Rut and Silje said: Saturday candy. *Lørdags godterie.*)

The true mind blow about this all, I kept thinking, was that these codes of conduct, this Nei Pact, was actually being kept by nearly five million people. And this trickled all the way down to the corner shop owner who would scowl into the shifty eyes of the six-year-old and ask if her parents actually knew she was doing this, trying on a dare, to buy a Snickers on Friday?

Nei. Oh, the beauty. Especially with percussion. That one stamped boot.

Never was *"nei"* heard as often and as loudly as during the political campaigns regarding Norway's entrance into the European Union. No matter how patiently prime minister Gro Harlem Brutland tried to sway the vote of a population anchored in generations of setting limits and stamping "Nei!," the country would not bend. This refusal to join the coalition has, as the world knows, helped the country to gain fabulous wealth (Norway is rated, per capita, as the wealthiest of western countries), which is due to centuries of living prudently before the discovery of oil and gas reserves in the North Sea.

And that, friends, is what you get from telling your kids candy is only for Saturday.

So the country must have limits. Check. And children must have limits. Check. And children must be allowed to be bored.

Unskyld meg? Excuse me?

Britt explained this softly, smilingly, when one day after a month or so of daily barnepark, I dared to ask what else might be on the pedagogical roster for the noontime brown bagger break at Blakstad. "Oh, nothing but the usual. Their sandwiches. Our song or two. We don't want to over-stimulate them." She'd even shrugged, nodding as if I already agreed.

I used one leg to shove behind my standing leg my big burlap bag of flashcards, Rubik's cubes and those overpriced finger puppets of all the living Nobel prize winners.

But Norway and Britt, bless them, weren't necessarily aching for a leg up, so to speak. "The children don't need too many choices," Britt advised me through the steam that rose from her coffee thermos. "Give them less," she eyed a boy jabbing the same spade over and over again into the same mound of grit-gray snow, "and they'll come up with more on their own."

Gradually, I gave in to not giving in to my children. I limited their choices. The goal, as far removed from American parenting as the Turn-pike was from the snaking two lanes of Oslo's freeway, E-18, was now to bore them. But to make sure, I kept coming back and back again to the chain link fence to keep an eye on how my two were surviving the yawn.

I'd drop by late morning, pen in hand, poised to take notes on meth-odology and pedagogy, when over a snow bank I'd see Parker negotiating, quite seriously and in native Norwegian, a better fort construction with Eivind, Øystein, and Magnus. Another day, early afternoon, I slipped by on my way to pick up fresh fish in Sandvika, and caught sight of Claire singing a Norwegian nursery song along with Thea and Madelene on each side. They were building four-tiered snow cakes on the bench, snap-ping at Henrik and Thorbjørn who thought they'd pound the creations flat with their rumpe brett.

Sometimes for a few minutes, sometimes for a couple of hours, I'd stand in hip-deep snow inside the barnepark's chain link fence observing life there, chatting it up with Britt, Anna, and Eva. That is where I really began to learn Norwegian, *å lære Norsk*. And that is where my children really began *å være Norsk*. To be it.

The ladies bring me newspaper clippings or (anti-Janteloven) gossip magazines, pointing to celebrities, politicians, the latest scandals, giv-ing me the dirt on this or that part of Norwegian popular life. And they wanted to know if grocery stores in America were really open in the mid-dle of the night (they laughed hard about that one), and if they were as

big as they'd seen on TV, if you honestly had to pay money to have a gall
bladder operation or *even* to deliver a baby in the States? If everyone in
Texas really had mansions, four cars, large plastic hair, and something
called liposuction. If there were many "*negroes*" in New York City?

And they wanted to know, after a month or so of daily chats, if I was
going to continue my singing career in Norway. Hadn't gotten my mind
that far yet, I sighed. Didn't I miss singing? they asked. Yes. I missed it
very much. Very much. Then could I imagine, they asked me, coming,
maybe, and singing a song or two? "Perhaps sometime?" one woman asked. "With the children?" another suggested. "During their lunch
break?" said Britt.

"*Tomorrow!*" (I think I might have sprayed some spit into Britt's
bangs.)

That I ran out that very day and bought a whole recorded collection
of "All Your Favorite Norwegian Children's Songs" and practiced them
all night at full volume, drilling the pronunciation, attests to something
being maybe a bit off, akimbo.

When that lunch break came, let me tell you, I was so in the zone, I was
hardly able to hold myself back. I worried I might belt the roof right off
that barrack. Eighteen round children's faces, including those of my own
two, encircled the picnic table like lights, shining on me. Every child was
un-parkdressed down to wool sweaters and tights, the curtain of red, blue,
and green parkdress hanging from low hooks on the surrounding walls.

"The mama of Parker and Claire has come to help us sing today,"
announced Britt, her big white teeth pearlier in my eyes than ever before.
"What do we say to the mama of Parker and Claire?"

"Good day, Mama of Parker and Claire," a ring of frost-bitten faces
with runny noses nodded and chanted in sing-songy unison. The elf boy
with whiter than white hair and Tom Sawyer freckles wiped his dripping
nose on his handknit sleeve.

"Children, she is a *professional* singer."

Oooooo.

"She has sung on a stage in New York City."

Aaaa . . . aaaah . . . ??

"In America."

Aaaaaaaaaaaaah!!

"We are going to sing as nicely as we can today for Parker and Claire's
mama. Can we do that? Sing for a professional? From *America*?"

Now, let me quickly insert myself here in the narration. Maybe you're
thinking my tone is mocking, that I'm condescending toward a barrack

full of little children and their caregivers. Oh, what funny little Nordic kiddies these types are, you might think I'm saying, and here I come, so important from the famous big city, and these Eskimo hillbillies don't have a clue, and I'm doing them a big favor to dip down and grace them with my—

Nope.

Not in the slightest. That they would have *me*, that I could show up and slip in and sit there and sing on *their* bench—sing *their* songs with *my* children in *their* circle—well, it was maybe one of the most important singing moments of my—

Stop. Let me just show you:

"Does anyone of you sweet children have a favorite song?" I ask in Norwegian. Already I'm feeling the stage fright of Carnegie Hall, and all because I've got Karolina and Louisa eyeing me cautiously, watching for a badly turned vowel. Or dementia.

"Anyone? We'll sing your favorite song together, how's that?"

Up from the corner a hand shoots as does a song name, "*Se min kjole! Se min kjole!*" It's Claire, and it's a song I know:

Se min kjole, den er rød som rose . . .

See my dress, the song goes, it's as red as a rose.

And I do see the red dress, or the parkdress, at least. I see all of these red (and blue and green) parkdresses hanging just like they had hung the first time I'd crept in here in my red boots. I see them and suddenly, I can't believe this all.

We sing a whole recital, those children and I, and the three other women, their red parkdresses bundled around their hips, hum the familiar melodies, swaying and clapping, too. Lunchtime goes longer than usual, long enough for the room to actually grow warm. We're all defrosted. It's getting steamy, even. The air in this little room feels and smells like wet wool.

On the last song, I lower my volume so I can hear, rising from either side of me, the voices of Parker and Claire. They are singing in perfect Norwegian and at the top of their lungs. Right there, American professional from New York City turns into a chin-quivering Mom with post nasal drip. And though we don't see it in the moment, all of us take a slow, deliberate turn toward becoming Norwegian.

6

VIKING MOTHER

O nly a couple of months into our life in Norway, we got word we'd have to move from our little rental house not in two years as originally planned, but in two months. The Norwegian owners were cutting short their own expatriate assignment in the States, coming back in the early spring.

Our "relocation assistance" at that time was handed to me by tall, beaming Turid, Randall's colleague at work. She said, as she gave me the local newspaper with its classified columns and nodded gently into my bewildered eyes, *"Kanskje kan du begynne her, Melissa,"* which sounded like "kahn shuh kahn dooo buhyinnah hæhrrrrrrrrr," and then my name, which all made me go arctic.

I had begun there, as Turid told me to, with those inscrutable want ads. This meant picking through each paragraph with a *norsk-engelsk ordbok* (dictionary), writing up my list of Norwegian greetings and questions on a legal pad, and following up with my imagined responses to imagined questions the imagined Norwegians on the other end of the line would ask me.

Sometimes I survived said call only to hear that the person needed to call me back. Which meant I had to answer the phone. The phone would ring and I would become a gerbil trapped in the bottom of a spinning barrel, twitchy, scrawny paws clutched at its throat.

Why so nervy? Because it's one thing to face a foreign language in person; you get all the benefits of eye contact, miming, props, that whole ornate context. But when you cannot even see your partner's lips, it's a whole other deal. The rich nonverbal subtext is absent and all you're stuck with is words, words coming at you like bullets in the dark, words and no way to fake understanding until something you really *do* understand—a conjunction, a "*ja*" or a "*nei*"—sails in to save you.

Ok, I *did* speak. And I *did* understand. Partially. But even shrugging my shoulders could break my concentration, and I'd be lost in the cute clatter of Norwegian that was hippety-hopping from the receiver into my ear. Once lost, it was hard to get my footing in the jig again. All that talk about *all* those Norwegians speaking perfect English? I knew they existed, those folks, and I eventually met them. But when I really needed them to help us find a new house, hey, they weren't dialing my number.

I might add that it's tough to get someone to rent you their house if they're convinced you've got the mental capacity and vocabulary of a two-year-old with a severe stuttering problem, and a high-pitched staccato delivery that might indicate a drug addiction.

I did survive the language gulag and the reward for the struggle was a house on the island of Nesøya right down the road from Nesøya Skole, which became the hub of our children's life, the root of major growth for us all. Significant growth begins, as wisdom has taught me, with pain. From my journal:

> *This year has marked the kids' surge in growth of all kinds. Parker's making great headway with his Norwegian, managing to converse like a native with his little school buddies and participating in the church program with a major speaking part. Wise Man #1. Type casting. At school for the Christmas program he's Troll #1. Is the universe trying to tell me something?*
>
> *Claire has refined a large repertoire of native folk songs, which she hollers and croons at all times and in all places. Both children are sturdy and active, joyous reminders to us of the vibrancy and hope of childhood. I can drone on and on about their energy and bright minds, how Claire loves all things theatrical, how Parker has a penchant for memorizing long texts. To be honest it's a little creepy, his ability to memorize. According to his teachers, they've never seen this kind of aural memory before.*

But. But. Adjusting to the whole local school thing has been hard work for him, for us all. HARD. I came close to crying in yesterday's school conference. As the school principal, Sigrid, was expressing her concerns about Parker's behavior, and his four teachers around the table were describing how disruptive he can be in class, erratic, uncontainable, sometimes explosive, I felt that salty wave climbing my throat. I was listening to the Norwegian terms for this boy— "strong character," "unchanneled energy," "sensitive to criticism"—I didn't say it but my internal voice was on loudspeaker, "This is too much for me! This is not covered by my skill set!!"

Well, bless her heart, Sigrid reached across to me when I guess she saw my eyes drop to the table top, and she put her hand on mine. "Think," she said, "of the adventure we'd all miss without his powerful presence in our lives!"

I managed a smile then. But hearing her words now in my mind makes we weep with confused but sweet gratitude for this boy.

Nesøya became our most essential, intimate Norway, and its elementary school figured physically and symbolically right at the heart of that experience. Eventually, both Parker and Claire spent extended school days where they attended something called Skolefritidsordning (SFO), an after school program led by a team of teachers whose job it was to provide a learning atmosphere that was *koselig*, meaning cozy and comfy like home. The SFO leader, Åsa, like the classroom teachers, was a serene woman, unflappable, practical, and creative and oversaw the program based in the large SFO room with its central kitchen and work island. There, parents who could randomly drop in would see their children making cookies or bread in September and oatmeal or soup in February. Lined along the walls under spacious windows were sofas with colorful pillows, and I'd often find either Claire or Parker there in a clump of friends reading books, sewing, or learning to knit, as koselig there as if in their own bedroom. In the winter, the children came in from the snowy or rainy playground and went straight into a dressing room where they hung their wet clothing in tall, heated drying closets. Then they'd slither around in their woolen stocking feet and if they were especially tired, they'd doze off on the corner sofa. Åsa made sure they weren't disturbed. School spilled into home and home into school, the boundaries blurring to a comfy, koselig wash.

I don't know what that does to you, but it makes me lick my paws and purr. It did something similar to Parker. He began relaxing, and eased into his new identity as a strong and enthusiastic class leader. In very little time his English took on Norwegian inflections, he translated idioms from Norwegian into English, and he often asked us not how to say things in Norwegian, but how to do so in English. Something similar was happening with Claire, too, and before long this duo began talking to each other in Norwegian as much as or more than they did in English.

The same was happening between Randall and me. Randall was making strides at work, which meant not only growing in his capacities as the leader of his function for this region, but doing so in the native tongue. He was the only non-native in any meetings, on any junkets, sending inner-office memos *på Norsk*. These folks who'd been learning English since grade school and had learned colloquial English by growing up watching American media with Norwegian subtitles, had to now suppress their strong English in order to teach Randall, at his insistence. That took lots of patience on their part.

An important step for him was giving presentations in Norwegian, the first of which came at him as a surprise when, six months into Norway and only fifteen minutes before the fact, the Swedish country manager told Randall that he and the twenty other Scandinavian professionals waiting in the adjoining room wanted to hear this particular PowerPoint in Norwegian. When Randall finished that hour, the whole table gave him a standing ovation. He was on his way.

That kind of linguistic grip doesn't just happen by osmosis or even from eating salmon every day, twice a day. It assumes commitment and consistency on the part of both the newcomer as well as the native community at large. We were lucky to have communities that always supported us in this venture. All of these friends—work, school, church, neighborhood—shared with us their time, traditions, and language, their boat trips, mountain cabins, family weekends, Christmas and New Year's parties, and summer vacations. They shared their kayaks, bikes, skis, herring recipes, and cures for pink eye and head lice.

They also sat around our long table more times than I can begin to count, mostly to eat and talk, but also to smooth out our gigantic map of Norway. Norwegians travel passionately, especially within their own borders. They use their land at every possible turn, gladly going to seclusion in their mountain *hytter* with their skis, fishing poles, a musket, and skillet. It was these friends who sent us to places with cute little clippety-cloppety names that made us snicker, places like Brikkstalsbreen, Hardangervidda, Jotunsheimen, Lofoten, Bodø, Flåm and yes, even Å.

But when we stood in front of its heart-stopping beauty, Norway had the last everlasting laugh.

It didn't take much to convince my family members and especially my brother and my parents to come along with us on our Norway discovery, and so they came for extended stays at least once but sometimes twice a year. As long as our families traveled to us or we all remained connected by the then steadily advancing technology, we didn't feel we were missing much of our former American life. I was no longer getting letters from theater friends, and I'd quite inadvertently let my three years' grace period as a member of Actor's Equity lapse. No, I wasn't even missing the east coast theater milieu all that much.

Quite simply, we were *feeling* Norwegian, each of us, which meant it felt normal to pay the equivalent of nine dollars for a gallon of milk, to eat raw fish on a dry cracker for breakfast and a hot dog topped with shrimp salad and wrapped in a tortilla (called a *lompe*) for lunch. It felt comfortable to wear a bright mustard-colored shirt to work, four layers of wool from November to April, and head to toe rubber from April to June. It hardly fazed us to think of cross-country skiing to church or grocery shopping. The roots were sinking. Life was full.

But not to the brim. We knew we were missing one thing. And so Randall and I decided to make a baby. The child would arrive at Christmas.

Christmas in Norway.

Three words, and my bones go all cheese fonduey.

This is because there is a special spirit to a Norwegian Christmas. With New Jersey's jingle-jangle still faintly clinky-clanking in one of my smaller brain closets, Norway's quiet spirit had caught me off guard, like this 5:30 a.m. phone call from Bente:

"*Fort, du må nesten løpe til fjernsyn,*" she is whispering, telling me to hurry—run!—to the TV. She's got no idea what she's asking, Bente. At almost nine months pregnant, running resembles a slo-mo animation of global plate tectonics, my pelvis held together by what feels like no more than three shredded rubber bands. But I waddle obediently down the stairs and dump my fertile self into the sofa.

Sitting breathless and alone in the darkness, I watch. In total stillness, the program illumines. It is one long, still moment until this crescent of blonde girls dressed in floor-length white gowns and with wreaths and burning candles atop their heads begins singing:

Night walks with heavy steps. . . .
Shadows are brooding. . . .
In every room so hushed. . . .

Whispering like wings. . . .

Sankta Lucia. The darkest night of the year, and in Norwegian, that means darkness of the underside of the blackest inkiest black. Something about that thick backdrop makes my anticipation for this moment and for this season more intense, intimate. I'm awaiting the Bradford child's birth, the Christ child's birth. The Unknowns; one under the taut skin of my belly, the other under the night skin of the universe, and this slow awakening happening in the orbit of my body, in the land of Norway.

Baby bottom gyrates up under a rib. A knee here. A foot print there. A head grinding relentlessly like a street dancer spinning on my bladder. Now he's rhythmically filing his toenails on my lowest left rib while he hiccups the effects of last night's spiced lentil soup. I push down with the heel of my hand. The lump bulges right back again, defiantly. Can he hear the television? Because he's pulled a lever on this recliner so he can lie spread eagle from my pancreas to my esophagus. I'm stretchy both in skin and in soul.

Bente has prepped me about Sankta Lucia. "If you want to really get *julestemning*, you must watch the performance live or at least on the live broadcast from Stockholm."

Julestemning is different from your run of the mill "Christmas spirit." It is not neon pulsing robotically waving snowmen in shopping malls, the slosh of musak in the dairy aisle of your supermarket, and Andy Williams rapping "Ole Saint Nick." It is deep, heavy, fresh as snowfall in the nighttime. I hadn't understood the term, really, when just a few weeks earlier at a Norwegian friend's house their young adult daughter was on the phone from California. She was there doing a year-long exchange in the land of Beverly Hills 90210, cooler than anything, you'd think. But from her end of the line I could hear she was sucking back tears, sobbing to her family, "*Det er ikke julestemningnen her enda!*" (There's no Christmas spirit here yet!)

But now I begin to understand. In our basement, in the dark, low in sofa, high in pregnant, I watch the television glow with angel girls singing about the weighted tread of darkness and the pending light, singing with innocence, their faces iridescent with the sweet liquid warmth of a musical sunrise, and I am lulled, nearly half-dozing. Before I can tug on the corner of the blanket that has slipped off my shoulder, I realize I'm draining tears from both eyes. Crying, for hormones' sake! Punch drunk on julestemning.

Bente, my formidable friend of the predawn phone call, later tutors me on it at length:

"You begin," her bright blue eyes widen enthusiastically, "with a thorough Christmas cleaning."

This means an on-your-hands-and-knees scrub down of every inch of pine. Dragging out a ladder to scour your ceiling. Polishing windows with vinegar and lemon. Beating rugs and bedding and mattresses and bushes. Flossing your banister. Tipping over the fridge. Wiping under it. Picking lint out of the wiry element on the backside of your appliances. With a Q-tip.

"Then you're ready for Christmas curtains," adorably girlish Pia schools me. She's also smiling.

"Curtains" means taking down all your everyday window treatments, washing them, folding them, storing them in plastic bags you've sucked the air out of, and replacing them with flouncy fabric in red and green. Holly berries, candy canes, bows, polar bears, trolls.

"So, where do you pick up these curtains?" I'm decidedly curtain challenged, except for stage curtains, which I'd never sewn or laundered.

"Pick them up? Oh no. You buy the fabric. You sew them."

"Sew? Curtains? For *all* your windows? For every Christmas?"

Was this even lawful?

"And after that, you do the *syv sorter*," Bente adds, still smiling. She is tall, has four tall children, and they all have peachy complexions with bright, winning smiles. I conclude it's a national mandate.

Syv sorter means making seven different sorts of Christmas cookies all in the course of one day. And there are prescribed sorts, I learned, of which Pillsbury ready-bake is not one, you sluggards. Real Norwegians like Bente are born to do seven sorts in a day and from scratch. But they are also born with peachy complexions, winning smiles, skis on their feet, a hockey stick in their fist, and something in their constitution that lets them relish slurping the teensy eggs out of the tails of raw shrimp. And still smile.

"And don't forget *kransekake*," Pia wants to explain to me, her dimples softening the blow. By now I'm feverishly scribbling notes. "You start with hand-ground almonds and powdered sugar and—you want to borrow my moulds?" She hands me her cast iron ring moulds for the traditional stacked wreath cake, then pulls me aside. "You can actually *buy* bags of the dough ready made." She lowers her voice, "But . . . *not a word*." I'd never seen darling blonde Pia look stern, but this time, she's glowering.

At Bente's, we all gather for Christmas Eve. We have come in our best clothing (Bente and Pia's children are in Sunday best and bunad, from 17th of May bunad) because, as Christian has told us, this evening will be "litt høytidelig."

Høytidelig. Also from the 17th of May, so I know this is code: please, pants with belts. Drawstrings and elasticized ankles turned away at the door or you will be screechingly out of place and forever labeled, "bumpkin."

We gather around Bente's table set with a great-great-grandmother's crystal, heirloom silver, china handed down generations. There are pewter warming plates and hand-tatted linens from another great grandmother. There are candles, an order to things, a program. A course followed by a verse from the Gospel of Luke. Another course, another verse. The menu includes substantial fare; traditional white sausage, delicately boiled potatoes, steamed Brussels sprouts, and caramel pudding and the crowning treat: stacked rings of the kransekake, each ascending ring decorated, as is the Christmas tree, with small Norwegian flags.

No paper plates, not even Chinet. No feet propped on the coffee table. No root beer floats in mismatched Mets and Yankees mugs. Not a single popcorn ball, corn dog or Snack Pack Jell-O Pudding. Nothing of that sort on this or any Christmas Eve there or anywhere from the Arctic Circle all the way down to the southern border. Of course that's just my guess. But it's one I'd stake my life on.

Christmas in Norway means gathering. That was why we'd bought our huge table. Our particular plank of pine has room for twelve; in a pinch, room for fourteen. Sixteen, if everyone dines armlessly. Even with the table as talisman, though, I never fully mastered the Norwegian Christmas. Maybe that's because it takes much longer than five years to do so, and maybe it's because I was a slow domestic study and had never felt that I really mastered many things domicilish. But I did amass all the traditional decorations, serve mounds of fish in every possible state at every one of my gatherings, and make vat upon vat of something called *gløgg*, an onomatopoetically named spiced cider that Norwegians consume without alcohol (as I do), or with. And when it's with, it's with lots.

I even perfected my own recipe for gingerbread dough, the very mortar of any true Norwegian Christmas. I learned all the local songs about the art and lure of gingerbread-baking, singing them with my children and adding choreography I can still pull off today. One year, I made enough gingerbread dough to re-shingle our roof.

It took the course of our Norway years for me to scrape off the biggest scabs of a crusty old-school strident feminism, the kind I'd studied in graduate school that had preached disdain for all things domestic. I managed to shimmy out of that brittle role model while also squeezing sideways past The Good Norwegian Housewife one. (I *never* tipped or Q-tipped my fridge, by the way. *Never once.*) But I took a swan dive into the one domestic task I liked: food preparation, or more specifically food preparation with the intent of bringing people together. I gave up Gloria Steinem for Rachel Ray and traded in Bella Abzug for Julia Child.

Child, as I've noted earlier, had her own meat cleaver-scarred Norwegian farm table with curved-back farm chairs similar to mine. Though our tables and chairs were nearly identical, Mrs. Child and I were not, which should surprise no one. I'm not over six feet tall, don't have an arsenal of kitchen knives, have never in my life made a *bœuf bourguignon* or, let's be honest, even a pot roast, and there's that small detail about her being a genius. Julia Child was also not blessed with children. I, on the other hand, was bursting with my third.

"*Nå kommer han ... Puste ... puste ...*"

Ellen, our midwife, whispered he was coming, our baby boy, and that I should breathe, breathe. *Puste, puste,* my head answered Ellen from where it was buried in the feather comforter squashed up between my arms supporting my prayer-time kneeling position at the foot of the double bed. I felt him coming, whoah did I ever, and had felt him since early that morning when Randall had braved late December's icy roads to bring us to the large, private natural birthing room in a quiet wing of Bærum Sykehus, our closest hospital.

Breathe? I'd been humming and grunting "Amazing Grace" all labor long as I circled this dimly-lit room with its adjacent Jacuzzi for relaxation and water births, its blue stability ball, ballet bar, apricot-hued walls.

And now I was at the last verse. Focused inward on a beautiful image of Christ, I startled for a couple of beats when, with a pop and a warm gush, my baby's orb thunked into my pelvic opening. Then just as I hit a high note, our purply-gray-pinkish, blue-eyed otter slid into this life.

Ellen—our *jordmor,* or "earth mother," or midwife—had a slight build and wire-rimmed glasses, a broad smile and pronounced front teeth, and though she was maybe no more than twenty-four years old, she acted the professional, scooping up every gram of the vault-chested, pudgy-limbed perfection and gliding him into my arms. No washing off or squirting in the eyes. She just placed him at my breast, this bright-eyed, wee wrinkled rodent of a son. Her voice never rising above reverent, she exhaled; "*Kjempegut. Og deilig.*"

A bruiser. And a delight.

The voluptuousness of heaven encircled us—Mother, Father, Child—and we curled up in each other in the oversized family bed against which I had just knelt asking for grace and relief. Ellen slinked out of the side door. From one wall to another holiness and contentment spread—no, not an entity and certainly not a vision, but a silent reassurance that this, this majestic being in our arms, was why we had come here.

Not just to Norway, although that was a given.

But to earth. Life. Given.

And that's Chapter One of the world of the Viking Mother.

Chapter Two is nursing. And nursing Dalton meant doing so every other hour on the hour around the clock. This child was draining the fluids from every inch of my being including my uvula, so my doctor suggested that rather than switch to formula (which was unnatural, so of course stridently discouraged in Norway), I rent a pump. Increase lactation, he said. Churn some serious cream.

This pump I got must have been a design joint venture between Hummer and Hoover. It sat like an idling dune buggy on the kitchen floor and when I strapped it on, I had to buckle myself to a piece of heavy furniture to keep from being yanked across the room. It could have sucked the chrome off a trailer hitch. As could have Dalton. After six months, I was ready to stop the nursing/vacuuming experiment because I noticed all my internal organs had been rearranged and pulled to the surface. (When I did wean him eventually, Dalton went straight to reindeer steaks, if that gives you an idea of what kind of appetite we were dealing with.)

Thankfully, Chapter Two was supported by Chapter Three, my *barselgruppe*, a typically Norwegian wonder that is an essential component of being a Viking Mother. *Barsel* is a word for birth, and your barsel group is a community for life. When Dalton was born, the state registered me along with five other freshly delivered mothers from my immediate geographic surroundings to be part of a support group led by a nurse/social worker who specialized in postnatal adjustment, family counseling and facets of early childhood education.

Every month in the nurse's station of Nesøya Skole down our street on the island, we mothers met with our supervising worker named Gunnil, shared snacks and stories, discussing our babies and ourselves.

Was little Morten sleeping? Was darling Kerstin on solids yet? Was Melissa's breast pump available to take a spin around the sand dunes or to vacuum out someone's garage? We kept this up for a year and then, as was often the case with these groups, ours took on a life of its own and we met independently at one of our homes, a coffee shop, or walking out along the fjord. It was not uncommon in Norwegian culture to keep these bar-sel friends for life. Lots of women I knew attended the marriages of the babies, now fully grown, whose births had brought their moms together.

One day at barselgruppe, we discussed milk. One of the newly-delivered mothers just had too much of it, she said. Constantly leaking all over the place, very annoying and inconvenient, not to mention messy and embarrassing, she sighed. So Gunnil suggested this mother bag all the extra milk her baby didn't consume, and take those bags to the *melke-bank*, the local annex of the hospital created expressly (no pun intended) for this purpose.

That new mother had a slight build, but was ample in maternally strategic places. She sat right next to a lanky brunette, naturally beautiful in jeans from about 1974, with capable large-knuckled hands that had milky unpolished nails, her manner cool and solid, like a big deep ceramic basin of setting mascarpone.

When I then mentioned I was becoming totally drained from being so totally drained, someone in the circle suggested I go to the melkebank. If there were deposits, there were withdrawals.

For dried up women. Like me.

"Maybe I'll take my extra milk there," another mother said. "I'm constantly soaking my shirts."

"And I've got too much, too," the mother sitting to my right added. "Mornings, my bed is drenched."

"Me, too!" a first-time mother of twins exclaimed.

"You know, with all my three babies it's been the same story," the brunette basin of mascarpone interjected, curling her long legs up under her hips on the couch. "I make more milk than my father's cows did. And that milk fed us five children when I was growing up. I've got cow DNA."

Laughter and sisterly eye-winking all around the room. Except me.

Because right then is when I started feeling about as succulent as the last potato chip in the bag, no more use to my hungry baby than a couple of medium-sized, plastic-wrapped, year-old fortune cookies. Without the fortune.

"Maybe you need to eat more," suggested Gunnil, motioning to a piece of chocolate cake.

"Some foods help stimulate production," a woman said, taking a big bite of the gooey dark confection.

"Foods like chocolate, I hope?" I asked, and bit deep into my piece of cake brought this time, as last time and like the time before, by the deep cheese brunette. I had noticed she always brought rich things like dense brownies and carrot cake and creamy toffee bars, so not only was she apparently our barselgruppe's crowned Dairy Queen, but she was the Treat Goddess to boot.

Maybe I had a mild case of milk envy. But you understand that I was, as I've told you, doing all I could but was still not quite able to keep the milk wagon loaded for Dalton.

"Funny," Miss Treat Goddess Milky Way spoke up softly, "I've never donated to the melkebank. All this extra milk, you know, I just keep it in my freezer."

"In your freezer?" the mother of twins, also helping herself to a second piece of cake, nearly laughed. "Why in your freezer?"

"Because it has so many uses."

Gunnil, putting aside her cake and licking her fingers, reached for her notepad and pen to take notes. "Uses? For example?"

"Well . . . " Ms. Lactose smiled as golden as a cube of chilled butter, "It's good, for example, for treating pink eye."

"Yes, I've heard this," Gunnil jotted a note. "Full of antibacterial properties."

"And for softening cracked skin," Yogurt Girl told us, those lean hands looking smoother than I'd noticed before. I took three big mouthfuls of cake.

"Yes, it's rich in emollients," Gunnil was nodding around the circle, hoping we were all listening to this perfect example.

"But really," our Lady of La Leche cut in, "I don't use it so much for that."

"Oh?" the mother of twins said, licking her lips.

"Oh?" the mother to my right wiped crumbs from her chin.

"Oh?" I swallowed my fifth bite.

"Then how do you use all your extra milk?" Gunnil's pen was waiting.

"I use it all in my baking," Curdle Girlie said, perky as a dollop of whipped cream. "Another piece, Melissa?"

7

Vi Er Norske

D alton Haakon Bradford. We chose the name for our baby because Dalton, as you've gathered, is my maiden name. And Haakon (pronounced similarly to "hoe cone," but that's where the similarity ends), is one of those big names of Norwegian royalty, much like Charles or George in England, Louis and Philippe in France. It happens, for instance, that Haakon Magnus was Norway's crown prince throughout our years living in that country.

Royal lineage, however, has nothing to do with why we wanted that name for our Viking baby. Personal lineage has. Haakon is an important name from Randall's maternal line. In the year of 1856, Haakon Aamodt, Randall's great-grandfather and the youngest branch of at least a dozen generations of farming family from the county of Østfold, Norway, joined the Mormon church. Summarily kicked out of the King's Royal Navy, he did what thousands of European Mormons of that time were doing. He took himself a wife, Julia Josephine, and emigrated to Salt Lake City, Utah.

Although you might not believe this, we knew nothing of Haakon's story until we'd lived in Norway for over a year. It's then we got a letter from Randall's oldest sister, who had more or less inherited the matriarchal and family history responsibility when their mother, Shirley, passed away suddenly, less than a year before we had been offered the job in Oslo. Shirley had been a charitable, humble, self-effacing person who shared few of the details of her upbringing, and even fewer of her extended family history. And so we all understood only that her heritage was vaguely Scandinavian, but the details petered out there.

So it came as a surprise when this oldest sister put two and two together and discovered that their mother Shirley was only three generations removed from a small community right in the middle of the endless rolling farmland of the county of Østfold, less than an hour's drive from our doorstep west of Oslo. It seemed that Shirley's father, Albert Aamodt, was born in Salt Lake City, Utah, to Haakon and Julia. Haakon's father was Christian Torkildsen, who lived on one of the many Aamodt farms in Østofld and, as was the way then, took the name of the farm, Aamodt. Our research told us that preceding Christian, there were at least ten if not more consistently linked generations from that one corner of Østfold. In other words, the Aamodt line *is* Østfold.

We figured it was a good place to start looking for family. So we packed up the kids and took off one day in search of the first church with a graveyard in that county. Not only did we find that church with its graveyard full of Aamodt tombstones, but a nice older couple out for a stroll that afternoon pointed us right in the direction of the largest Aamodt farm where, they promised us, the owner would love to chat. He was quite interested in genealogy himself.

An hour later I was playing with the children on ancient wooden farm equipment surrounded by goats and cows while Randall waved at me through kitchen windows. Inside, he was seated next to the family's long pine farm table where he and other Aamodts shared glasses of cider pressed from their local apples. This American son talked family matters with these Norwegian sons.

All these generations, and there Randall stood, right on Haakon's very patch of natal soil. Serendipity, a professional stroke of luck, and we believe Shirley's quiet celestial lobbying had landed us, an uprooted American family, less than an hour from the roots of Randall's family tree. Using Haakon's name for our child born in his country, a country he never set eyes on again after emigrating for his faith from the verdant fjords to a chalky expanse of an unknown desert, was our small way of gratefully closing the family circle.

Dalton Haakon Bradford. The string of firm, double-syllabled titles seemed to fit his dense, big-boned build. A strong, heavily-connected appellation for a strong, heavy boy.

But the Norwegian government would have nothing to do with it.

After submitting the name to the Civil Registry, we got a note back saying *Haakon* was great, but *Dalton?*

Nei, det er ikke lov.

Not allowed. Our choice was "unacceptable."

Unacceptable?

Unusual, maybe. I could accept that. But *unacceptable?* Pshaw. This legal stuff was simply unacceptable.

We read on. There were several points detailed in the nice shiny brochure they'd enclosed which outlined which names one must avoid in Norway. I recall some vague guideline about not giving a child a name that would be "disadvantageous" to him in adulthood. Here, I suspected they were thinking of Chastity, Moon Unit, or Dweezle, and any number of American smash-up names meant to evoke father, mother, eye color, and astrological sign in one fell swoop.

Marvellabluvirgo, for instance.

Furthermore, the pamphlet instructed that parents were not to use as a given name the mother's maiden name (our first infraction), nor any last name for that matter, to avoid doubling up on names when one marries. Messing up the genealogy charts and stuff. An Olson Olson. A Carlson Carlson. Marvellabluvirgo Marvellabluvirgo. Oh, the effrontery.

But wait! You're thinking (as we were) that Dalton was, 1) a boy, so he would not, given the tradition, take on the married name of his Norwegian bride with the family name of Dalton and become a freakish and stuttering Dalton Dalton, and, 2) the name Dalton is not Norwegian in the first place, so the chances were less than zero that there would be someone in this vast country named Dalton.

Randall whipped up the phone and brandished his finest, most professional Norwegian, which was by now and in this moment of frustration polished and gushing at full force like a 300-meter Norwegian waterfall after thaw.

"This is the Norwegian Civil Registry. I'm Snorre at the office of Name Laws. May I help you?"

"Yes. Good day, Snorre. I'd like to name my baby what I want to name my baby."

"Let's see . . . are you Norwegian citizens?"

"Nope. Neither is the baby. We're temporary residents in your lovely country. So of course we can't be subject to your Name Laws."

"Let's see . . . let me transfer you to my colleague."

"Hello, this is Odd."

"Hello, Odd. I am Randall. Neither my newborn baby nor my wife nor I are Norwegian citizens and we want to name this baby what we want. We've decided on Dalton Haakon. Is this going to present any problem for your office, your country, King Harald, and Queen Sonja? And if it does, what if I name him anyway? You going to confiscate him?"

(Goodwill snicker.)

No snicker.

"Actually, Randall, in order to receive a Norwegian birth certificate, you have to comply with our Name Laws. If you do not comply, no certificate. No certificate? No passport. And your son is then officially illegitimate."

"Alrightee, Odd. May I speak with your supervisor?"

"Hello, this is Hrothgar, office of Name Laws. You might want to consider putting your son's second name, Haakon, first, and just putting Dalton second. This is a good compromise, don't you think? According to this footnote, you *can*, in fact, use a family name as a *second* name. But not as a first."

"No, Hrothgar," Randall said, "I don't think we really want to compromise on our child."

"Then I'm afraid I can't help you. We at Norway's Name Law want to protect the children. If he one day marries someone Norwegian with the last name Dalton—"

"Time out, Hrothgar. First, help me understand, would you please, how many people with the last name of Dalton are currently living in Norway?"

Pause. Computer click-click-click sounds.

"There are . . . hmmm . . . six. I see there is . . . um . . . one Dalton on an island off the southwestern coast. And one Dalton . . . let's see . . . yes . . . northeast of Hammerfest near the Arctic Circle and—"

"Right. Okay, so what's the probability of this little baby Dalton Bradford one day marrying one of these Daltons and then crashing Norway's entire genealogical data system by taking *her* name and becoming Dalton Dalton?"

Silence.

"Well . . . Randall . . . there is still the other issue."

"The other issue?"

"We just can't be sure that Dalton is an acceptable first name. I've checked, and it's nowhere on our Acceptable Names list. It is normally a last name, your wife's last name, am I not right?"

"Hrothgar, may I speak with your supervisor?"

"Hello, this is Beowulf. You are calling about the Name Laws, aren't you?"

"Right, yes. Okay listen. Dalton is a fully acceptable first *and* last name. And to make everyone happy, I'll personally see to it that our son not marry a Someone Dalton from the Polar ice cap. In fact, I won't even let him *date* anyone from there. Can we just name our baby what we want?"

"For this exception, Randall, you will need to provide a letter of intercession from your native government. Then, you will have to be able to show proof that this name Dalton is acceptable. Solid, tangible proof."

So did you know that you can, if you really have to, receive via FedEx vintage bubble gum cards of the New Orleans Saints football player, Dalton Hilliard? A CD cover featuring Dalton Baldwin as accompanist? And title pages of every last one of Dalton Trumbo's screenplays?

A fortune for all that plus a paltry bribe of one packet of El Paso Taco seasoning for an Embassy affiliate, and we got the obsequious letter begging for the right to name our baby as we, and as his great-great intervening Norwegian grandfather who must have been smiling somewhere, wished.

Grandpa Haakon had been a sailor in the Royal Norwegian Navy. And even though Randall grew up in landlocked Utah never knowing a stern from an aft, something of that salty sailor's blood made it into his veins anyway. I saw proof of that when one freezing winter day we found ourselves sailing over the North Sea.

Randall's work routinely invited employees and their partners on occasional trips somewhere in Scandinavia. The most memorable of these for me was to the dramatic beauty of the Lofoten Islands north of the Arctic Circle. It wasn't, however, the dramatic beauty of those picturesque black blades of angry granite shooting out of the silver plate of sea that made the trip memorable. There was other drama awaiting us.

Before we board for the intended six-hour hydrofoil ride from the mainland to the islands, a crew member with a cleft chin, missing teeth, and a closely cropped red beard announces casually that this will be a rough ride. North Sea. Midwinter. Choppy waters. Brace yourselves. Grimly, mechanically, the crew is moving about, battening down hatches, slamming doors shut, unbolting and then belting life jackets and life preservers.

Norwegians, for all their virtues, will not hear that any *thing* is supposedly rough or hard. Because, naturally, *they* are what's rough, *they* are what's hard. Everyone on board is elbowing the next person as if to say, "The chap said, what, *choppy*? Rough? Ho-ho! Bring on some rough."

Our friends Oskar and Mette are seated right behind us. While the engines rumble and the vessel jerks and crunches into position, these two share snacks from their hand luggage, giggling, chortling. There are other friends of ours everywhere we look, too, lusty, hunky-dory travelers, who ignore the engine grinding into full ear-slamming throttle and the muffled crew member's advice over the intercom: *We're heading out. Best to be seated. Waters are especially lively with the wind coming down from the northwest. We'll be heading straight into it. Please sit down. Really.*

So these Norwegians, too cool to be told this might test their Norwegianness, reluctantly find their seats. A few guys are slapping backs and sniggering, rolling their eyes like high school seniors who've just been told by the squirrelly substitute teacher to return to their seats and listen to the lecture like all the other nerds. They're just about on their cushions when, in the space of 0.3 seconds, the vessel lurches from a perfect standstill to mach speed and I'm slammed into the headrest, cheeks fluttering, gums exposed. I can't even peel my scalp from the chair. A collective *Whuuoooh* rises from the passengers like a wave and out my little porthole to the left I see we're slicing like a power saw through a deeply grooved and teethy horizon, gun metal razors spitting silver shavings every direction into the air.

With each hump of air we sail over, we're airborne, a good half-foot above our seats. I'm whehing and eeeewing and ooohing like everyone else, flopping wildly up and out of and slapping back down into my seat. At first this is funny. We all move like synchronized swimmers, hair flying, limbs rubbery. But the roller coaster's not ending like any predictable amusement park ride. It doesn't let up at all, in fact. It gets worse. We're strapped on the back of some rabid cosmic bronco, all hundred or so of us, being randomly whacked and thrashed until our jaws are unhinging, our heads on the verge of being snapped off.

The mood gets heavy. Only a weak laugh or two—Ha. Ho. Ha-ha.—just a couple of die-hard one-liners from a log-throwing type back in the corner. And then instant and complete cricket chirp.

Chirp.

Chirp.

Chirp.

And the rhythmic slosh of ocean slapping metal.

Slosh. Whish. Whoosh. Slosh. Whish. Whoosh.

"Oh, Lord," I hear Oskar mumble. "Make me pass out soon."

And then from the silent spaces between the whish-whooshes of steely ocean being cut by the walls of our steely vessel, someone hurls. Someone hurls in that hacking, open-throated, intensity that cracks the tomb and immediately fills the air with the raw sting of bile. We are quiet, so quiet, so deathly quiet, and the flopping and chopping of the water keeps mocking, kershlocking our insides.

I can ride this, like labor pains I can ride this, yes, and ride it through, ride it out, I can, I know I can, yes, ride this, riiiiide. But my whole interior feels whoosh-sloshed and my brain is whishing soupily in my skull. Someone grunts, "I need air," and a bunch of people follow his drunk-like tread out through the ship's back door. Randall, who's looking in the pink, nods to me, motioning that he'll go around to see if anyone needs help. "Go!" I say to him just as I'm slammed right back into the lowest bowels of Odin's wrath.

Mette and Oskar are still behind me, groaning and grousing, and all at once Oskar, (who's a big guy with friendly jowls and a thick neck), projectile vomits. Something damp lands on the back of my ear. "Oh, come on, Oskar. Do you have to be so loud?" Mette retains a fair dose of tenderness as she chides him. After all, they are newlyweds. I happen to have sung at their wedding just a few months earlier, and therefore feel a certain investment in their marital bliss. "Do you need a piece of gum?" I would say. "A Tic Tac?" In other circumstances, yeah, but for now, forget it, I can't as much as open my bag to get them anything if I had it to offer help, though I do manage to turn halfway and wink, I believe, wink spritely while I feel an ochre-toned sludgeness glurping from my lower limbs up through my torso, spreading like rancid pancake batter across my whole being, up, out, upward, outward toward my esophagus and tingling toward my trachea. My jaw goes totally slack. I try to schlurbble some pathetically upbeat word to Mette, but I'm caught in that half-winky turn, unable to turn back to my seat, afraid to move at all. Helplessly I watch Mette, who has her hands wrapped around her head, her head between her knees, and her knees drawn up to her chest, rocking softly. There is no sound coming from her. And Oskar's friendly jowls have gone Alfred Hitchcocky and melted into moroseness, the shade of recycled cooking oil. Mette's hair, I note, has been in the line of Oskar's fire. But she's oblivious. She will not yet lose patience with her puking new husband. For this moment, they're doing splendidly.

So I turn away and pin myself to my porthole, begging inwardly for Oskar to at least keep his vomit in his aisle.

The red-bearded crew member is striding by, casually doling out these tidy, pint-sized white bags. He's just riding this Perfect Storm, this fellow, riding it like you ride a parade float on freshly spread asphalt. Cruisin.' He hands me a bag, and I smile in thanks, but I sense my lips are horny toad lips and I'm coming undone, becoming amphibious. *Focus, focus. Concentrate, concentrate. Just sit right back and you'll hear a tale . . .* Out my porthole is the horizon, so cruelly removed, so placid way out there, so unconcerned, conceited, so stuck up, that horizon. I drill my glare right into its line and start Lamaze breathing. I am becoming one with the horizon. It is in me. I, in it.

Horizon.

Horizen. Zen.

Ohmmm.

Is that Oskar softly crying?

My back is turned from the grisly scene where I know everyone's hacking, groaning, buckled over and falling sideways into seats, legs slumped in all directions or curled into the fetal position. Someone's spread eagle on the grimy Astroturf floor, her fur coat speckled with someone else's (I assume Oskar's?) vomit. More people are heading outside, trudging over the limbs of the vomit-coated victim in the middle of the floor. Each time the vessel takes air, she's a centimeter or two off the floor, and then comes thumping back down again limply. Barely a whimper.

I need to escape Oskar the Spewer, so I rise from my seat like an arthritic head of state, ready to address my executioners, eyes closed, shuffling blindly toward air. Along the vessel's railing outside, there's a lineup of rear ends above half-buckled knees. A couple of bodies are even on their knees, arms strung through the railing, grips loose or clenched, heads tucked into their chests.

Per Olav, tall, barrel-chested, normally gregarious enough to do rollicking Elvis impersonations at company dinners, stands in the middle of the crouching cluster, where he's letting out a low, sonorous Gregorian chant of a growl. His lips are chalky. His eyes are sunken and red. His pockets are bulging with neat little white vomit bags. Then his head's in a bag he holds with two colorless fingers, he's convulsing twice, filling the bag, and then he throws the thing into the wake like a trucker throws his twelfth cigarette. "*Jeg haaaaaater Lofoten!*" (I hate Lofoten) he yells, a mucusy gurgle lubricating each vowel.

The woman next to him isn't so well prepared and, with a half cry, vomits, too, but into thin air. Into thick air. The chunks and juice make a swirling, fireworks kind of pattern and drop on the chest of the pasty-looking man to her right. Neither she nor the man as much as flinch.

I return to the tangy interior and, eyes half closed, finger my way to my seat. Back in deep meditation, I'm getting smug, convinced I might actually end up being one of the superior two or three übercreatures here who survives intact, without spilling or splitting my gut. I'm all calm, all peaceful now, and by sheer force of will I'm all hummy-dumming something to my mind in this moment as my eyes, blinkless, channel the sea gods. A small circle of my forehead is melding with the cool, steady glass of my porthole window, and I see nothing, know nothing but the steady, perfect serenity of the horizon. I am that line. I am the line. I am a line. I am in line. Line. Line. Line.

Then the unthinkable happens. A tap-tap-tap on my shoulder. I grit my teeth so tightly I can't speak, can't respond, and though I do not want to turn—no, I can*not* turn, glued as my skull is to the glass—I'm chronically polite. And I turn. The way people freshly set in neck braces turn. I tuuuuuurn my head while peeeeeeeling my eyes off my line. There, Randall's blue eyes. "So . . . how you doing?" he whispers sympathetically, leaning close to me.

That he's able to rip out and open one of those white bags in time to catch the perfect upward arc of my vomit, remains to this day a moment of matrimonial wonder. And he never even winces when that eruption comes with the same sound and force you get when you rip a whole gymnasium's carpet off of super adhesive on cement.

Six virulently fetid hours later, the world stops beating us up, the sky settles down, the hydrofoil shudders into harbor. I smack my lips, drag my trembling fingers through my sweaty hair, and look around to see that every last one of us has just stepped out of the ring with the Destroyer. Folks have bruises and abrasions, clothes are torn and soiled, hair is plastered into gummy, geometric shapes, someone actually has a gash on his face, and Anita, dear Anita, Randall's assistant, has broken her ankle.

The huddled masses yearning to breathe free stagger into the linoleum-tiled entry port at Lofoten Islands. I am relieved to see Mette and Oskar limping together, even if the young husband is leaning heavily on the young wife, and the wife is looking with disgust in the other direction while handing the husband his wadded sweatshirt, which he takes in one hand as if barely coming out of full anesthesia, and uses it like a towel to wipe off the last drips of bile clinging to his chin.

8

SONG OF NORWAY

Wouldja listen to me? Whatever you do, do not do weddings."

The brunette soprano in fishnets and a body microphone was schooling me, wagging her polished pointer finger my direction. We were in our dressing room between the acts of the Tuesday matinee at the Westchester Broadway Theater, a bunch of the cast half in costume, half in costume change, chatting about agents, 8 x 10 headshots, and all the details of musical theater careers.

"No fun'rals, eethah," piped in the fiery belter with a red wig and a killer Bronx accent. "Soon's ya go Equity, mine as well stay outta churches altagethah."

Translated, that meant that as soon as you were a member of Actor's Equity, the union for professional stage actors, all that kind of work—funerals, weddings, bar mitzvahs, clam bakes—was beneath you, even illegal, a breach of your Equity contract. When you got your union membership card, my friends agreed, you did the Big Time, nothing else but. This was our solemn sisters' pact.

Now what could I do with this fancy schmancy Equity card of mine? The one right there, tucked in the pocket of my fleece-lined anorak? I'd left that theater trajectory to follow my husband's career and, I'd hoped, to offer a big world to our little family. But now I was frozen in my tracks, literally and professionally. My identity was in crisis. Last thing I'd heard, though, there weren't any Big Times coming any time soon to my tiny island.

No funerals. No weddings. No clam bakes. No gigs underneath a hyacinth trellis with a Latvian accordion player doing Lionel Ritchie. And like the Bronx gal had said, I had to stay out of churches altogether.

So what did I do? I started singing in every last church in sight.

My own church was a small but hardy Mormon congregation in a place called Sandvika. Had I looked no further than that one community, I'd have already found more than your average number of better-than-average musicians. Terje was a full-time music teacher and fine accompanist. And when Terje was busy, Thor could sight-read just about anything you threw at him, from Grieg to Gershwin. Karin was a flutist with the orchestra for the Norwegian Opera. Her daughter, Heidi, was an unusually gifted Mozarteum-trained violist. Anneli was a world-class concert pianist. I was the undercover defector from Equityville. We all made loads of beautiful music together.

Then there was Bente. You remember her from the 17th of May, seven types of Christmas cookies and antiseptic appliances. But what I didn't tell you about then is that even more than julestemning, this woman had music in her veins. When I found out she had a lifelong love for the American musical theater repertoire, I just about leapt headlong over her grand piano and right into her arms. We hit it off, Bente and I.

Together, we did Broadway evenings in church, at schools, at private recitals, and at corporate events. She rollicked at the ivories while I wailed my favorite spirituals. She dug out every Swedish, Norwegian, and German folk hymn she could and found audiences for these programs. When I had an audition for the chorus of the opera or for a gospel choir or for an upcoming regional musical, she hopped in as my willing piano sidekick. Bente and I never performed more often than at Christmas, which holiday in Norway is synonymous with making music.

Besides with Bente, though, what did I sing, with whom, and where? Let's just say the range was eclectic. Among the most memorable holiday gigs was Händel's *Messiah*, staged in a dilapidated barn hidden deep in the mountains. A glacial manger. The small baroque choir and our bunch of soloists stamped boots in brittle straw covering the upper loft of this barn where we crowded together, trying to generate some heat without utterly desecrating Händel. Our vibratos were like machine guns. Our faces were tinged with smoke and our hair was almost ignited by the small live torches we were given for the heat as much as for the light, since there was no electrical source but for the shizzing generator into which a Yamaha keyboard, our only accompaniment, was plugged. I was so jittery that the nicest audience member, an older gentleman with a beard to his belt, lent me his floor-length, fur-lined World War II army coat. Then he tossed me his hat. The head-to-toe getup kept me from getting whiplash or chipping my incisors from all the chattering, although, strangely I did expect everyone to salute me when I finished.

Talk about atmosphere. All that candlelight and singed hair, that residual laryngitis, and the walking pneumonia until April. Still, I smile when I recall how the legs of the keyboard began shaking then slowly folded in on themselves, and neither the pianist, still pounding away, nor the vocalists, still singing, missed a beat. The keyboard sank to the floor, the conductor crouched, following the pianist's fingers, the closest baritone scrambled to his knees to recover the conductor's sheet music flying all over the place, our voices mounted higher as we neared the dramatic end of the chorus, until everything, keyboard, conductor, sheet music, reached the floor with a thud. And just as we landed on that last, sustained, triumphant "Ha-leeehhh-lu-jaaah," this conductor shouted at the top of his lungs, "You're never going to forget this!"

And I haven't.

On another night, it snowed heavily over Oslo, but I was toasty inside. I stood in the fully restored Holmenkollen kappell, a stave church overlooking the Oslofjord, a place entirely of wood and lit with candles so it glowed like a jewel box. It was packed to capacity. From where I stood at the microphone on stage, whom did I see seated front and center? My family. And behind them, Bente, Jan Åke, Børre, Pia, and a whole pod of friends from church and Nesøya and work and school, also family. There, as a soloist with Norway's beloved Big Chief Jazz Band, we did a program of American holiday favorites, "Chestnuts Roasting on an Open Fire," "Have Yourself a Merry Little Christmas," and "I'll Be Home for Christmas," and got the whole audience swaying.

The founder of Big Chief became my agent and within a year, and as a means of launching what was going to be a concert tour of the country, got us a spot on Norway's talk and talent hour called "Wesenstund." It was a Sunday evening broadcast, so that day at church, our congregation was patting me on the back, wishing me the best.

"Make us proud," Stein Håvard nodded at me.

"Don't wear pearls. Not enough jazz in them," advised Trond.

"*Lykke til!*" Karin said, smiling, her thumbs up for "good luck."

I got those miniscule fifteen minutes of fame, had a blast singing my heart out with Big Chief. I did keep a tape of the broadcast, and have watched it exactly once so my parents could be proud. I'll bet my great-great-grandchildren will one day find it an inconceivable hoot.

There was a moment when I sat alone waiting in my tiny dressing room at the NRK studios, after makeup and hair and tech people had done their preliminary rounds and all the members of Big Chief had patted "*lykke til*" on my back and gone out a side door for one last smoke. I sat on a black naugahyde bar stool in front of one of those mirrors with white bulbs all around, sat there watching my backstage television prompter up in the corner, waiting for Gro to knock on my door with a two-minute signal, watching myself mouthing the texts for two songs we'd only decided on two hours ago when we'd done light and mic checks. It was there and all at once that I was oddly in another far-away dressing room. In that other dressing room there was a big band overture signaling a second act. I was in a green robe and body mic and had just gotten off a backstage phone call with Randall. I was pulling on my platinum '40s wig and shoving my feet into my heels. And though I should have been mouthing texts and mentally going through choreography, in that moment in that other dressing room I was mouthing something else. My mind was fixated on a glowing, noiseless sight of a green John Deere snowplow and a clear pathway cut right down the middle of a world of snow. There, in a low, dreading mumble, I was mouthing to myself, "*Norway?*"

"*To minutter igjen,*" Gro chirped, leaning into the door. She smiled from behind her rectangular, neon-yellow-rimmed glasses, giving me the two-minute signal.

And my whole chest cramped with such a vise grip of gratitude I was out of breath when I stood up, stroking flat the wrinkled fabric on my thighs, shaking my shoulders to loosen things up, humming up and down the scale to warm my cords. I walked through that shadowy, curtainy darkness every stage person knows so well, thinking the whole time of my little family lined up in front of the television on their small knees and in their jammies, watching impatiently through the first parts of this Norwegian talk show they now actually understood word for word, completely. Waiting to see their mamma sing.

There would be many other singing engagements over the two years that we would remain in Norway. There were months when I was learning new music every week, my children wandering in and around the piano or sometimes around other vocalists or orchestra members. I was recruited to sing at every kind of function. At the library's opening social, a fiftieth birthday gathering, the kindergarten's closing social, the local book club, a corporate midyear social, a neighboring town's Late-Winter Song Evening, another town's Early-Spring Poetry Reading, a high school's mid spring chamber concert, and the frequent American Broadway potpourri. Breach after flagrant breach of the sisters' pact.

When invited with three other female American musicians, Barbara, Marilyn, and Deborah, to perform at the US ambassador's residence, I took along nine-year-old Parker, who sat primly in his navy suit and bow tie, his hair parted on the left side and slicked flat like a confederate soldier.

"You have to sit right in that seat, honey," I told him, pointing to an upholstered chair in the front row, "Because in one song, I'm going to give you the signal like this," I nodded once, "and then I'll come get you with my hand just like this, and bring you on stage. Then I'll sing right to you. Right into your eyes. Got it?"

"Got it. I don't have to sing, too, do I?"

"No, you only have to listen. And you also have to help me not mess up, buddy. Can you do that?"

It was Stephen Sondheim's "Not While I'm Around," a lyrical, haunting piece. When I pulled the little boy with a bow tie and confederate hair to my side and knelt on the stage and sang right into his eyes, I nearly abandoned all efforts at composure. I nearly forgot about the respectable audience, the professional distance. I almost forgot about Mr. and Mrs. Ambassador sitting right over my shoulder in a suit and gown. Instead, I was composed; "Nothing can harm you," I sang to my child, "Not while *I'm* around." And I finished, as I remember, with a smile, my head tilted, squeezing his skinny suited shoulders, giving him a peck on the cheek, and dismissing him with a tap on his rump, clapping for him, nodding to audience, "Now isn't he just so cute?"

There are those minutes in life which you ache to redo or even, if by magic, somehow inhabit again.

I didn't take the children to all of my performances. One such, I described in my journal:

> *Flå is a small arts community tucked deep in the folds of Hallingdal. Flå had invited me, the "American Broadway Singer," to appear at their annual Arts Days celebration.*

I stood in a glitzy American gown on an outdoor stage with microphone in hand and sang three hours of show tunes and big band standards flanked by twenty-five somewhat rigid but nevertheless warm-hearted and well-amplified members of Hallingdal's civic "Big Band." The locals, robust and impossibly well-scrubbed, wielding sausages and wearing boiled wool knickers, stomped patterns across the pavilion's dance floor till all the Aquavit ran dry and the moon peered over the rough ridges of Hallingdal's towering walls. I went through everything the band had in its repertoire; Benny Goodman, the Andrews Sisters, Bing Crosby, Glenn Miller, even Neil Diamond.

Then there was this last number, a traditional Norwegian Sæter tune I'd prepared just for this event. When it was announced, five band members, rosy cheeked, woolen knickered, flannel plaid, stood to join me, and three of us sang first with Ole the accordion player, then six of us sang in a cappella harmony, arms wrapped around one another's waists or shoulders, howling like mountain sheep herders under the moon's perfect spotlight. I don't think it gets much better than this.

Unless you're doing a screen test for a Norwegian television commercial:

"Fine, fine, that was just fine, Melissa. Let's just try it one more time, and this time even more enthusiasm. All right?"

"No problem. Enthusiasm? Got it!" I responded in Norwegian. I'd gotten the script just that morning from my agent and had drilled it in the car on the way to this recording studio on the northern edge of town. I cleared my throat, messed up my hair a bit (my enthused look), stared deep into the black hole of the camera, and started afresh:

"Now I dare to try on *whatever* clothes I *like* on *whatever* day of the *month!*" Beaming, I picked up a small, imagined cardboard box from an imagined counter off to my right and flirted with the camera, adding, "*Always Ultra Feminine* pads *with wings*. So you can *really fly!*"

"Super! Cut!" someone called out, and the man holding the hanging microphone let his arms drop with a grunt.

A woman in a sound booth stepped out, and all I saw in the shadows were her denim skirt and boots. "Now remind us, Melissa, you're from . . . let me see . . . Trømsø? Or was it . . . " she's flipping through some papers, "from Bodø? You're from the north I can tell; am I right?"

"From the west. The western States, actually."

"Hmm? Really? Interesting. Hey, can we put some more on the tape here?" the lady asked. "Like, I don't know, Melissa . . . Uh . . . Can you sing?"

"If you'd like me to, yes."

"Give us an American song, is that good?"

"Sure, uh, let's see. What's *your* favorite American song?"

The microphone man, the one who was no more than a shadowy shape in green Converse All Stars, was quick with a favorite song. He starts whistling it from the dark . . .

By "rainbow, way up high," I'd taken over because, like millions of people, I knew this tune by heart. I sang it a cappella into the baking but also calming heat of four huge spotlights. I sang it all the way through. From "there's a land that I heard of" to "why, oh, why can't I?," under all that text and simple melody, I was scratching my inner head, laughing a bit to myself, asking *How did I get here*? But also feeling like I had fully awakened in this country, that "there's no place like home."

At the same time, my agent was deep into plans for that full country concert tour the next year. We'd done publicity photos and a demo CD. He was contacting venues. We'd had preliminary meetings to pin down calendar details. "You must bring your husband and children, too," he'd said, "It would be a great cultural experience for them. We'll let that son of yours play on the drums."

Also at about this same time, Randall's company was discussing a possible transfer back to the States or a transfer elsewhere outside of the States. Randall and I, however, were lying next to each other in bed at night, in ever longer and more animated sessions of Ceiling Talk: "And what if we just stayed here? For good?" and, "Do *you* also just want to stay here for good?" and, "What do we need to do to *stay here* for good?"

In good faith, I had long since signed up Dalton for the barnepark down the street for when he would turn three, and had him in a biweekly play group where he was beginning to speak sandbox Norwegian. I'd planted tulip bulbs, we'd bought Parker a drum set, and Claire was on the roster to start horseback riding lessons in the fall. Great-grandfather Haakon Aamodt's investment in getting his progeny back to his roots, we thought, was certainly paying off. So why not close the circle and simply graft the branches back to the roots?

Grandpa Haakon's county of Østfold lies about an hour southeast from Oslo's talk show and television commercial studios. In the middle of that county is the village of Ski, and in the middle of Ski is a tiny white stucco chapel. There, on one of those brilliantly blue-skied, late-spring days, Sigrid, the daughter of a prominent local farmer, is getting married, and

I've been drafted to serenade the day-long traditional farm wedding. What will unfold before me, the only non-Norwegian on hand, is like a movie so enchanting I feel I'm unprepared to be adequate as the soundtrack.

I arrive early by car, ready to run through the program one last time. The church organist arrives on his road bike, skidding into the gravel parking place, and, with no more ceremony than the nod of his head (which he keeps wiping as he continues to sweat), launches us into a breakneck dash through our program, tearing through four Norwegian love songs at the same speed with which he arrived on his bike. "Well now," he says, slapping the organ bench, "I think that'll about do it," and he's running over a hill to hose off at a nearby farm. I'm still catching my breath, leaning against a pillar in the choir loft, when I peer down to see a procession.

A thick, inching sea of deep color seeps into the chapel's all-white interior. Figure upon figure, couple upon couple, family upon family file in gracefully, cautiously, as if the floor were made of the thinnest sheet of glass. There are mostly heavy, black wool skirts that swish nearly to the floor, barely exposing the occasional edge of white stockings, which meet the edge of black shoes. On the front of the shoes, ornate, pilgrim-like silver buckles.

In some of the many regional versions of bunad, the skirt fronts, as the bodices, are gathered into the waistline with the smallest pleats— dozens of pin-tucked pleats—that make architecture out of wool. They're encrusted with clusters of embroidered flowers, the sheen of which looks like jewels in the early afternoon light coming in through the high windows. Everywhere there are balloons of starched, white linen sleeves tapering to lace-trimmed cuffs and, on some women, wrist wreaths of silver coins which tinkle and glint, the sunlight flitting on their surface. There are brooches, some larger than your palm, clasped at the top of the bodice near the collar. Some women wear small, embroidered woolen bonnets tied under the chin with ample satin bows. And there are small handbags made of matching wool with iridescent embroidery, affixed to a silver chain draped at the waistline. Some dresses, a dozen maybe, aren't black or deep red but are clear cerulean blue.

The men look like they've arrived on the last commuter train from Brigadoon: velvet knickers, embroidered vests, white linen shirts, black leprechaun shoes. Some children, just a handful, are there, too. One mom indiscreetly yanks her Karl-Andreas or Anders-Håvard to attention, and directs him into the pew next to her as she tugs down the bottom of his red vest and re-tucks the bunched hem of his starched shirt. He's sullen. Thirteen. Has spent the morning bailing hay or milking his own goat,

I fantasize. Or skateboarding, my inner realist corrects me. Here is old Norway, but again contemporary, now-a-day Norway, History and The Present, in all its splendid finery and well-mannered neighborliness waiting reverently for a *høy tid*.

My organist has traded in smelly lycra bike shorts for full bunad regalia himself, and ashamed that I'm just in my best cream silk suit and heels, I slip behind a marble pillar. At the same moment, the organ opens up all pipes announcing Sigrid's arrival. The groom, vigorous looking with muscles everywhere (even in his jaw, which he's clenching, like his fists) waits at the altar.

Sigrid, also blonde, fresh and freckled, poised in a simply-cut white satin gown, proceeds up the aisle: a cool, tall glass of milk. I'm staring at her while I take a deep breath and begin singing: "*Kjærlighet, varmeste ord på jord . . .* " Love, the warmest word on earth.

When the ceremony ends, the new couple clambers up into a handsome horse-drawn carriage which, trailed by other horse-drawn carriages carrying parts of their bunaded entourage, clops over the rolling hills of Østfold toward Sigrid's family estate. The parents who've invited me to sing, Solvor and Lars, lean down from their carriage to give me road directions, complicated automobile directions, I'm told. It's much more direct over the fields. I'm in a tailored suit with stiletto pumps, driving a motor vehicle with a CD player and automatic windows. Obviously, I've missed a road sign and driven into the middle of the wrong century.

This family's farm has got to have its own zip code. Lars escorts me up to a crest beyond the limits of the groomed property that radiates outward from the central manor house, and there points to a place on the horizon that I'm sure must be Sweden.

"It's just the easternmost edge of the property," he smiles softly. Then he swings his arm in a full arc in the other direction and, those specks over there? Those prominent hills a few kilometers away? "Also the edge of the family domain." It's deep green, the entire expanse of it, abruptly tree-rich in spots, deliciously farmable in general. Lars seems too soft-spoken to own a whole county.

"It's my husband's family's soil, too, you know," I tell Lars. "Aamodt, Haakon. Thorkildsen, Christian. Farmers going way, *way* back. Do you know the names?"

"Then," Lars puts his hand on my shoulder, "somewhere not more than a century or so ago, we were family, your husband and I."

Back at the manor house, people are starting to arrive, leaping down from buggies, off single horses, or out of Volvos. Solvor wants me to see the house and doesn't hesitate to escort me, room by room, through its every antique corner. The place is a fortress with massive oak staircases flanked by oak banisters so big you'd need two hands to grab the circumference, leaded-pane windows dating back three hundred years, lustrous floors of wide, worn planks bulleted in place by chocolate-colored dowels, hand-tufted carpets brought from Sweden, and hand-woven linens from Denmark. Huge family portraits with their oily sheen on pallid, stern visages line the walls above a stone fireplace that cuts a garage-sized hole in the front salon. Everywhere I turn there are signs of The Hunt, and rounding a bend a bit too frivolously, I nearly lose an eye on a low-hanging reindeer antler.

The men look ready for a barn raising, but tonight they're only reinforcing the orchestra pavilion in the courtyard, and moving into rows the long, decorated banquette tables where wine, breads, and dried meats are already being laid by a troop of diligent women. I'm handed a pewter platter of cured venison and a wooden trough of sculpted pickles and radishes to put on a table somewhere and make myself inconspicuous (in my twentieth-century silk suit and patent leather stilettos) by being industrious like every last body around me.

Suddenly, the farm's cutting loose. There's the metallic commotion of cowbell ringing and wild whooping, everyone around me chanting something in unison, something that's accelerating, something that has us all stamping our feet and clapping our hands at once. I dive in full throttle, although I end up almost falling over when I jab all four inches of my stilettos into black-brown farm soil.

The bride and groom have arrived.

A large woman, Inger, redheaded and white toothed, clinches her fleshy arm around my shoulder and shoves a glass of wine in my hand, hollering and stamping still. Since I don't drink, I wrap my arm around the shoulder of the next guy, Ingemar, white haired and red cheeked, do a little holler and a light stamp, and shove the glass into his hand. He downs it in one hearty swig like water, establishing the drinking blueprint for the rest of the night.

People stay primarily sober for at least the first two hours of the four-hour dinner for two hundred guests, a spread of gelled vegetable aspic, smoked salmon with scrambled eggs and sour cream with dill, crab, and coriander salad, cucumber salad in a light vinaigrette, lamb, and tender little new potatoes, all served in a grand hall downstairs in the central house. I sit on the middle table, not far from Lars and Solvor, who are poised under an enormous stuffed black bear head that looks like it's belting a high note.

After dinner and under a sky of polished cobalt, we all dance and sing like barefoot children. *Really* like barefoot children, because somewhere between the hired band's Johann Strauss and Bee Gees, I've kicked off my shoes like everyone else. Has grass ever felt so cool? Has the moon ever been so close? Have I ever not lived here, not loved these people, not wanted to sing at every single one of their weddings?

Around four in the morning I watch the delicate, black shadows of horse-drawn carriages tiptoe over the far ridges, disappearing in a rising sun: spiders crawling into a flame. Motors cough and hum, the trumpet player Hermann is packing it in, and the lead singer Nils drops another empty Aquavit bottle onto a pile of many other empty Aquavit bottles. Its "cli-shink" makes the mottled cat dart under a cleared banquette table. Solvor comes at me from behind and, putting one arm around my waist, strokes my hair, and draws my head to her shoulder. A mother's touch. A new sisters' pact.

Weddings. Messiah barn burnings. Feminine hygiene product pitching. New Orleans Jazz. Embassies. My own Mormon church. And then at last, a biblical musical.

Josef Og Det Utrolige Farvet Drømkåpet needed a lead narrator. Barbara, my multitalented musician friend, was already directing the musical's children's chorus and doing orchestrations from a massive keyboard, working her big circle of local music talent to build the band. She was overbooked. Since I'd already done the English version, *Joseph And The Amazing Technicolor Dreamcoat*, in New Jersey, the producers thought I might be able to do it here. So I said yes to play the narrator in Norwegian.

Then I became the show's artistic director. And choreographer. And even found myself backstage in one of the performances, training dogs. (They were the biggest hounds I had seen in my life, cast in this show as Ishmaelite camels.)

The closing night of *Josef*, I walked out into the parking lot, costumes in a suit bag, humming one of the show's tunes. When I stood next to my car overlooking Oslofjord, I stopped abruptly in my tracks. I looked straight ahead. I shook my head. Had I not noticed before? Across the road and down one block was a small barrack painted barn red. Next to it, a chain link fence. There was a gravel parking lot and four swings, a simple metal slide, a teeter-totter. I'd known it all first under a couple of meters of snow. There I stood, still in my stage makeup, congratulatory roses in my arms, and suddenly I recognized I was only feet from where

I'd once hidden behind the steering wheel of my parked car, thermos of peppermint tea in my hand, scouting out this intimidating but enticing new world, contemplating the dangers of Blakstad barnepark and the foreignness of this cold, impenetrable land.

Somewhere in the middle of the postshow cast party, I felt the same vise grip I'd felt in that dressing room at the television studios. The whole Bradford clan, Melissa, Randall, and their three children, and a dozen of the main players in the cast were gathered around our long Norwegian table, watching taped footage of our closing performance of *Josef*. Claire bopped up and down in the lap of Anita-Marie, Parker was with Tormod and Per Trygve, who'd played Jacob's oldest sons, Reuben and Simeon, doing phrase-by-phrase translation from the Norwegian text to its English original he had learned when I'd done the show in New Jersey and this nine-year-old son, then three, had memorized the whole script. Dalton, now toddling sturdily, raided every last refreshment platter. Randall did crowd control and video machine duty while dispensing casual Norwegian one-liners to all our guests.

Here were the faces. Faces of real people whose language I spoke and whose humor I caught, whose regional accents I could identify, whose families I'd eaten with and worked with and sung with. Folks to whom, I knew it by that time, I was soon going to have to say goodbye.

In our many Ceiling Talks over the months leading up to the show, Randall and I had had to make some difficult decisions. We'd asked each other hard questions about work and family and education and growth. The conversations got granular when it came to discussions about identity; who were we? Who were our children? We were, in the end, non-Norwegians, no matter how blonde or blue-eyed or fluent-in-the-tongue or fast-on-the-slopes we aspired to be. Yet we were not really what we used to be before Norway, either. We were, we concluded, something else.

This ambiguity took a firm shape, which was then drawn with some tension when Randall got an offer from his company (again, sort of out of the blue) for a position based in France. He was asked to come to Paris for preliminary interviews. When he called me on what I remember so well was one of the most heartbreakingly fruitful Norwegian spring afternoons, his voice was cautious and almost apologetic. Still, I thought I sniffed a bit of suppressed sparkle. "Hon, you know what?" he said. "There's a great big world out here."

And that's all it took. I didn't need a green John Deere snowplow. I didn't even need a nudge. I knew that despite everything, despite all we had scraped and scrounged to build a new and thriving life in the land of our forefathers, despite all that, we were *something else* and we were going to head *somewhere else*, and that somewhere else was going to be the setting of another chapter of our family's growth. Great big world? We just had to join it.

Which tinged with tenderness this moment of postmusical celebration with our Norwegian friends. They knew nothing about our pending move. And so they probably had no idea why, when they brought me a thank you gift, I welled up and had to apologize for my emotions. *A thank you gift?* They said they wanted to thank *me* for helping with their show, for serving them? I tried to tell them *nei, det er ikke lov*! No, that's not allowed. And that they *forstår ikke*. You don't understand!

I tried, I really did, but I know I never managed to tell them or Johanne or Britt from barnepark, or Bente or Pia or my whole loving church family, or Barbara or Sigrid the school principal, or Ellen my *jordmor*, or Gunnil from barselgruppe, or the nameless conductor on the sinking Yamaha keyboard, or little Karolina or Louisa who'd checked my grammar as well as my sanity, or strawberry-blonde Jesper who'd just needed toilet paper, or my neighbor who'd hiked over my head and shoveled off my roof, or the many nameless but not faceless others who filled our Norway years—I know I never managed to tell them and that *nei, nei, nei*, I had not done a thing for them. It was they who had done *everything* for my young family and for me.

9

L'Arrivée

Moving from Norway to France meant trading in one splendid extreme for another equally splendid, but strikingly antithetical one. It was a move from north to south; from Nordic to Latin; from a calm island to the bustling Île de France; from the tundra to the Tuileries; from craggy fjords to the sleek Seine; from the untamed spirituality of Lofoten to the crafted symmetry of the *Jardins de Versailles*; from the Land of the Midnight Sun to the Land of the Sun King; from stark homogeneity to vibrating variety; from two kinds of cheese to 378-plus; from hot dogs to *haute cuisine*; from IKEA to Louis XVI; from the comfy lilt of the economic Norwegian tongue to the highly stylized lavishness of *le Français*; from cooperation to competition; from the community to the *moi*; from rigorous obedience to *la Révolution*; from no-nonsense androgyny to the religion called *la beauté*; from muddy parkdress to starched parochial uniforms; from sandals to Christian Louboutin suede platform pumps; from innocence to experience.

From Eden to the world.

Or more specifically, to the old world, since we began our French years in Versailles.

You know of Versailles. I had known, too. I thought. But I had not known that for the French, "Versailles" is as much a concept as it is a city or a château. When the French refer to Versailles, they are referring to *la vieille France*, or the old France and all that implies: nobility, Catholicism, traditions, and families who today live in the same home their ancestors built back when the *Place Hoche* had a guillotine for public executions. "Versailles" as a concept means, for one, extravagantly gilded and velvet-heavy furnishings. Things overwrought yet serious about it are *très Versaillais*. The concept also means five or six children dressed in navy skirts or knickers and white knee socks, trailing a mother with a practical chin-length bob locked in place with a navy hair band. That phenomenon is also what my neighbor, in a whisper, called *très Catho*, or übercatholic. *Versaillais* implies *le patrimoine*, which has much to do with the preservation of historic France as it has to do with lineage, which is signaled by the family names beginning with "du." The city's slogan, if you asked me to come up with one, would be, "What was, is." As commoner newcomers to the kings' court, we were about to learn what "was" was.

Around the corner from the *rive droite* train station was a renovated turn-of-the-century home with a white stucco façade and an oval window smack dab in the front. If you opened up the navy-blue, double-front door, you could look directly through the depth of the house (it was one room deep) into an enclosed backyard with four small round bushes placed like thumbtacks in each corner of a table cloth of green. The house had a bright white interior with emerald-green trim throughout and tasteful tiles in its bathrooms, a kitchen with glossy yellow walls that reminded me of Provence, a side view straight onto the dome of the Église de Sainte Jean d'Arc, and a back view onto the local synagogue. It was a fifteen-minute walk to the *place du marché* where the biweekly open market had stood since the thirteenth century. And only a fifteen-minute jog down *Boulevard de la Reine*, crossing *Boulevard du Roi*, and through the gilded gates of the sprawling *Château de Versailles* and its even sprawlinger *Jardins du Château de Versailles*.

Like a movie set. Except for the hordes of white-athletic-shoed tourists who could have been extras out of costume in an otherwise-period film. They came directly from the train station or in enormous buses that parked in what used to be the royal horse stables.

With time, everything in Versailles turned out to be a former "royal."

The home was also directly across the street from the private Catholic (or *catho*, if you insist) *École Hulst*. From all appearances, this was the most prim and trafficked preschool in *toute la France*. Fascinated, I peered through my kitchen window, gulping and plotting, rubbing my hands together guardedly, hidden behind my potted rosemary, thyme, and basil the way I'd hidden behind the steering wheel of my car looking over Blakstad barnepark. I applied my same methods of observation, wanting to be part of it all and considering sending little Dalton there, until I learned I would have had to have put his name on the waiting list the hour I found out I was pregnant with him.

Okay, so Hulst was in demand.

But it was demanding. At least for a loosey-goosey, fresh-from-barnepark mother-and-child duo, like us. Watching the children scooting in and out every morning, I could have sworn they all came from the same navy-blue gene pool. Dalton, in contrast (and I, for that matter), seemed to lack that certain oui-oui chromosome needed to slip in without causing a sea change.

Granted, that could have all been in my perception, but to be honest, I was too intimidated by what I observed as the school's "was-ness"—its exacting French A-lines, the one boy in a blazer and velvet knickers, all that crispness—to enroll my son. Not without at least a few months in a preliminary crisper.

I went around the corner and down the Rue Remilly to l'École Maternelle Richard Mique, which was public, ecumenical, and visibly less crisp than Hulst—comfortably wilted, let's say—and I set my sights on enrolling Dalton there. Following my barnepark method of attack, I stalked the Richard Mique premises in off hours. I then loitered at corners during drop-off and pick-up, noting the habits of local adults. I listed the children's gear, shoe styles, haircuts, behavior. I then made eye contact, greeted mothers and fathers, took Dalton there by the hand twice, just to practice the trek. And to build nerve.

Eventually, I dared approaching a real person on the street to question her about the school. I'd selected her, actually, over a few days scoping for The Most Open Face in Versailles. Her name was Rita. She was wonderful. She became a friend. With four young children herself and relatively new to Versailles, too, she could instruct me in Anne Sullivan French about applying a month late to the school, as I was doing. And wouldn't you know it. Like Johanne from Norway, Rita told me to go directly to the main office the next day and request a place for Dalton. "*Mais vite, vite*"—but hurry!—her wide eyes insisted.

There was no chain-link fence around Richard Mique as there had been around Blakstad barnepark. But there were serious-looking walls and gates that were padlocked at all hours but the fifteen-minute intervals at morning drop off, lunchtime pickup and drop off, and afternoon pickup. Timing it precisely, I was able to enter and find the *directrice's* office, where I was greeted by a brunette woman who resembled in no way but hair color our dear tante Britt. There was no snow-blown look or red front-zip barnepark jumpsuit. No thermos of coffee. No messy hair and ruddy cheeks. Instead, this delicate woman wore perfume. And pearls. And a fitted skirt. And heels. And she sat behind a large desk sipping a porcelain cup of tea. I felt myself suck in my gusto and make myself as absolutely prim as physically possible without turning a shade of puce and approached her with soft, alluring steps. She was not ready, I'll bet, for my attempt at French, but she was genteel and was used to working with people a tenth her age, so when she spoke to me with single syllable words and those large semaphore movements, I was able to discern enough to know what she told me.

Rendezvous. Need of one. Speak with school director. Come back with another faith.

(Whuh?)

Oh. Right. Come back another *time.*

So I smiled, thanked Madame, scooted spritely on my way, and went home to re-wax my legs, starch even my underclothing, and prepare my speech for the next morning's private audience with *Madame directrice.*

"Madame Bradford," the directrice smiled warmly at me the next morning, addressing me in French. "Our school has never admitted a non-francophone American child. But if your son *were* to be admitted," she leaned forward on her elbows, removing her glasses to look me in the eye, "I would assign him to the most skilled *maitresse.*"

Oh sheesh. I heard my squealy American voice circling, its hands on its forehead, eyes low, circling circling like a crazed crazy voice. *I've been here before,* it squealed from the pit of my brain. *We know exactly how this is going to go. They don't know our type. We're doomed!*

"Thank you, Madame," I said like Catherine Deneuve or any other glamorous and unrufflable movie star without sweat beads on the upper lip or a voice squealing against a wall in the pit of her brain. I adjusted myself on the wooden chair facing her desk, knees together and feet flat on the floor, schoolgirl style. A whiff of my own Chanel perfume brought me to my senses and gives me courage. "I am entirely grateful for your solicitude."

Words I would never use in English, in case you wondered. But in French they were somehow *entièrement* fine. No question, I was feeling a tad grovely.

"I will assign your son—what is his name? Dalton?—I will assign your son to Madame M., an excellent pedagogue," said the Madame directrice, as she smiled again and wrote something on a form she then handed to me. "She will help your son *s'adapter*."

Forms. *Pedagogue. S'adapter.*

These three words, though I had no idea of it that morning in the school director's office, foreshadowed much of our early experience in France. Indeed, one could say they are central to life in France in general.

In addition to the form I was given that morning to complete, there were also two letters of recommendation, two forms proving legal residency, a form proving Randall's employment, four forms from the office of the *Ministre de l'Education de la France*, three dental and doctor's records including proof that Dalton was inoculated against tuberculosis as well as verifiably *propre* or potty-trained, his copied passport and, just in case anyone doubted he had indeed been born, his birth certificate. Those forms, as well as two more interviews with *Madame directrice* and an *exemplaire du graphisme*—a writing sample—and three-year-old Dalton was admitted to the public Maternelle Richard Mique of Versailles, France.

My education in forms and formality, like my Viking son's formal education, had begun. Formally.

Bureaucratie is a French word, of course, and France won't let you forget it. Getting Dalton into French school was not my first encounter with French bureaucracy, though. As soon as we'd landed in Versailles (Friday), unpacked our suitcases in a hotel (Saturday), gone to church (Sunday), and Randall had flown off on an extended trip to Karachi (Monday), all my days thereafter, it seemed, were filled with sorting through French forms.

Just a detail: I did not speak French. I had not studied French law. I had no background in governmental negotiations, neither did I have anyone to help me peel off those pesky official royal wax stamps without losing the whole middle paragraph in the process. I had three young children, no child care, twelve suitcases, and, the week we finally moved into our home, I had a flooded basement that turned to mulch thirty-four cartons of irreplaceable mementos. For that baptism by basement flood, I had a skinny Portuguese plumber with his Polish Sancho Panza. How the two ever understood each other, how I ever understood them, how they ever understood me enough to clean out the mess without being electrocuted by the live wires dangling above the soupy reservoir that just the day before I'd stocked with all my storage, remains to this day one of the weirder mysteries of my life.

I also had a deadline. There were two weeks before school started for me to get everything up and running. For those two weeks, Randall would be absent, establishing his first connections with his direct reports in the Middle East, an area which, along with Europe and all of Africa, made up his new area of professional responsibility. If I ever wondered how he was doing in Islamabad, Karachi, Cairo, Beirut, and couldn't reach him, I just turned on the news. As you know, interesting things were going on there. And, as you can guess, this was not the Calm Pill a wife and mother needed. Ah, but he had gone to that two-week-long personal security course at Langley. Here he learned how to effectively wield a kubaton, how to identify a sniper and roll for cover, and how to drive a getaway car at high speeds and from the floor of the passenger side with only one hand on the pedals. This, of course, made us all feel much, much more relaxed.

All this on my mind, I'd find myself taking those forms in a big folder to an endless string of offices, dragging three restless bodies with me, essentially crawling through French legalese with the help of a frayed dictionary and flailing arms. Mine and the children's. One of these many offices, I was sure, held the mystical keys to unlock the entrance to this new world. It seemed they didn't want me there, these alarmingly uncharming French. Well, unless I was willing to be their circus pooch and fling myself through the endless hoops to jump. My three children, my stressed-out self, hopping through hoops, standing in offices, beseeching what felt like a whole pageant of unsmiling officials behind glass walls in cigarette-smoke-filled bureau after bureau after bureau.

Today I wish I'd kept a tally to share with you how many times I arrived at some office, a sweaty wad of forms in hand, barking children at my ankles, ready to get the coveted stamp so I could proceed to the next stamp-dispensing venue, only to be told I was missing one signature, one blood sample, or a birth certificate. (And this was just to install a clothes dryer.) The American in me who values convenience and accessibility, the German in me who prizes efficiency and order, and the Norwegian in me who extols simplicity and cooperation, balked in one groaning triad at the convolutions of our new host culture.

The children took the big tangle of inconvenience in stride, though, only because they were too young, probably, to realize what we were doing fingerprinting them every week. Parker, though, had his own run-in with forms when he discovered the basketball hoops in a sport center in Rue Remilly around the corner from our home in Rue René Aubert. Parker loved nothing as much as he loved basketball and was going crazy not playing. So, I was almost ready to let him scale the fence to shoot some hoops there once in a while in the middle of the night. But the fence was high, and I am a rule keeper, and there is an after-midnight no-noise law for Versailles, so we waited until we saw a live person inside the gymnasium one extremely hot August day. We went in to seek shade and to plead our case.

"*Bonjour, Monsieur,*" I said with as much confidence as I could muster without donning combat gear. The middle-aged gentleman in a small office at the entrance of Gymnase de Remilly looked up at me, nodded, released a puff of smoke, and flicked the ashes from the end of his cigarette.

"*Bonjour Madame, jeune homme.*" It was Boris Karloff's long lost French cousin, I swear it.

I'd brought Parker, my *jeune homme,* to help me plead and, if necessary, to impress with a three-pointer from the back court with his eyes closed. To convince a potential gatekeeper of just how much this boy really loved basketball and how, maybe, his engagement in their Versailles Club du Basket (I'd seen a sign advertising tryouts) would benefit them as much as him.

"Excuse me. I disturb you," I start in, taking the same lines I'd first used on Britt at barnepark, only with slight modification. "We are Americans. We inhabit house not far." I say this pushing nine-year-old Parker in front of me. "We are hot."

Which is not the right thing to say. In French, *it,* meaning the weather, *makes* hot. But *you* are not hot. No decent Mormon mother of three, at least, is *hot* or announces that she is. And not on a first encounter with Karloff's cousin.

"And you have the air," the man responds, his face as unmoved as the heavy heat wave that is making parts of me, like my brain, liquefy.

I *have the air*? Well, in fact, I didn't have the air. I had none. Which is why I thought I was going to faint on the spot. I didn't have enough air, that was for sure, but this guy, the guy who is smoking and therefore giving me less air, is accusing me of having it. Only weeks later did I learn he had just been saying, "You sure look like it." But right then and because I had to be a wee bit obsequious, I told him what any hot, needy newcomer would: "I'm terribly, horribly desolated."

Things in that moment weren't going precisely as I'd hoped, and I began aching for a woman with half a red jumpsuit and a coffee thermos to walk in from around some corner back there and sing, "*Hurrah! Komm in!*"

But there was a door. And it had a plaque. And the plaque had a title. And all this, I thought, belonged to this cigarette-smoking Grinch, a man clearly leaving me to my own devices.

"My son plays the basketball," I bulldoze indelicately over my string of unwitting faux pas, trying to recall the phrases I'd written on Post-it notes and studied on the walk here. "Is it that you have perhaps a place for him, Monsieur?"

"*S'il vous plait?*" Parker peeps.

The man then lifts himself from the chair, tosses his cigarette into a trashcan, and stretches his shoulders. "*Shwee pah coach,*" he says with a shrug. Which meant nothing to me at all for a full minute.

Then a light goes on, and it had to do with what I now saw are the man's janitor's clothes and the broom he reached for. I get it. He isn't the coach.

The coach, when we did meet him on our next visit, was animated, even gregarious, and completely keyed about an American boy named Parker as in "*Tony Parker!*" he shouted, who, the man boasted, had grown up playing basketball in Versailles. He shook the hand of the boy who'd just moved in around the corner, the one who had a Norwegian mom, the man always thought, the boy who loved more than anything, *le basket*.

But being France, there was a certain protocol. Only after several forms, mug shots, blood tests and fingerprinting, was Parker allowed to wander in there as he pleased and shoot away. Some months later, he would become a full-fledged member of the Versailles CB (Club du Basket) where he played three times a week on a team of resolute French players who spoke no English except the essentials even I could understand: "dribble" (pronounced "dreeebl") and "Parker," pronounced "Par Cœur," as in "by heart." The motivation to make that switch from Norwegian to French got some traction. And in no time, he improved his game while picking up loads of local basketball lingo. Alright, so not quite French of the court of Versailles. But French of *a* court of Versailles.

Like *bureaucratie, formation* is also a French word, and like its etymology, comes from "form"—all those papers, tick boxes, and triplicate copies with an official rubber or wax stamp. But "formation," the French word used to describe education, has to do with making the broadness of humanity fit into one established form. It means there is a norm that people (in our case, our three-year-old, Dalton) should meet. There is a form into which people (again, our preschooler) should fit.

"Madame Bradford," said Madame M. at our first parent teacher meeting, "Let us discuss how Dalton *s'adapte*."

"S'adapte." Namely, my son zadapting. Even in the cool of a late afternoon in late September with all the other children gone home and Dalton amusing himself on the playground equipment outside the window of the classroom where I sat with Madame M., even in that positively pastoral setting, the very mention of *s'adapte* made me hot under my Hermès. I pulled it off, twisted it around my hands, then began pressing it flat, stroke-by-stroke, across my lap, while soft-eyed Madame M. gave me the particulars.

We were both sitting at two of the twenty-three preschoolers' small wooden desks, my skirt was tucked under my thighs since my legs were at a nearly vertical angle, and we were speaking French, which, after my month in Versailles, was gathering gentle momentum. But it still felt like too-tight glass slippers.

"Yes, how is he doing? Does he have friends? Is he learning French songs? Does he smile at school?" My questions were somewhat limited to the vocabulary I had at my disposal, but they showed my primary concern: Was this son of mine a happy boy?

"What we must concentrate on, Madame Bradford, at this crucial point in his formation," (that word) "is your son's ability to follow lines." Madame M.'s voice was velvety, yet upholstering solid wrought iron. A crimson Louis XIV settee.

"Lines?" I wondered if I'd misunderstood. I stroked the scarf, which I now tugged down to cover my knees.

She pulled out some sheets of paper she had apparently collected for this interview. "You see here," she pointed to a series of cursive letters—lowercase "Qs," I recall vividly—which were preprinted as dotted-line templates of the letters.

Q. Q. Q. Q. Q. Q. Q.

The children, I gathered, were to be tracing the letters.

"Right here," she pointed at a slightly large upper loop, "and here," a somewhat pinched lower loop, "there is a problem. Your son is not able to follow lines."

She stared at me. There was a trace of sadness in her eyes, as if she were the doctor giving me The Diagnosis.

"Yes? I see. He cannot follow the lines. This is . . . bad?"

"I propose that you practice these letters with your son at home so that he can understand the exactness with which he must execute these letters."

"At home? So the letters look—"

"Perfect." She was nodding, encouraging me. "Don't you agree?"

I agreed this was serious business.

"And his colors," she went on, sifting through the collection of papers with "Dalton" written in blue ink in the upper right hand corner yet with

an unfamiliar cursive—the "l" loop crooked, "a" and "o" a bit pointy—
which cursive he had learned at school, certainly not from me.

"His colors," she continued, "go outside the lines. You see here?"
She shared with me a tidy little lineup of preprinted fruits—"*pomme*,"
"*orange*," "*pêche*"—colored in pastel chalks of red, orange, and peachy
pink. Colored as a three-year-old colors, which means with verve and,
yes, an occasionally juicy apple, orange, or peach spill.

"This must be controlled," my son's teacher explained, stacking several
papers with two hands. "At this stage in his formation, he must learn to
follow the patterns and copy forms."

"Copy forms," I echoed, as if taking mental notes.

"If he fails to do this, he will not be ready to enter Say Pay, a very big
step, Madame Bradford."

Now you're wondering what kind of a cockamamie campaign "Say
Pay" is. I had wondered, too, when I heard the mothers chatting about it
one of the times I trailed them on the street. They were throwing around
the term with great vigor, batting it, so that I heard it bouncing up over
their conversation like the magical birthday party balloon you're trying
too hard to keep from touching the ground.

Say Pay meant *CP*, and CP meant first grade, still three years away,
but unlike a US first grade, CP is truly a big step. Unlike a Norwegian
first grade, it was the beginning of the end of equality. Class ranking, carried year to year, begins that year. Competition was encouraged, essential
even, to assure the excellence the academic system aspired to. Curious
and nervous, I started entering in those parental conversations with that
magical CP balloon, and found out the discussions always had the kind
of weight one usually grants to an upcoming national election or a military maneuver. CP was *très serieux*.

"I will work with him at home," I promised outwardly with dutiful
head bobbing and with an inwardly-directed browbeating. All those
winter days in Norway? Why had I not been drilling his loops and
lines? Why had I just been taking him on forest walks, singing songs,
examining snow crystals? Why had I been so lax? Not thinking pedagogy? Living in La-La instead of Oooh-La-La Land?

Here is the crux of the issue: In Norway, nature is bigger than man.
The elements rule, man bows to them. In France, man is bigger than
nature. Man rules, subdues, and commands nature. As an extension of
this, the nature of mankind himself—of a three-year-old man in Dalton's
case—must submit to an imposed form. The point of education, then,
is not to stimulate the natural man (or preschooler) into whatever his

nature might compel him to be, but to form him into a standard shape. "Formation" is not about growing innate or individual gifts, but is about cultivating and elevating from the crude elements and refining them.

For a visual of this contract, think of a field of Norwegian wildflowers, like a hillside of gangly, twisty, fluffy, neon, crew-cut dandelions.

And then think of the Versailles gardens.

The point is: Keep nature in line. Well within the lines.

Tante Britt would have shred her jumpsuit to pieces.

I got an even closer look at the meaning of *formation* by volunteering as a parent representative of Dalton's class, which, by the way, was Rita's suggestion, and required that I spend hours with my dictionary, you guessed it, reading and filling out many, many French forms and preparing for meetings and counsels. But I'll forgive Rita for that, because it also meant that I made immediate connections with other mothers of children in Dalton's class, which soothed my anxiety, grew my French, and in due course benefitted our entire family for many years to come.

Under the caring pedagogical hand of Madame M., Dalton did learn to work in a quiet and concentrated manner, mastered certain techniques, and understood protocol. His reading? His writing? His appreciation for colors, line, form, and perspective? They all improved. His French? Today I go to him for corrections on my written grammar.

But it actually wasn't until subsequent years, when little Dalton became a bigger Dalton and our family moved into Paris, that I learned how pervasive the idea of *formation* is in France. At a parent-teacher conference at Dalton's French bilingual school, *l'École Active Bilignue*, one teacher announced that for her writing assignments, she did not care a whit about form. It was content and ideas that count. I feverishly took notes, underlining the teacher's profile as *Franco-Canadienne*. Which explained what sure seemed to be an unorthodox stance regarding form; Form? Meh.

I tucked away notes, scooted out my chair, and walked through the door to the next mini lecture, this time given by a Parisian French teacher.

"I could not possibly care less about content," she announced in crystal clear French. "Let them write what they will. For me, it's form and appearance that count. Margins aligned. Paragraphs indented. Loops uniformly open and well-rounded."

She then pivoted on her high heels from the observing parents and to the chalkboard, where she demonstrated the execution of even loops and the pleasing curve of a meticulous "Q."

Q. Q. Q. Q .Q. Q. Q.

The smallish desk I sat in had something to do with it, I'm sure, but for some reason I was instantly back in l'École Maternelle Richard Mique again.

And instantly choked up when the teacher then turned to her desk, retrieving a couple of handwritten student papers to hold up as examples.

"This," she dangled the sheet with two fingers, close enough so all the parents could see the slightly cramped letters, the one or two words that exceeded the margin, and the red teacher's writing in a diagonal slash— "not at all satisfactory"—and the child's name in the upper right hand corner, "*This* is what I do *not* appreciate very much."

A mother in the front right-hand desk drew her hand to her mouth, then dropped her eyes, letting out a sigh of shamed disgust. The teacher eyed her, "Madame, you might want to work with Frédérique before exams."

The mother nodded from her child's desk, arms clamped tight to her sides, knees pinched together, head still low.

Then the teacher pulled out a second sheet. I felt the whole room of mature adults—mothers and fathers with advanced degrees, corner offices, bank accounts, and beeping Blackberries—I felt everyone brace themselves.

But this time it was an example of good *graphisme*, as the teacher called it. She held it with both hands, taut, wide, a veritable billboard to the wonders of penmanship.

"This," (I was already jealous of the parents of the Chosen One before the teacher even finished her sentence) "is the work of a concentrated young man. Regard the cleanliness, the order, the beauty!"

In the upper right hand corner were the perfectly even, round fountain pen forms of:

D-a-l-t-o-n.

I dropped my head in relief and wonder. She might as well have knighted me on the spot.

10

L'ADAPTATION

You can hardly believe the beauty of the Grand Canal of the Versailles gardens at dawn. If you come right at gate opening to take a long jog, as I do this Saturday morning in early September, you can jog right past the grazing sheep of Marie Antoinette's faux Austrian village Universal Studios stage set on your right, past the turn where you could go right into Le Petit Trianon, the private mansion built for *this* Louis's mistresses and *that* Louis's reclusive queen, and after a broad colonnade of trees, hop off the cobblestones about where, on your left, the public toilets and bike rental place are set up. Then you take a sharp right past La Flotille, the outdoor restaurant (still lifeless at this hour), and whooshk! You lose your breath at quite a sight indeed.

It's the perfect symmetry and stillness that gets you, the great gray sheet of water like a liquid landing strip, with one swan here, a mallard there. Oh, and the enormous fountains back there since you can't help but turn completely around and jog backwards with baby steps just to take in the panorama. The magnificent gardens lead up to the château itself, which comes into view, rising from the earth, as it was designed to appear to be doing, either ascending to heaven or descending from it, as its Sun King claimed he had. The biggest monument to vanity since the

Trump Tower. Yet with much better jogging possibilities and finer aesthetics. And, if you ask for my opinion, much more beautiful.

Back to those paths, I make it all the way around the Grand Canal that spreads its arms in a crucifix and, passing back out the big golden garden gates, check my watch to make sure I'll hit our neighborhood *boulangerie* as the pretty ladies there open its doors. Hot baguettes. Warm croissants. *Millefeuilles aux amandes.* We've already got our list of favorites.

La boulangerie Jean Michel Bigot in the Rue du Maréchal Foch is soberly majestic. It has golden doors, a deep purple interior, quietly attentive women behind the big glass counter, and, as I am to learn that day, a *versaillaise* clientele. There can't be better tradi to be found (the sourdough loaves made according to some "traditional" recipe, hence, their name) especially when found in that freshly birthed state, crust perfectly dense and the sourdough insides a mass of spongy comfort you can't keep your hands out of. Tradis have become our daily staple and we have become daily customers at what is an impeccable house of carbs.

Tradis, specifically, are all I'm after at the end of my jog, when I run right up to the door in the same getup I wore just a few weeks previously to jog the loop around our island in Norway: my favorite Yankees baseball cap over an unwashed ponytail, its brim tugged down snugly over an unmade-up face; black Lycra leggings; a neon-yellow long-sleeved t-shirt; an old blue nylon jacket tied around my waist. (I was so hot, I tugged the jacket off over my head and tied it tightly over my hips at about the third bend around the canal.) My shoes are muddied because I wasn't not been able to resist the forest (typical), but they are at least still tied with their fluorescent purple laces and are holding up with my pace as I sprint to the shiny golden façade of Bigot.

I'm also listening to music. It's happy and loud, an energizing program of Duke Ellington, The Style Council, Garth Brooks, and Placido Domingo doing Verdi arias. I've timed my entrance well by sprinting full throttle the last block or so, and am panting as I tug out my earphones and shake out my legs in front of the polished glass doors. You know how it is when you run and only start to really sweat like you mean it when you stop. Well, this is where I start to sweat in earnest. The doors are sweat sensitive, I gather, because it's right then they slide open automatically, which I hadn't quite wanted yet, since I was gasping and this was so early and so quiet and so French. And I hadn't yet silenced Placido (or was it Garth?), who was slung over my shoulder inside these earphones of mine, still making loud music like a drunk, hanging around my neck, wailing away. Everyone within a given radius heard him.

And that is maybe why a lady, the last in line and dressed like a clear-cut Madame du Quelque Chose, turns slowly toward me. I can feel her swift censure like I feel the swiftly closing glass boulangerie doors barely miss my head. *Swush.* I scoot back, fumble to turn off my music, lick my lips for moisture, swallow, try to draw up a bit of spit. I reach in my jacket pocket for gum, pop in a piece, and chawnk on it like any good trucker, hoping for some juice, then, still chawnking, trot merrily into the shop. Where I *fais la queue* behind not only one Madame du Quelque Chose, but four of them.

How four middle-aged women can look so meticulous, smell so fragrantly feminine, be so coiffed, and have manicures, too, at an hour when I still have bedsheet road maps on the side of my face, is sobering. One is wearing pearls. Another, matching shoes and handbag. Another, patent leather heels. In midnight violet. *She's dressed to match the bread shop interior?* And it's with that thought and while standing right behind them, trailing crusts of mud from my raggy Nikes and wiping drips of sweat from my jawline with the sleeve of my scratchy nylon jacket, that I then realize that without knowing it and certainly without wanting to do so, I have morphed into The Spectacle.

The sweaty, stinky, Spectacle. The muddy, Lycra-y, Garth-y, Yankee, boulangerie Spectacle. The one who thinks she's just going to crash this joint and be allowed to buy, like these four powdery Mesdames, a tradi or two.

Upon my bee-bopping entrance, these elegant early birds drop their quiet conversation midsentence like they've all flown beak-first into a plate glass window. It is so quiet, and I am so loud (or at least I feel I am) and immodest, and foul-mouthed even with my wad of Wrigley's Extra Ice, and they look mildly traumatized or entertained, I'm not sure which. But I am the newbie again, unaware, still, of all the codes. Just want my fresh French baked goods, s'il vous plait, if I might grab some. And *run.*

No! Walk.

So I shuffle, head down, to the gilded counter, grab my baguettes from a blonde woman with movie star beauty complete with a manicure that still looks wet—just your average bakery gal!—did the required flourish turning to all sides, to anyone who will hear my muffles: "I am so sorry, Mesdames, please excuse me, please forgive me, I apologize, thank you so kindly, Madame, yours are the best tradis in all Versailles. Have a lovely day. Everyone. Tout le monde. I am a beast."

Actually, *je suis bête* is the phrase I use, which means, roughly, "I'm a ding dong." But bête, besides meaning ding dong, also means beast.

I know this already because I'd ordered Disney's *La Belle et La Bête* for language practice the day I found out we were moving to France. The fact that Disney's beast was a *la*, by the way, and not a *le* and was therefore feminine, not masculine, caused some consternation for Claire, which we ironed out over time. But that whole tangent is beside the point here. What I'm telling you is that in this embarrassing culture clash moment, I do in fact feel 100 percent—no, 200 percent—bête.

I trudge home and take a second look at my gaggle. Tousled, all three. Fresh from the rough-and-tumble world of the northern wilds, rambunctious from being uprooted, mismatched and wrinkled from living out of cardboard boxes while I still try to figure out how and where to buy closets. (There are none in this turn-of-the-century house.)

What a week ago in Norway looked natural and healthy, now seems grubby and unkempt, and to make matters worse, they are sporting what I suddenly realize—had I not seen this before?—t-shirts with slogans across the chest, for Gucci's sake. But my trio resists being "spruced up a bit," as I put it. They need more than ever in this state of confusion (and who can blame them?) koselig (cozy). And I feel like we need a cordoned-off area.

Clotilde, Clémence, and Clara were not only as lovely as their names, but as fashionable. They also happened to be in Dalton's preschool class at l'École Maternelle Publique Richard Mique, the closest cordoned-off area. So I enlisted them, without their knowledge, as my fashion coaches. When they arrived in their little aubergine or ruby or emerald wool felt coats in late October, with their flare skirts and lace stockings with coiffed bobs and velvet hair bands, I wanted to line them up for a photo shoot. And I wanted to dig out all my own childhood photos, the ones where my hair is greasy or tied with yellow yarn or both, and my clothing fits like a cheap barbecue grill cover and is about the same color. I wanted to hunt down all these snapshots with their splotchy heavenly-blue school photo booth background and make a bonfire with them in my bathtub.

But you're saying, it's not the girls with the high-style IQ but their parents, the crazed ones who were dressing their children up like puppets. Not so. I watched these girls greet each other every morning at the doorway, with their four-year-old assessments of each others' ensembles;

"Oh, your hair bow is a very nice red," "A beautiful barrette, so classic!," "Ah, your boots and gloves, so pretty," and "Why not a pop of neon with all that brown?"

They also knew somehow instinctively, it seemed to me, what was *not* beautiful; "This box of tissues (this felt tipped pen, this silver glitter, this sheet of construction paper) is not beautiful *at all.*" And all the little girls, pursing their lips, releasing a sigh, nodding with confidence, would concur: "No, it is not beautiful *at all.*"

I trusted them. And was back to crawling on all fours again like I'd done in Norway while figuring out how to dress children in ekte vintertøy, eavesdropping now on French conversations, not only to learn some slick colloquial turns but to catch the latest fashion trend. And if you think it's just the girls who dressed stylishly, think again. The boys showed up in their pea coats and corduroy knickers, their pressed button-down shirts and cardigans, their haircuts that showed no sign of Mom's kitchen-shears fiasco. They lived up to what their teachers called them as they shook hands one by one at their schoolroom door: *les jeunes hommes.*

Young men.

Against this backdrop of pleats and Peter Pan collars, monogrammed shirt sleeves and—wait, were those cuff links?—a boy in rubber, purple overalls or even his fanciest bunad is going to stand out. I took a look at Dalton and decided he looked mildly dilapidated. He needed a wardrobe overhaul. On second thought, the whole family, I declared that night at dinner, needed a wardrobe overhaul.

So we began at the feet. I learned from Rita and other Mique mothers that my son needed to be *bien chaussé*—well-shoed, literally, or well-heeled, as anglophones tend to say. Being bien chaussé ruled out both the clunky functional rubber boots of barnepark as well as the self-lighting, neon-soled tennies of New Jersey.

Dalton and I arrived at a little local shoe store in Rue de la Paroisse, Versailles' main shopping drag, ready to slip into whatever was on sale. I thought of Synnøve at Sportshuset and wrestling my way into a killion Kroner worth of ekte vintertøy and was sure this was going to be much easier. However, I learned in no time that shoeing my child, like parkdressing my child, was going to be a science. Shoes were the very foundation of being *bien formé*. Shoes—like penmanship, like coloring apples, like buying baguettes—were serious.

The shoe salesperson/fashion consultant-cum-child psychologist instructed me while placing Dalton in front of a mirror, circling him while judging his form.

"He is *assez costaud* (fairly stocky), your son," she declared in French, "and has slightly rolled arches."

Dalton stood in the middle of the little shop, eyes darting, like a stiff troll with shocks of blonde hair, dimples you could lose a silver dollar in, and stocking feet beneath a solid little body—a bright Scandinavian delight.

"This would mean that for his *morphologie* you might consider this shoe, this shoe, this shoe, and . . . that one. You know? In order to *équilibrer* his appearance," she said, touching her eyeglasses which hung around her neck on a thin, golden chain.

Neatly on the floor was a lineup of shoes: one navy with red trim, one navy with white trim, one navy with green trim, and one navy with navy trim.

"But I don't like navy blue," Dalton muttered in English while the woman laced tight the first (navy) shoe.

"What does he say, the young man?" She tilted up her head to me and slipped the eyeglasses up on her nose, as if to see the situation more clearly.

"He does not like navy blue," I said. And raised my eyebrows in a searching smile.

"Ah, but *bleu marine* is a good color, a classic color, young man," she said, patting his bottom and scooting him toward the mirror.

Dalton could understand just enough French at this point, but like a troll, he preferred grunting to strangers over speaking to them.

"I do not like bleu marine," he whispered to me in English, his face as unemotive as yesterday's tepid oatmeal.

"What do you say, young man?" The woman put her hand to her ear as if cupping it would amplify this young man's voice.

"He says, Madame, he finds the other shoe the most handsome. This brown one."

I picked up a solid-looking brown leather shoe with a high-top, its sturdy Vibram sole and Velcro tabs great, I thought, for easy access.

"Very good, Madame," her tone flattened. "Let us try the brown one. Perhaps not as classic as the bleu marine. And not such a beautiful cut. But if the young man wants to consider it . . . "

I could see the effort she was making, unwrapping the tissue paper, lifting out the brown hulking bootlet, pulling open those Velcro tabs whose noisy scratch sound grated against the shop's total silence and her nerves. Not classic at all. Ragtime jazz, actually.

Dalton stood stalk still in his one brown shoe. "I want it," his half-smile said, making a dent in just one of his dimples.

I put my hand on Dalton's shoulder.

"He wants it, Madame," I sang to her.

"Although it is not . . . not as classic as the bleu marine, young man? Although it is not cut to make his foot look . . . a bit more elegant, Madame?"

"Although it is not as classic, yes. Although it is not as elegant. Yes."

"Yes, well, very well then," the woman sighed, clearly disappointed.

I had obviously selected precisely the shoe that would not flatter my three-year-old's morphologie, and would therefore mark him for life.

"One must decide, I suppose, Madame," the saleswoman said, putting her glasses back on her nose, "if one wants to teach one's child that mere comfort is more important than one's classic, elegant appearance."

She rang up the total with a briskness that meant this transaction was final-final, then, handing me the bag, added, "In the end, though, one never regrets an elegant appearance."

One had to decide. What one will regret. And this one decided for comfort, Velcro and brown.

Dalton ended up being the only boy in his entire maternelle with brown high-top shoes with Velcro tab closures. His new little friends (all in lace-up or buckle shoes in a classic bleu marine) called his shoes *les chaussures américains*. Even if they were made in France.

The shape of a shoe, like the lines of a Q, are emblematic of something profoundly French; the attention to beauty and aesthetics, the tribute to man's dominion over nature. It fascinated and seduced the New York City me, but also frightened and exasperated the Norwegian me. Norway, too, had paid serious attention to beauty, but to raw beauty, and to preserving, not controlling nature. That stark contrast was evident in a conversation I had a couple of years into our life in France.

It was a friendly lunch among women friends from different cultures. Only one of us was French. And I was the one American. The others were from Eastern Europe, the Middle East, the Near East, and the Far East. The conversation had begun with a discussion about the values we thought drive our cultures. Everyone had strong opinions about what values they felt drive the United States, and everyone had even stronger opinions about what values they felt drive France.

"Intelligence and beauty are *the* dominant French values," my Polish friend Irena said.

"History and beauty," thought Joumana, my Lebanese friend.

"No, no. *Pleasure* and beauty." My Indian friend Ashima was sure she was right.

"Beauty . . . and beauty?" my Japanese friend Nao shrugged.

And my French friend Florence, what did she think?

"You're all right," she said. "Wit, history, pleasure, beauty." She then took a sip from her glass, set it down on the table where she also poised her elbows, then laced and unlaced her fingers two or three times, thinking. Then she smiled and added, "*And* the beauty of wit, the beauty of history, the beauty of pleasure, and of course the beauty of beauty."

Darned if the whole sentence, as she said it in French, wasn't witty and beautiful.

Since the days of Marie Antoinette, the world outside of France has assumed that beauty is a French commodity. And have you noticed? France isn't doing much to quash that perception. But there's *la beauté*, and there's beauty. So I wanted to poke around a bit at the assumed perceptions of both.

"Ah, those Norwegian women," I started in there at the table, throwing my head back, sighing. "Don't you think they're beautiful? You know, that striking bone structure, the coloring, the clarity of the eyes?"

"Beautiful, maybe," Joumana of the many bracelets and strong lipstick said. She'd gone to school in Paris. "But what about *l'appearance*?"

"You know what I'm talking about," I said. "Their legginess and toothiness. Their strength, their natural, wholesome look." My friends' faces were a wall of nonresponse. "All the muscles from cross country skiing and hiking big, snowy mountains."

Florence cocked her head. "And . . . this . . . is *beautiful*?" She let out a spurt of a laugh.

"Without a trace of makeup, hair a mess," I grew even more enthusiastic, "Right off the ski slope, right off a fishing boat, just so . . . what should I say? *Ravissante*."

"But what about *la présentation*?" asked Nao, who was studying design in Paris, and was wearing all black, ballet flats, only a whisper of makeup, her manicure, skin and hair as glossy as a magazine cover.

"Right, la présentation," added Ashima, who's married to a Frenchman, "You can be as beautiful as the Pyrenées, but it does you no good if you can't present yourself cleverly."

"Presentation, yes," Irena added. She'd obviously absorbed Paris through her invisible pores. She was dressed in a black-and-white, houndstooth suit worn like a second skin, and her cream silk blouse was unbuttoned right to where her double string of pearls dangled. "Presentation is the bigger part of beauty. Beauty itself, only the rudiments of presentation."

As you can guess, Norwegian beauty lost.

And as you can guess, la beauté (which had never warranted such a serious or philosophical discussion in my whole life) proved to become a governing presence during our French years. But I have to add a disclaimer that la beauté isn't only about a woman's physical appearance, although it undoubtedly points to that, too. I'm referring, instead, to beauty in general, all kinds of beauty to which my senses were awakened thanks to France.

I've tried—and what writer hasn't tried?—to capture and then convey something of the beauty that was a dominant feature in this new French life. But every time I've tried—for this chapter, as an example—I've ended up slack-jawed and slouched as if my spine were melting, draped, and pained and dreamy over my computer keyboard, slavering and longing, a mess and worthless for an hour or so afterwards.

Or shivering. Zinged as if trans-zapped by a mild electrical current that inevitably runs through me when I let myself get too deep into reminiscing about it all. It's as I told a friend once, "France ruins everything," which meant that living in France meant absorbing a new standard for many things and that nothing that would follow, no matter how hard that thing would try, could ever quite measure up.

You know I was only partially right about that. France does set a new and *seemingly* unattainable and *seemingly* unsurpassable standard for what *seems* to be just about everything. It's maybe fairer to say that France defined beauty in new terms, redefining so many other facets of my life as a result. It spawned a new vision of things in me so that I wouldn't just be asking, as I had for years in Norway, "Will this thing here work?" or "Is this article of clothing/this roof/this hairdo weatherproof?" or "How durable is this construction/material/body?" or "Can I open this in the middle of an avalanche, a flood, a moose attack and with frostbitten hands, with ski poles attached at my wrists, or on a hovercraft commute out to the Lofoten Islands?" Now, I would be asking other questions like, "Is this a well-wrought line/poem/bouquet of dahlias?" or "Are these proportions harmonious/balanced/classic-without-being-stodgy?" or "Is the color discreet/good with my skin tone/going to be on this spring's runway?" or "Is this color too restrained and therefore passé/garish and therefore passé/lifeless and therefore needs a splash of chartreuse?"

The new focus on beauty for beauty's sake turned something as banal as picking out a head of fennel or selecting a toilet paper dispenser into a serious exercise in aesthetics, an exercise reserved in other cultures for things like buying a painting to repainting your entire home. I began weighing and measuring things with my tongue, fingertips, ear, nose, or eye, always judging things for their beauty, be that beauty in taste, texture, sonority, scent, or appearance. That's a lot of aesthetic exercise. I was becoming an Olympic aesthete.

You wonder, maybe, why bother? Why make the effort for beauty? Why not just allow for beauty if it happens to pop up in nature (like a robust, well-formed dandelion), but force it (like a sculpted topiary)? Why plow down a whole inner city for beauty, as Baron Haussmann did in order to transform Paris in the early nineteenth century from a congested, fetid medieval city into the model, bourgeois, flaunty Paris it is today? Why? Because, for one thing, human nature responds to beauty. It needs it. It could be that we behave differently in a beautiful place from how we behave in a fetid one.

And this all translates into a lesson I learned from my girlfriend who was gravely particular about the bed linens she chose for her son Ludovic's bedroom. She refused anything with images as grotesque or aggressive (both directly translatable words in French), in other words images as *moche* (ugly), as she called them, as cartoon images of dinosaurs or superheroes. All this because such grotesqueness and aggressiveness, she explained, can be absorbed into our subconscious. Into our dreams. Just as we drift off to sleep. And especially when we are little. Like two years old. Like Ludovic.

Why prioritize beauty? I can answer that best with a short gallery, if you'll indulge me and if I can pull this off without ending up like a mound of melted butter oozing into my keyboard. Or frizzled straight up with the zing of high-octane delight.

There was a certain note, implausibly tender and suspended like a single strand of spider silk, sung by a beautiful soprano at the end of her third encore of a beautiful concert held in a beautiful theater. There was the fluidity of a ballerina's arms, so liquid-like and translucent, I could hardly tell her limbs from the chiffon of her ankle length skirt that rode the air like a child's breath. I think of the last crashing notes of Beethoven's Ninth Symphony where a stage full of over 300 performers representing many nationalities sent thunder vibrating beyond sound waves and, the second the music ended, the audience to its feet, erupting in shouts of "Bravo!" flooding the hall with a thunderous gush of beauty.

I think of the razor-fine precision with which the trees were groomed along the boulevards, and I think of the tottering figures under them, the fragile old ladies in their brave coral-red lipstick and moth-eaten hats and gloves, pulling their outdated shopping *caddies* over cobblestones to buy their fresh food for the day.

There's that corner you can turn into Avenue de l'Opéra where out of nowhere the Opera Garnier springs into view, its green roof and golden statues both magical and magisterial. You can take the stone slope of Rue Foyatier leading up to Sacré Cœur, stand on the steps in front of that white wedding cake basilica atop the highest peak of Montmartre and see nearly 360 degrees of Paris with her domes and spires and grit and sheen, then step through the big doors to see ahead and above you, in bright mosaic, Christ's arms spanning the breadth of the cupola.

There are all the stacks of well-used street-café tables made of one iron pedestal and a round marble top. The disheveled bird and antique and book and art print and flower markets. The bridges over the Seine, especially the Mirabeau in its rich avocado green and the Pont Alexandre III in its gold leaf opulence. The crowds of African faces teeming through the roads around Tati, the overflowing discount department hub by the Gare du Nord. The vast and vaulted main floor of the Musee d'Orsay. The sandblasted façade of the Conciergerie just opening its eyes to the wash of sunlight at 6:21 a.m., about at the end of your morning run to the Jardin des Plantes and back. The dignified curves of the lamp posts in the Place Dauphine on the Île de la Cité. Stacks of pastel macarons at Ladurée. Steps of the Église de la Madeleine carpeted with red geraniums. Century-old script on the Marais shop fronts. Mosaic tile floors. Fountains. Chairs in painted metal, green lacquered park benches. Pigeons. Men in green or yellow driving automated street scrubbers along the curbs. Women in fig-colored pantsuits and severe hair checking parking meters. Frescoes. Trocadéro late afternoon, view across the Seine to the Eiffel Tower, street musicians beating drums, tourists and locals alike dancing their hearts out, shoes off. The gigantic slip of the Tricolore, the French flag, dancing, too, in the arch of the Arc de Triomphe, visible from the Place de la Concorde at the entrance of the Tuileries gardens, which sit at the bottom of the Champs Élysées.

And all you can *not* see of hidden inner courtyards, thirteenth-century stairwells, stuccoed ceiling appliqués, stained glass in cracked plaster walls that hide a whole wealth of quotidian, urbane beauty.

Then on this day there's the moment when I've broken a real good sweat and have turned to view a huge monument to a single man's vanity. A monument—can we agree on this?—also to beauty itself. A monument to the beauty of wit, the beauty of history, the beauty of pleasure, and of course, to the beauty of beauty.

11

La Gastronomie

When Dalton stayed full Mondays at maternelle, it meant he was invited to dine with his entire class in the cafeteria. Dining meant just what it sounds like: four courses, linen, silverware, straight backs. No plastic utensils, trays, or cups. No nuggets and ketchup and canned corn. No sandwiches, certainly, since how can one eat a sandwich with utensils? Even *les pommes frittes*, or French fries, should to be eaten with a fork, we learned.

The value in dining, explained Madame M. as she and I stood outside the *cantine*, peeking occasionally through the porthole window in the door to watch how Dalton was doing, was to *élever le palais*. This phrase threw me at first. Was this some kind of telekinesis, lifting up palaces or something? What it meant was to educate (or refine) the palate.

"A child," Dalton's cheery pedagogue explained, "must not be given food that will degrade the palate. If early in life he develops an appetite for bad food—fast food, cheap food, tasteless food—how then will he distinguish later in life what is truly excellent?"

I peered at the preschool children sitting straight in a row, linen napkins across their knees, utensils held firmly in each hand. My Dalton, his back to me, was eating *les épinards*, or spinach, quiche, and sliced fresh fruit with yogurt. In a blue ceramic dish was a small salad with mustard vinaigrette, I was told. He and his classmates would be offered a selection of cheeses after that course before the small square of chocolate to finish off the meal. He drank water from a glass-glass. A woman in a white frock and orthopedic sandals touched him on the head and pointed to his napkin when he wiped his mouth with the back of his hand. He used the napkin. And looked both ways as he then pressed it flat across his lap.

"This, Madame Bradford, is as important a part of *la formation* as is anything else your son will learn. The French, you know, consider food to be about much more than just eating. *La gastronomie* is an art and a science and," (to this day I recall these words with the sound of a background gong) "the sign of an evolved culture, of an evolved human being."

Whuh-o. I felt her statement like an indictment, though I'm sure gentle Madame M. didn't mean it as such. But I cringed, and while cringing, felt my back instantly hunch over, hair cover my face, and my knuckles hit the ground. All those barnepark brown bags of a single slice of bread and goat cheese? Eaten with bare hands? All those Norwegian birthday parties with a set menu of tepid hot dogs, chocolate cake, and red punch or the Norwegian office buffet for Randall, which, over the years, never changed from sliced tomatoes and cucumbers, two sorts of cheese, bread, and a platter of room-temperature canned herring? What about the one and only brand of milk—its carton said, simply, *Melk*—that first year we lived in Norway? And the two types of cheese—goat (brown) and cow (yellow)—compared with the 378-plus types in France? We'd kind of *liked* that approach to food. It left so much time for . . . for not thinking about food.

Going back even further, what about all those New Jersey vending ma-chine hoagies inhaled during the mad dash across campus, the Slurpees downed in an elevator, the extra large fries scarfed behind the wheel and handed, fry by greasy fry, back to the toddler in the car seat? I'd not only been eating the wrong food, I was now starting to see, but I'd been eating it *all the wrong way*—mobiley. As my Parisian neighbor Lauren would tell me some years later, eating while running, taking an elevator, while driving, while watching TV, while doing anything but eating was, well, "*Un peu comme les barbares*," or a wee bit barbarian.

We barbarians, we knuckle-dragging types, had some things to learn about the art, science, and religion of French food. In private, I hit the books. You might be thinking recipe books, but that wasn't where I start-ed, since recipe books alone constitute only the smallest fraction of the centuries of French food literature. Volume upon canonized volume (more than in any other language, I'd bet) describes and codifies how and when and where you meticulously select the finest ingredients. Then how you painstakingly clean, peel, julienne, chop, boil, sauté, or whip them. Then how you pluck, skin, debone, dehorn, detongue, de-entrail, de-eyeball, baste, braise, layer, stuff, twist, or set afire the rest. Ultimately, how to present.

The presentation itself is, as my neighbor Clotilde told me, 50 percent of the task, and 90 percent of the joy of feasting. Preparing and sharing in food, I learned, was above all a sensuous endeavor. This she explained while ladling steaming, fragrant bouillabaisse into the scooped-out heart of a grilled potiron (pumpkin) the color of Utah's red-rock country. Before serving it to four of us gathered for a simple midweek luncheon, she swirled in a minicyclone of crème fraiche and planted, right in its center, a single elegant sprig of rosemary grown in her garden.

So this was it: French cuisine was a big chunk of science, yes. All those books I'd lugged home and tried to read with a French-English dictionary said so. But Clotilde and other friends like her demonstrated how cuisine was so much more than that, so far beyond steely engineering. Built on a gridwork of science, maybe, but alive and abloom with art, passion, inspiration, and topped with one fat dollop of whimsy. The purpose of food is not to fill our stomachs, Clotilde and others taught me, but to feed our minds, bind our relationships, stir our emotions, and even enliven reverence.

The alchemy of science plus spirit. This might be what distinguishes one chef from another, and when you're the most distinguished of the alchemists, you earn your place in the chronicles of Michelin-star fame with your one, two, or three stars. Having a star elevates chefs to celebrity status, making names like Bocuse, Ducasse, and Robuchon every bit as legendary and worthy of worship in French culture as are the names Yves Saint Laurent, Dior, and Givenchy. A great chef, like a great couturier, lives and dies for the art.

The story of François Vatel is a case in point. Named head chef for Nicolas Fouquet, who was superintendent to Louis XIV, Vatel became frantic when his elaborate feast for two thousand, staged at the Château de Chantilly in honor of Louis XIV, did not go exactly according to plans. When an order of fish did not arrive on time, Vatel saw the event and in turn his entire reputation ruined. He went to his chamber to thrust a sword through his heart.

The pressure to be an alchemist of gastronomy is fierce. Deadly, even.

The spirit of Vatel hung over my new life. On the four days a week when I would arrive to pick up Dalton for lunch, the mothers and babysitters were all gathered around the school gates discussing lunch menus. You're going to braise endives? And she's going to sauté chicken livers? And she over there will whip up a soufflé to go with the fennel salad with chunks of Parmesan and toasted walnuts? It seemed everyone wanted to know what was on everyone else's menu for the fifty-minute lunch break to which they would treat their three-year-old cherub.

I just held tight. It was somewhat destabilizing to listen to everyone's fancy menus. I was feeling challenged enough merely figuring out what was on those shelves in the grocery store, where to get things if what I needed was not there, whom to ask for help to find something as basic as salt, for starters. That whole food-on-the-table thing was, with everything else going on, all I could handle, but I listened closely to the women's talk. I was starting to understand whole swaths of French, so I was gathering courage. But in the next instant, I realized the severity of my utter culinary ineptitude. Slap together a floppy ham and cheese? No prob. But pull out an actual pan—or three?—and baste something? Why, that would take more effort than the eating, which equation just didn't make sense for me. So I listened in on but never actively joined the Lunch Menu Chat Group. Never did I dare admit that my own son was going home to a vulgar, cheap bowl of microwave canned ravioli. In a Barney dish.

Mondays were (after canned ravioli can you blame him?) Dalton's favorite days. And it didn't take long for a pattern to establish itself. I picked him up. By the turn in the corner I would have asked, "Your day, tell me, was it fun?" As we crossed the street he would start in, "We had cordon bleu and les brocolis." And I'd ask, "Was there a sauce? Bernaise? Hollandaise?" By the time we reached the next turn he had detailed every dish he'd eaten; "A sauce on les brocolis, yes." We waited, then we crossed at the light. "And salted butter with plum jam on the croissant." By the time we reached home I had all the notes needed for the next night's family dinner.

Although I wasn't conscious of it, we were in fact mirroring a normal part of French life. When the French are not buying, planning, whipping, stuffing, basting, or glazing food, they are talking about it. Food—not its quantity, but its quality, diversity, authenticity, whimsy, sensuality, and sheer beauty—food matters. Food matters enormously.

This truth was magnified a hundred times over when, four years later, we moved into the heart of Paris. We could count the steps (seventy-three) out our door crossing south over Rue du Colonel Combes and following down Rue Jean Nicot, further across Rue de l'Université, beelining it to our favorite patisserie that served Dalton's favorite pastry from our love affair with Bigot, a *millefeuille aux amandes*. From that *boulangerie* to the next one that baked Claire's preferred *baguette*, thirty-one steps. To Parker's favorite *chawarma* served up by Belghazem, the Tunisian guy at the Greek "resto" *Apollon*, twenty-five backwards. To my favorite steamy bowl of *pad Thai* slurped from a bowl at one of the three 12 x 12-inch tables at *Chez Do*, twelve steps more, same direction. To fresh Lebanese *tabouleh* at *Marrakech*, ninety-four steps around the corner (trying to ignore the lurid-looking Pizza Hut) and past the façades of Moroccan, Algerian, and three authentic Italian places, including *Il Pupi* run by Giancarlo and Vincenzo, brothers from Sicily. You passed sushi, kimchi, and litchis, before coming to *L'Ami*, meaning *L'Ami Jean*, the neighborhood's best-kept Basque secret whose up-and-coming but down-to-earth chef, Stéphane, was featured scowling in black leather in one of the town's celebrity magazines.

We had no idea, but another culinary celebrity lived right down our street, right through the block from L'Ami Jean. To us, this figure was no more than the father of our boys' friends, the husband of Catherine, one of my girlfriends. To the French, however, he was Monsieur Constant—Christian Constant—who had three restaurants in St. Dominique and one in the southern French town of Toulouse.

And he had a Michelin star.

He also had a recognizable southwest accent, which he'd retained along with his saltiness and savvy. He worked long, hard hours doing what he'd been trained to do from the days he did kitchen at the Crillon and the Ritz. In those days, Catherine told me they had called him the Pitbull. But I'd never suspect it greeting him in our entryway when he came to pick up one of his sons, or when I'd drop by his Café Constant to pick up my elementary school-aged son sitting casually at the bar, shooting the breeze with the staff.

Constant's turn on the science-and-spirit of cooking? Sitting in his lively Cocottes de Constant, you know it immediately: sharing good food should be invigorating, interesting, and intimate. And any good dish should amuse, not ambush, the senses. I've eaten a common salade niçoise I don't know how many times in my life, but never did that simple dish grab me by the lapels the way Christian's did.

Constant's resto row and all the surrounding variety were found in just one small corner of the big city, one minuscule speck of Paris. Venture a few steps beyond our streets, and you'd have Russian caviar at *Petrossian*, classic bistro fare at *Thoumieux*, alongside Indonesian, Mauritian, and Maldivian tables. There was *Le Divellec*, the somber dining fortress of the political elite spilling out of the Assemblée Nationale and, a stride or two away, your average but very good dozen or so *crêperies* and *brasseries*. From our windows you could almost see the customers at several gastronomic pilgrimage sites like Michel Chaudun's corner *chocolaterie*, Bellota-Bellota's dried meats from the Pyrenées, Marie-Anne Cantin's famous *fromagerie*.

And what had once been Jean-Luc Poujauran's but was now Stéphane Secco's pale-pink temple to baked goods was a place where the women at the register grew to know our whole family by name. Secco's croissants were so renowned, people drove across town to wait in long lines and sneak off with four for a late Saturday breakfast. But our neighbors whispered tales of regular customers like Jacques Chirac, who was reputed to have been a *client fidèle*, requiring the feather-light, butter-rich load be heaped into a large, flat, woven basket strapped on top of the blue and pink *camionette* and trundled across cobblestones to the Palais de l'Élysée.

About such culinary variety, Charles de Gaulle, a Chirac predecessor, once asked, "How can one govern a country that has 246 varieties of cheese?" (Actually, there are closer to 400; more than one for every day of the year. No wonder governing France was harder for de Gaulle than he'd estimated.)

But I'm telling you, after all that variety, all that walking around hunting for just the ambiance, all that comparison shopping for the perfect dish—after all that—like you, I'm completely worn out. And overwhelmed. So I hobble off to slop together an omelet. This I eat straight from the pan, standing, with salt, and using the same fork I whipped it up with.

I felt like that sometimes. Paris is the gourmand's capital of a gourmand country, a place where food, both sacrosanct and common, covers every ethnic and epicurean twist and turn. This wealth of diversity can turn something as banal as catching a quick bite into a religious rite loaded with all the hallelujahs and hellfire that dogma can stir up in a hungry soul. With so much, there can be an initial temptation to unbutton the inner glutton. But the bigger temptation, as I lived it, was to grow agitated if we ever ate mediocre or even normal food. I'd look down at whatever I'd made for dinner—the pesto pasta, the grilled cheese (even if it was a cheese from Marie-Anne Cantin), and groan to myself, "We are in *France*. We can *not* eat like we're living in just any old place."

Unless, of course, I was on the road with the children, there was an epic downpour, and it happened to be an off-hour for dining, which means any time before noon or between two o'clock and seven. Get hungry then, and you're doomed to listen to your stomach grumble. (Or your children howl.)

So there was, I'll just admit it up front, this one time I sat smiling contentedly in a Ronald's Playroom in the countryside outside of Rouen. Now, Rouen is a fine Norman town whose name is sometimes incorrectly pronounced by foreigners as "ruin." And it's not quite like "rain" either, although some foreigners, trying for a good accent, miss the linguistic target with a nasal, "rain." Neither "ruin" nor "rain" are correct for Rouen. Normally. But for the day I was there to visit an important cathedral with my youngest two, ruin and rain were prophetic words, nothing less.

The Rouen cathedral was made famous through Monet's several canvases, each painted repeatedly in a different state of weather. (Had I never noticed most of those weathers were the mist of post-deluge?) And the day I ventured there the deluge would not let up. I drove and drove looking for refuge, and as the children grew hungrier, I grew more anxious about finding a bite. When there, on the horizon and rising from an industrial park outside of town, I spotted them: golden arches. They shone with exceptional brilliance through the gray sheets of a midafternoon storm, pulling, as it seemed, my front bumper like a mega-magnet. We zipped right into a parking place. In Rouen.

Rouen lies in Normandy, one of the food-loveliest parts of a food lover's country, a place from where the richest creams and cheeses and the most delicate apple tarts originate. And I'd been working really hard to wean my kids from the lure of any kind of fast food. By this point, I'd done exceptionally well at demonizing anything served through a window, in Styrofoam, and with sauces you have to tear open with your teeth. Rarrrrrgh.

Yet. Here I was. Outside was this plexiglass sheet of rain and ruin. It was 3:00 p.m., a very bad time to be hungry in this country. (You couldn't get served in a restaurant at that hour even if you owned it.) The children were restless and grimy after several hours on the road, bad groundwork for hushed dining. We all needed a toilet badly, and I insisted this time around that my toilet be the sit down kind, not some Latin rest stop contraption, an apparent holdover from the inquisition, pungent enough to make your eyes burn. This was no time for a Frisbee-sized table crowded with clinking crystal, burnished silver, and white linen, where the reward at the end of an arduous forty-five-minute wait is a plate full of something you can neither pronounce nor whose ingredients you can identify. (Although it will undoubtedly have a recognizable sprig of parsley.) Neither did we want to wash it all down with a goblet of fizzy, lukewarm water. This was just a really late lunch or rather early dinner for a ragged band of famished vagabonds, not the ultimate search for gastronomic ecstasy, so I was thinking: fast, unruly, cheap. What I needed was a virtual miracle in France.

I sat in an orange, plastic swivel seat, pen in hand, listing in my notepad all the reasons I love McDonalds or, as the French call it, *Mac Do*. I waxed rhapsodic: Pot of gold at the foot of two gleaming arches. Never mind that the McNuggets are made from unidentifiable chicken parts. My children got their potty break, we all had hot water and soap for our hands, they ate, *and* as important, they enjoyed a sweaty and effervescent cultural encounter with Jean-Baptiste, Amandine, Pierre, Raphaël, and Clarissa, all in a warm, dry, padded ball room.

I, meanwhile, sat and shot the breeze with all the children's parents. Françoise and Martin were pro-American, and though they spoke no English, they loved Beel and Eelaree Cleenton, as did the eighty-four-year-old mother-in-law who, while seated as I was at a kiddie table, and with her veiny manicured hands, carefully patted the corners of her ruby mouth while polishing off Le Wrap, Le Muffin, and Le McFlurry. Where else but in a McDonald's in France could I get five hours of easy cultural exposure in safe, hygienic, and liberating conditions for less than the cost of two Parisian street crêpes eaten under a dripping awning in a downpour? Or without the bitter cloud of cigarette smoke giving me secondhand lung cancer? Or without having to remind my children to sit down, keep it down, put the candelabra *down*?

It was holy time, my one day at a Mac Do's outside of Rouen, proof enough for me that life doesn't have to be one perpetual strand of pearly *haute cuisine*. That just now and again, while raising one's palate, it is in fact permissible—even advisable and culturally desirable—to *descender le palais*, to lower that palate, along with the plate, all the way down to your lap.

12

IL CRACHE, IL CRASH, JE CRAQUE, LE CRASH

La langue means the tongue, which tongue, in this context, means the French one. And that's exactly the part of me that was tied in a sailor's knot when I sat staring into the large liquid brown eyes of Madame M.

IL CRACHE

She had called a special conference with me after school hours. I'd spruced up, throwing on pearls, ironing a seam down the front of my pantyhose, and brandishing killer heels. I came quickly, mincingly.

"Your son, Madame," said Madame M., "*Il crache aux enfants.*"

Although the heat between us told me right off this was serious, I had no idea what "*crache*" meant. So I took a stab (which you should never do in French unless you're fencing) and guessed it meant the obvious: my child was crashing into the other children. Head butting. My three-year-old, towheaded fullback.

"*Il crache?*" I asked in falsetto.

"*Oui, Madame,*" she dropped her eyes, pain wrinkling her forehead. It was very touching.

"*Aux enfants?*" I winced, burying my chin in my chest, my shoulders drawing up to my earlobes.

"*Oui, Madame.*" She exhaled audibly. "*Aux enfants.*"

We sat for five seconds in silence. She stared into her lap. I stared at the part down the middle of her hair.

"*Vraiment?*" I said, double-checking if this was true, since Dalton really wasn't a violent boy at all. "*Il—*" and I made a head-butting, full-back movement. *Crashing.* Into imaginary other children. "*Il crache?*"

Madame M. looked up at me, perplexed. Then, like floodlights flipping on over a soccer pitch, she said, "Oh, *non, non, non.* Madame Bradford!" Then she laughed.

I laughed, too, relieved. Thank *heavens* my son wasn't doing something as coarse and as *crude* as head-butting.

"*Non, Madame, non, non.*" She then cleared her throat and straightened her skirt. "*Il crache!*" said lovely Madame M., as she drew herself together to demonstrate what was meant with the words.

And with that she spat.

She spat left, right, and right at me, her eyes widening, nostrils flared, bottom lip glazed with spit. "*Il*" (spit, spit, spit) "*crache aux enfants!*"

"Oh. *Voilà.*" A slight tide of nausea swept over my torso.

"When the children try to speak to him, he backs into a corner," this kind pedagogue said, "And when he backs into the corner, the children try to coax him out. It is all meant in fun, I am sure. But the closer they get, the more he refuses, and when they get close enough, Madame . . . "

I interrupted here by spitting, my brows drawn up, questioning if I got it right.

Dalton, my *crach*-ing son.

What I needed to do, I decided, was expose my little boy to more French environments besides just his preschool. Take him out with me on errands, let him meet people who don't corner him or poke colored pencils into his tummy when he can't respond with the right verb conjugation. We were in Versailles, after all, which means every corner was a mini culture capsule manned by authentic locals with whom I could certainly try to speak my baby French. And my baby would of course follow suit. Ease in. Quit the spit. I had a great plan.

So I started the next day at the grocery store.

IL CRASH

It was noontime on a day other than Monday, when Dalton otherwise would have stayed all day at maternelle to dine in the cafeteria, and so my husky three-year-old was with me at a midsized *alimentation*, helping me stock up on essentials, which now included a flotilla of bottled water, endives, fennel, radishes, only two cans of ravioli, eight types of cheese, and an artillery of yogurts in *parfums* that for some reason made me think of Christian Dior working a butter churn.

With my back turned on him for a split second, Dalton tried to scale the outside of the full cart and flipped it over on himself right in the middle of the frozen hors d'œuvres aisle. The echoing crash drew a crowd of women, all in their sixties and seventies. They flocked near us, encircling the momentarily winded, saucer-eyed boy clobbered by an impressive heap of Evian and produce. Dalton lay motionless on the tiles. The Roquefort and Gruyère lay smushed quite definitively under his splayed arms.

Heads bobbing, the ladies discussed this *évenément* between themselves, then offered me their *conseil*. Madame should not move *le pauvre* (the poor guy) because the blow might have damaged his spine. Madame should knock him a sound one on his derriere for having smashed such fine endives as Madame had selected. Madame should rescue her Roquefort from underneath the tins of *petit pois* and, by all means, get the dairy products home before they spoil. Madame should take a taxi to an emergency room because Madame cannot drive with the invalid in her arms, and as it was noon, none of the eight doctors' offices surrounding the market would be open for three more hours. Ah, oui. The inevitable and interminable lunch break.

Mumbling whatever few French responses I could muster, I gathered the bruised bundle of child (not radishes) in my arms and left my monument to la gastronomie in an indecent sprawl, the women shoppers gawking and pecking at it, at each other, at the mother and child genuflecting their way out the sliding glass doors.

With my handbag shoulder strap creeping down my arm and sweat dripping down my front, I headed straight for the closest hospital, Hôpital Mignot. Dalton's human siren accompanied us all the way.

The doctors at the emergency room, after searching for internal injuries with an ultrasound, found none. (Then I told them to check my son.) They discovered that the grocery avalanche had broken my boy's foot. My Viking, they told me, was finally going to get his armor: a knee-high cast. The kid was going to be cobbled. And *Madame la maman*? She was instructed to keep her invalid completely sedentary. For the next month.

Could *Monsieur le docteur* write a prescription for traction? Tee-hee-hee? Not even a smile.

After one week, Dalton was wielding that cast like a judo instructor, and by the end of the month-long chrysalis, we had chiseled it off with butter knives because it was so battered, it and his leg were decomposing. During that whole time, of course, he couldn't attend maternelle since, according to Madame M., his cast would give the other children even more reason to cajole and Dalton more reason to crache.

JE CRAQUE

He was dragging that cast along the floor conversing with Monsieur Patate, a big Mr. Potato Head I'd bought the week we'd dropped into our new French lives (and who was a plastic, French-speaking Nathan Lane; "*Je suis content que tu sois là!*"), when I got a troubling phone call from the main offices of ASP, the American School of Paris. It was a request that I come in at my earliest convenience—"Like, can you make it in an hour, Mrs. Bradford?"—to meet with a school administrator and some teachers. ASP is where Parker and Claire were newly enrolled.

Backing up: Upon that initial arrival from Norway, we'd decided to enroll them at ASP, although it hadn't been our plan at first. The other school of our choice, the Lycée International in St. Germain-en-Laye, could offer them French immersion, which we'd thought we'd do in France just as we'd done in Norway. But when the Lycée tested their written English, they found it substandard, not "mother tongue" enough to justify it being their official primary tongue. Their Norwegian, though, the Lycée said, was right on age level. So they could enroll at that school if we agreed to enroll them as Norwegian students. This would have meant that in addition to taking most classes in French, they would have taken core classes (language and literature, history, etc.), in Norwegian. Nothing, not even *Anglais*, in English.

After deliberation, and keeping in mind that we'd probably only be in France for a limited stay of two or three years, we decided it was most important to get them up to speed in English. We chose ASP. This is all a long preamble, I know, but I share it to describe one of the costs of having integrated so well in Norway, I guess. At that juncture, had we been able to predict that we'd ultimately end up being in France for a total of eight years, and that Parker would finish all of his schooling there, perhaps we would have chosen differently. Put our two oldest, who at seven and nine were still well within that magical language acquisition window, into local schools. Just like we had in Norway.

But we didn't.

And the ASP alternative ended up being a blessed one. Maybe even one of the best choices we've ever inadvertently made.

Although never in a trillion years could you have convinced me of that when I drove, already blue lipped after that phone call, to the school that day.

A certain school administrator in particular (shall we call him Napoleon?), new in his job and sitting at the head of a table to which I had been called along with three other teachers working with Parker, was threatening to expel my boy from school that week. If he didn't expel him, this man wanted to at least put him on indefinite probation. Along with other color commentary on my child, commentary I'd rather not immortalize in print or remind myself of in the process of printing it but which has something to do with "pretending to not understand things in English," and "demanding too much of his teacher's attention," this administrator accused me and my (absent, in Marrakech that week) husband of being misguided, whimsical, unpatriotic parents, having not offered our children the American way all along. The other three teachers were visibly deferent to Napoleon, but I at least was able to meet their eyes. I could see they weren't wholly in agreement.

I stammered something about this administrator maybe not completely understanding about our having been deeply integrated in Norway, about our kids speaking better Norwegian than English, that the Lycée confirmed it, the Lycée had been our first choice anyway, that I would work with Parker, I promise, and that he and all these caring professionals could be reassured I was competent to do so because, um, well, I *had* been a college English and language instructor. And, as a side note, I was also this boy's mother.

I also remember having "Not While I'm Around" start playing on my inner stereo: "Demons are crawling everywhere nowadays / I'll send them howling, I don't care, I've got ways," and the image of Parker as I was kneeling in front of him, singing into his eyes in the concert at the US ambassador's in Oslo. In a land, by the way, where folks loved my son, where they'd fought for him, incidentally, and where a Napoleon, you, sir, would *never* have been *let* across the *border*, let alone *into my child's school*!

Once in a great while, I've got this meddlesome, amped-up inner stereo.

But it sometimes leaks out quite soundproofed. Because what I also remember is apologizing out loud, perhaps even effusively. Saying I was so sorry for myself, for my son, for our existence in the universe. I do remember well that appalling apology reflex.

The administrator continued looking around the panel of teachers for consensus. What, he asked, could have been redeeming about our family's experience in Norway? Look how it obviously screwed up your son, Mrs. Bradford. And why, in heaven's name, were we dragging our children to Paris now, he wanted to know. The cachet? The romance? Just *some expatriate assignment*?

His eyes bulged so much as he made his point that I had a hard time not mirroring him involuntarily. Maybe I did, come to think of it, because I remember he made a point of leaning forward slowly on the table on his elbows and asking, "You find this amusing, do you? Mrs. Bradford?"

Silence and heat. From where they were knotted in my lap, I felt my hands grip each other as if gripping something else. I looked into my lap then out the window to see children swinging side by side on the playground, trees greening, the sky floating along all blue-like and sky-like without a single care. And in that telling moment something clicked, and I mustered courage and confidence and decided to be bigger than this man across the table, to stay self-contained and charitable, but to not let a stranger's misjudgments and insults slide off me like water off a duck's back. I decided I would gird myself and not acquiesce to this man. To take this moment firmly in hand. To stand up, tip over the table, and roar.

Fiction.

Truth: I was trying hard to not cry.

I don't suppose anyone could have scripted a wilder barrage of hurts than this administrator did. I was incompetent, irresponsible, whimsical, selfish. My child was demanding, conniving, vagrant, unwanted. The very thing that had cost such a bottomless investment of effort and commitment and communal support was utterly lost on this man who was, ironically, an expert in international schooling. That whole long tale beginning with Britt and Eva and Anna? Synnøva and parkdress, Frogner Park and the monoliths? Sigrid and the Nesøya teachers, Skolefritidsordning, homemade troll costumes? Walking in a sea of children wearing his very own black, embroidered wool bunad and waving his very own Norwegian flag at Harald and Sonja? A king and a queen? Who then, note this, *waved back*? For crying out loud?

This man had no idea.

And I sensed he had simply no interest. Which not only puzzled me greatly but sizzled my nerves. Had he not in his whole career in the international school racket ever encountered lots of other families like ours? Those who move, dig in deeply, move again, and take a healthy layer of the last soil with them? And then they need some assistance in adjusting? Planting in new soil? Never?

I countered him to no avail. Parker was going to be put on probation unless he showed "remarkable progress, Mrs. Bradford. *Truly extraordinary* progress."

I remember the threatening words. I remember his eyes. I remember my crackling shame and simmering self-incrimination. I folded up my notepapers, stuffed them in my bag, got Dalton from where he'd been toitering around in his leg cast in the adjoining room, shook hands repeating my commitment to make this work, and left.

And all the way home behind the wheel I shook silently in sobs of defeat, exhaustion, and fear.

Jumping back in our history a few years, we have to remember that the Norwegian school system has some wonderful strengths. But pumping out skilled mathematicians, scientists, spelling bee champions, or rhetoricians by third grade isn't one of them. So we'd shown up all tousled, blue-eyed, and Nordic at this private international school, and for Parker especially, that entry had been a challenge. Not only was this all in English now, but even at his early grade level it was a kind of structured academic approach he wasn't used to.

I only understood this far too late in this France Arrival Drama, but Parker was frustrated and overwhelmed by . . . well, I could write a long list here. It's enough to write *everything*.

Whereas Claire wept daily and begged to go back to Norway where she could just "play at school like normal kids do" (she turned her pathos inward), Parker responded by stirring up excitement in his classroom (he turned his pathos outward). His behavior was erratic, according to his homeroom teacher. His reactions were disproportionate to whatever a given situation was. He seemed to be on fire or at least boiling with unbridled energy all the time. That force of nature came out in emotional spikiness, sometimes gleeful. Sometimes not. A tad Tigger. A touch Terminator.

Well, of course. I shouldn't have been surprised. In fact, I probably should have anticipated this. This was a transition, and as during the transition phase of childbirth, it's not exactly the moment to have your glam photos taken.

I'd seen some of this spikiness at home, a bit of it, but I usually thought it was a reaction to my own stress, my own sense of feeling overstretched, overwhelmed. And maybe, on some level, also being uptight. It felt like I was constantly running, constantly having to gear up for the daily basics.

That there were a million daily inconveniences—not broken feet, flooded basements, fire ant invasions and the like, but countless other picayune demands (connecting the phone, getting a driver's license, buying school supplies, filling the house's subterranean fuel tank) that I had to execute, 1) in French, which I could not possibly learn fast enough, 2) with a child lugging a plaster leg perched on my hip, and 3) alone. Randall was traveling from Monday to Friday to places I had to look up on the map, and so I had no backup. No reprieve.

When Randall was in the country (which was less than twenty percent of the time), we were in and out of conferences for our two children on a weekly basis over three months. When he was away (and the whole month of October he was hopping between three continents and dropping in at home for five dinners only), I had the rich task of getting my kids speedily up to American and French snuff. I was sleeping fewer than three hours a night, eating fewer than three real meals a week. Going gray in hair and skin, eyes and clothing sagging.

It became clear to me only at the end of one especially long evening of tutoring and coaching, how little these two knew about things their American teachers and you, Anglophone reader, probably take for granted. I'd gone through some simple math problems with Parker and had left him on his own at the far end of our Norwegian long table to finish the rest. Meanwhile, I was singing for Claire a bunch of stock American nursery rhymes ("Ring around the Rosie," "Humpty Dumpty") for a writing project she had to do, since she only knew Norwegian equivalents like mushroom songs and ditties about trolls. From the other end of the table Parker was showing signs of tetchiness:

"I can't *do* this one, Mom. I just don't *get* it," he grunted. "*How* am I supposed to *do* this? It's *impossible* to understand."

"Just . . . please . . . just finish it up," I said. "And please, *please* just quit grumbling. Okay Claire, let's try this one more time from the top: *Here we go loopty loo, here we go loopty lie* . . . "

I was so worn out and threadbare, you could hear my soul through the shredded fabric of my voice. Claire had her head in her hands, singing monotone to the tabletop.

A minute later I perked up in my best answering machine voice:

"Don't keep telling yourself you can *not* do it, Parker. You're smart, honey. You *can*."

I extended a hand to touch his shoulder, "I just *know* you can."

"Yeah, Parker. *You can do it*," Claire backed me up.

We must have sounded like Mousketeers. If he'd had any idea what those were.

He shook off my hand and snapped, "*I can not!!*" then slammed his pencil down on the table so hard it went flying off into the far wall. "I don't even *know* what they're *talking* about in this *stoooooooopid* math book!!"

His pencil rolled along the floor as he sat there, huffing, looking straight ahead, not at me. I looked at that round nose, nostrils so small but flaring. His chin, puckering and twitching while he ground his teeth.

I just stared at him. I'd run out of options.

Then, after Claire and I gave each other the eye and the *shhh* sign, Parker squeaked, "So . . . so what *are* deem-ahs . . . and kwahr-tairs . . . anyway?"

"What?"

He looked down at his workbook lying open on the table. With one finger he signaled a general place on one of the pages. "*Deem-ahs,*" he dropped his head and mumbled, "and *kwahr-tairs.*"

"Let me see this thing," and I dragged the manual over to where I sat.

I looked at the page.

I swallowed. I closed my eyes and shook my head.

I looked back up at my glaring, nostril-flaring, confused son.

I looked back at the book and recrossed my legs in my son's direction.

Then I scootched much, much closer to him and put my hand on his arm.

Deem-ahs are what you get when you are Norwegian and read the English word *dime.*

Kwahr-tair is what you get when you read *quarter.*

"Hey, sweetie. So, does your teacher know you don't know what these words mean?"

"No. I haven't told her all the things I don't understand."

So guess what. I did. I went back into the school and tried to make it clear to that teacher and to the others who worked with him that we were building from ground up. I even brought the math workbook and pronounced the whole problem as if reading it as a Norwegian child with no idea of English phonetics or coinage. From all of them, except from the administrator, I got nods of recognition and kind encouragement. That was enough to keep me this side of nutso for a while.

When not doing read-a-thons and math-a-thons in English to help Parker and Claire integrate, we were doing the same in French, to help Dalton do the same. There was an evening (really, I could have used you there) when I had one child chanting, "When two vowels go walking, the first one does the talking," another child worried sick about a boy named Jack who's broken his crown, and another belting "Sur le Pont d'Avignon."

In between them all, my soul was pushed on its knees in pray-a-thons, begging for all the heavenly intervention without which I knew we would all be deported.

To their credit, the two oldest dug in and absorbed all they needed so that teachers and administrators were satisfied. Dalton, the spitting tee-totaler, won himself a girlfriend named Marie-Celestine. And though our three were always energetic and outspoken, and the first two still used Norwegian idioms translated awkwardly into English, and the young-er for a while made up French words like "zee cozee peellow" and "zee grand scoop d'ice cr-r-reem," they ended up doing just fine in their new schools.

That first autumn, then, we'd had three children enter new school systems, one in French, which meant learning a new language, and two in English, which meant relearning an old language. Our heater broke down during an unseasonably early October freeze, we had no closets, we had no personal parking places for our two cars, we all got the flu, all of the *Île de France* got the flu, we had a bat problem (I forgot to men-tion that?), I had back problems (I forgot to mention the spasms and bed confinement?), we had a broken foot that kept one child from school for a month, and we had a real-life encounter with a Napoleon, who, I heard months later had been quietly exiled.

In the midst of all this, we'd figured out banking, basketball, and baguettes. We'd found new doctors, plumbers, and dry cleaners, and a fishmonger. New ways of walking, greeting, shopping, running in the gar-dens but not running in the streets, dressing, eating, breathing, existing.

LE CRASH

Then winter, the dead season, started early. Streets were slippery. And one Sunday morning, I nearly killed my children whom I'd buckled in their seats before dashing to pick up a babysitter who'd called last minute for a ride to church. One moment of poor judgment and poor visibility, a frosted-over sign, a bad turn, speed on ice, another motorist whipping up the opposing road while going over the speed limit, and the sound of metal against metal and glass splintering like a galactic trash compactor. Our small car spun three times, then punched its nose into a parked car.

We'd been struck broad side. The other driver was uninjured, though he'd been coming at over fifty kilometers per hour. There were cuts and minor lacerations to my children, chipped teeth, a deeply gouged tongue, and a nasty whiplash to the babysitter.

I knew the instant we hit that I was completely at fault.

"Two weeks earlier," the mustached police officer whispered to me in a French that was oddly crystal clear in the blur of sirens and a crowd of bathrobed onlookers on the street, "at this very corner and at this very hour, another driver did the same as you, Madame. And he was not as lucky."

I was lucky? I felt toxic, lethal. The Wormwood totem. This was the last straw.

13

La Langue

How does one recover from stress-induced depression? And who dares admit in the first place that this is legitimate depression, serious enough to send you to bed for a week with debilitating back spasms, down ten pounds, heart heavy with self-incrimination so stereophonic, even three pillows crammed around your head don't muffle the sirens? How does one face the fact that one has had too much, that it's beyond one's ability, that one is done for?

Boy, do I wish I could tell you.

As it was, I was unable to admit that this all—and by "this all," I mean everything from the last chapter plus literally hundreds of other stressors I simply don't have the room to write about and I know you won't have the patience to read about—that this all was *too much*. Especially to my perfectionist satisfaction.

Whoa. Who just said that? Who just snuck in here and wrote "perfectionist?" Granted, I have high expectations for life. And I do tend to push myself. But perfectionist? I'd rather use the words my friend Valérie said when she walked toward me as I stood there shaking at the reception desk of *les Urgences* of l'Hôpital Mignot. My sweet Valérie, with her arms wide and eyes as compassionate as Edith Piaf, said, "Mélissa, sometimes you place the bar too high. Take it down. Lay it on the floor for a little while."

Her voice was soft and steady as she put her hand on my forearm and coached me: I didn't need to put certain pressures on myself. I didn't need to feel I had to do everything in the French language, and just as the French do. Or twice as well as they do. I didn't need to take on more responsibilities than the bare minimum. Bare minimum responsibilities like, oh, breathing. I should focus on slowing down, on getting balance, lowering that bar. And while I was at it, buying some closets.

Randall swore off travel for the month of January, which gave me a bit of breathing room so I could regroup. Valérie and other friends I'd already made at church, enterprising and fragrant and compassionate French women—took me to their favorite vendors on Versailles' *Place du Marché*, gave me tips on how to elegantly but effectively rock the cars in front and in back with my van's bumpers so I could parallel park with panache. They introduced me to the mysteries of peeling tomatoes for my salads, buying edible gold leaf, identifying a decent truffle, and whipping up a gourmet dinner using the magic of Picard frozen foods. They generally rallied to fill in the cracks just about everywhere. All while my back and the titanium knot in my emotions unspasmed.

Important: They, like our church friends back in Norway, all agreed to the language rules we swore to. They would be our personal itinerant French tutors, which they seemed to love. So everything (even those tricky telephone calls, emails, handwritten birthday notes, appeals to high level French courts) had to be by edict *en Français*. I supplemented by taking biweekly conversation courses at the Berlitz center in the second floor of the white refurbished eighteenth-century building off the Avenue de St. Cloud down from the château and set up my own unofficial *Let's Go French!* dot-to-dot route through all of Versailles.

It looked something like this in my pocket notebook:

- Dry Cleaners/Teinturerie: Show lady Rs. pants. Vocab. **Melted zipper, stubborn spot, hanger.** Ask good shoe repair place. *Cordonnerie.*

- Shoe Repair/Cordonnerie: Give man D's brown shoes. Vocab. **Dye dark blue.** Ask remove Velcro? Add laces? Ask good hardware store? *Quincaillerie.* Very nice guy. Uncle lives NYC. Yankees fan?

- <u>Hardware store/Quincaillerie</u>: Moroccan man. Vocab.
  **Eyelet. Shoelaces. Pliers. Power saw. Mouse trap. Bat
  trap. Ant poison. Flood:** *Inundation.*

And so on. For months. I filled many notebooks. I'd make my literal
or mental notes while interviewing people in the street or in their shops.
It was my pattern in France the way interviewing Britt and Anna and
Bente and Idar had been my pattern in Norway. As long as I began with a
tumble of apologies (which, believe me, I felt) for the fact that I didn't
speak French, for the fact that I was born and raised in the wrong country
with the wrong language to begin with, then the way was paved to free
French tutoring. I walked flat-footed all over their *Français*, I'm afraid, and
spoke flat-tongued all over their sacred ground, but as long as I was polite,
deferent, and curious, they were polite, delightful, and even extravagantly
complimentary.

You've seen examples of the opposite of this, I'll bet. Cases where you
were in some foreign country (like, say, France), and someone, a foreigner to that country, foreign like you, marches up to a counter in a, oh let's
say a *Mac Do's*, stares down the thin girl with a brow piercing standing
behind the counter, then opens up rapid fire like this: "Hey, hi, okay so
me and my buddies'll have two Big Macs with three extra large fries and
four large Cokes, a double cheeseburger on the side, and while you're at it
back there why dontcha just toss in a coupla milkshakes?"

This Foreigner smiles at the girl, smiles in a friendly way, rubs his
hands together, lifts his brows, licks his lips again, waiting. Waiting for
her answer which, I suppose, he imagines is going to come sailing back
to him in his language.

But she's still just standing there.

She stands there, the girl, flaccid as a refrigerated fry, then lifts up one
unpierced brow as if to say, "*Quoi?*"

The Foreigner repeats the whole monologue, this time much louder,
a bit slower, with full corporeal involvement, while pointing to the panel
above and behind Counter Girl's head. He turns back and chuckles to his
buddies (*Will you get this chick?*), then he stops for a moment to just let
his last rendition sink in. Then he adds, "And we'll be needing lotsa them
little ketchup thingamajigs. Ten-four?"

Needless to say, someone (maybe this someone is you?) in line behind
The Foreigner leans forward about now and suggests in a warm whisper
that the girl speaks another language. Given that this is another country. Given that in another country people sometimes speak something
other than English. This amazing thing: you cross a huge ocean, you get

your passport stamped, and lo and behold! the people have their own language. It ruffles us foreigners every single time.

Or maybe you've seen what I did on a bus in the center of Paris. It was one of those resplendently picturesque late spring days that give flocks of tourists just the right crystalline sun bouncing off the domes and statues and Seine. The bus was full. The hour was rush. The bus stopped to take on a woman who was, as I recall, wearing yellow clam-diggers, a matching visor with a red flower on the brim. She was visibly out of breath and at the end of her rope.

I instinctively moved my bag to make room for her so she could sit right next to me and I could fan her and maybe make soothing conversation, or I could even ask her to hop off this bus with me so I could stroll her around my neighborhood, give her a break, a glass of water, and some courage. It can be rather tough to be a tourist in Paris, although that doesn't seem to deter upwards of eight million of them from coming to the city every year.

She had a map, this one-of-eight-million, which she crumpled and rolled up in one hand, baseball bat-like, as she addressed the bus driver. He was a wiry guy with black hair, a moustache, and nicotine teeth. I'd been watching the back of his head for a few blocks. He did not hate his job, neither did he revel in it, but I'll tell you this: he could have done all the streets of Paris with his eyes closed, he was that jaded.

I said the woman addressed the driver. I was wrong. She addressed the entire bus:

"I'm sick and tired of getting on and off, on and off these stupid French buses of yours!" she barked. "Already been on, what was it? Number eighty-two? Then *it* went the wrong way, then had to get onto, can't remember, think it was sixty-nine?" She was uncrumpling her map by now, trying to smooth it out on her thigh, which she was poising midair, grabbing on the pole, her visor sliding back on her hair.

The bus driver folded his arms, watching silently. The whole bus folded their arms, watching silently. My anticipatory smile kind of melted right then, I have to say, into flat but pained unease. She kept at it in a sputter, "This system's so wacked up, buddy. You just *gotta* help me out here. Where the devil's the Eiffel Tower? I'm losing my mind, I'm telling you. *Losin' it!*"

There was this pause where all we heard was the sound of this poor woman's eyes stretching wider and the bus driver's mind winding up for a fastball. Then, in one placid movement, he put the bus in park and pulled on the emergency brake, turning deliberately in his seat to face the woman straight on. And in the most even-tempered, well-aimed, machine-gun-like French ever spoken on a public bus or elsewhere in the world, this bus driver said something almost exactly like this:

"Madame. You have climbed on my bus. This is a French bus, a bus in Paris, France. I am a Frenchman. From Paris, the city with the marvelous Eiffel Tower you have flown very far, I imagine, to see. In Paris, in France, on my bus, we speak French. We do not speak English. We have our own borders, which you've crossed, and our own culture, our own. If you want to see something else that is very tall but insist on speaking English, then you must go to London and see Westminster, or New York City and see whatever it is that you see in New York City. And the *Eiffel Tower,*" he said as she backed away from him, shrinking, "is *juste là,*" and he pointed through the bus window. No more than two blocks away. "You can go by foot, Madame, *si vous le préférez.*"

He was civil. He was smiling tautly. And he held the doors wide open for her.

As you can see, the moment seared itself into my cells. To this day I regret that I didn't climb off that bus with her and just stroll alongside her to the tower, translating as we went—mistranslating, actually—everything this driver had said. Telling her how much he, too, loathed the wacked up bus system and loathed the folded city maps and loathed that the Eiffel Tower was sometimes, if you happened to be standing on the wrong corner as she had been, hidden behind trees and buildings.

How acutely I regret I did not do that. As it was, I watched her step off and huff away, her yellow sun hat with its red flower getting smaller, receding down the colonnade of leafy shadows along the avenue, the yellow like an awkward smile that one holds in place although the shame is burning, the red like a single piece of oversweet candy. Or a little puncture wound.

Language, if you turn it right, is a critical key to entering any new culture. But in France, as experiences like this taught me, language is *the* critical key. And that's why, when you turn the key of French wrong (and I did so more times than my ego can bear recounting), it was a gaffe, you were gauche, and you wanted an oversized bag to slip over your entire being. Let me show you how big that bag has to be:

When Dalton entered Richard Mique, the French government required he be vaccinated against tuberculosis. The French call that vaccine the BCG, for the Bacillus Calmette-Guérin. The BCG was unheard of in either Norway or in the States, and I did not want my son vaccinated. Though I contested the safety or necessity of the BCG, I could not get a waiver. I was told I had to submit my child to it if he was to enter a public French school, which, in a sort of catch-22, was the best way we knew he would learn French and we would integrate.

So the month after our arrival, and with no French under my unmistakably unfashionable belt, I went to a pediatrician to have Dalton immunized with what I was told by the *directrice* was a BCG vaccine thingy. Nervous to negotiate this in French, I pronounced to the receptionist as regally as possible exactly what my son needed to receive.

And the woman looked at me blankly, shook her head, telling me softly that my son did *not* need that.

I blushed, summoned my nerve, cleared my throat and said that, *mais si, si, Madame*, according to the preschool's regulations, he in fact *did*.

She repeated that he did *not*.

I straightened my corset, repeating that he *did, malheureusement*, require that BCG, that though I was *philosophiquement catégoriquement contre* it (I only managed cognates rather well, so I used as many of them as I could), I wanted him to be part of the school and, *hélas*, this is what the direction said he would need.

Especially as a foreigner. The mystifying BCG.

I still remember how the receptionist smiled at that point, and then instructed me, her eyelids half closed but without mocking me, on the difference between a BCG, which was a vaccine, and what I, *Madame*, was saying:

BCBG

BCBG?

"*BCBG, Madame Bradford.*"

Qu . . . quoi?

BCBG, just so you can note this for your next vaccine vacation to France, stands for *bon chic bon genre*, a common colloquial term used to describe those folks with unmistakably *fashionable* belts. The upper crust, stylishly preppy crowd. The "right" neighborhood, *BCBG*. A "go-to-be-seen" café, *BCBG*. A handbag, a way of walking, of smoking a cigarette, of tilting your big, black Bridget Bardot sunglasses, a way of sweeping your hand nonchalantly through your sun-kissed hair and letting it fall over your left shoulder. All *très BCBG*.

No, as funny a joke as it would make, there is not, at least the last time I checked, a vaccine against genetically inbred French stylishness.

At least that experience initiated me early on into the world of vaccinating in France, which, for an outsider, can be enough of an ordeal to send your unvaccinated hide back to the fatherland on the next steamer. It went like this: make the appointment by telephone for, let's say, a chicken pox vaccine. Arrive at the doctor's office for said appointment and have child diagnosed—"Yes, your child indeed needs a vaccine." Be told to go to find a pharmacy to buy the vial of the vaccine itself. Call the doctor for a follow-up appointment. Return for appointment. There, doctor dutifully injects your child with vaccine. You are rewarded with a baroque-looking signature and an even more baroque-looking official stamp. Throw into that mix an ordeal with language, which is exasperating, as is Parisian traffic. Far worse than traffic, though, is Parisian parking.

Anyway, it's wise to remember that whether you have keys to a Suburban or to a Smart, if you don't have the French key at all—if, for instance, you don't even have a miniature key like a neat little *bonjour* greeting, or a simple *pardonnez-moi* key, a key the size of your diary key when you were eleven, that kind of key, hanging there on your language key chain—if you didn't as much as *try* to turn the French key at all, then *hélas* all over again, you are in for trouble.

What happens, then, when you brandish your teeny French key and, *zut!*, it still doesn't fit? Well, I'll tell you. Sometimes it's enough to make a grown woman weep.

My friend Marsha, a family doctor in the States, had left her practice to follow an important career move for her husband to Paris. They had brought with them two daughters, and as is often the case when you have to enter new school systems, both had to have their vaccinations updated before a certain deadline.

Marsha was, needless to say, a competent and even scorchingly bright woman. Medicine was her domain. But she spoke no French, especially no medical French. She had, however, understood at least enough in her appointment with her own family doctor—"Yes, your child indeed needs a vaccine"—to know that she needed to go buy the vaccines herself.

This is where I enter the story.

"Can you just come with me, Melissa? Just to spot me? Just to the pharmacy, in case something French happens that I can't handle?"

By this point, three years into France for me, I was glad to play the quasi competent one for once. I'd gotten the fool thing down long ago.

"*Bonjour, Madame,*" a pharmacist greeted Marsha, who strode up to the counter ahead of me, determined to maneuver this one alone as we'd planned. I was prompting her in my hidden wristwatch walk-ie-talkie from my position back in the throat lozenge section. Seriously, she was going to do fine, especially given the fact that there were now three white-frocked French pharmacists facing her. I saw this as a plus:

they'd assist her. She saw it as a combat: they'd outnumber her, out-French her.

"*Bonjour*," Marsha responded. "*Je voudrais acheter les vaccines pour mes deux filles.*" Which, technically, was just right. She wanted to buy vaccines for her two daughters. All the words were there. In the correct order. Conjugations spot on. She had practiced and perfected her line. And although her pronunciation was somewhat off, I swelled with pride. *You go, fille!*

There was silence. Apothecary silence. Three pharmacists stared at Marsha blankly. This made me nervous. It made Marsha more nervous. Okay, her pronunciation was not precise—Tex-Mex, maybe—and maybe she had swallowed the word "*vaccines*," I still don't know. But this formula wasn't quite working. The French panel in white smocks just looked, turned to one another, cocking their collective head quizzically.

So Marsha tried again, louder this time, taking one step closer to the counter. One woman, youngish with streaked brown hair and serious eyes, repeated Marsha's words back to her with a question mark at the end. To which Marsha said, "*Oui. Les vaccines.*"

I can't explain what the mechanics of this misfortune were—perhaps she needed to say *vaccinations* or *innoculations* or the precise names of the vaccines needed—chicken pox, flu, measles, mumps, rubella—instead of general *vaccines*, but oh glory be, this Phrench Pharmacy experiment was phalling phlat.

As it did, I was tempted to step up and cut in and just place my hand on the counter, rip off my best colloquial French terms, and get this one over with. Instead, Marsha, gathering her very sharp wits, lifted her hand pointing to herself and said, "*Moi. Médecin.*"

"Me. Doctor."

But the pharmacists, overcompensating, I guess, for the language limitations of the customer standing before them, must have thought she was saying, "Me. Medicine." I'm not entirely sure, since I've replayed this a few times, trying to understand where the snag was. They must have then wondered if whatever she wanted (Vaccines? To be vaccinated right there? Some other medicine altogether?) was not for *deux filles*, now, but for her. Medicine. For the adult woman. *Me. Medicine.*

And you see where this is going. I felt Marsha stiffening her spine, squaring herself with self-respect, *Hey, I'm one of you! In the land of medicine I'm no foreigner. Somewhere else, if you can believe it, I'm the one who writes the prescriptions!* But we were in a knot, then another knot, then another knot. It was knotty in every way, and all of this in what without the language element could have been, should have been an easy, run-o'-the-mill, friendly five-minute exchange.

The three now turned to each other, heads tucked low, conferencing in hushed tones. Marsha repeated her words, in case she had not been loud or clear enough the first time. "Moi!" pointing emphatically to her sternum, "*Moi, médecin.*" In the same moment I shifted on my feet to step forward, I won't soon forget what I saw. This woman—a doctor of medicine, a woman with a bevy of patients and attending nurses in another hemisphere—started shrinking. Marsha took a too-deep breath that heaved her shoulders to her ears. And then she dropped her chin to her chest. The three pharmacists stood still, puzzled, as Marsha then drew up her head and turned around to find me.

There were tears just beginning to form a moat in her eyes.

I wanted to lunge a mega-vaccine right into the Eiffel Tower.

We left, as you've already guessed, with vaccines in hand and apologies all around. It had been *un simple malentendu*, a simple misunderstanding, and the pharmacists were genuinely regretful to have caused any stress. Then they were interested in hearing all about Marsha's family practice in America, wondered how she could have ever left it even if for just three years. And then how totally different the process is for getting vaccinated in the States, how much easier, more efficient. Then how Marsha's attempt at French was many times better than their English (they all concurred, heads bobbing), so *le docteur* should be proud. Amazing how a grown woman well past her growth spurt can grow two inches in height right before your eyes.

So in the end her girls got their shots in the arm. And Marsha got hers.

14

LE PETIT PRINCE

Respectable women do not make demands of the medical system. This is what I was picking up in my conversations with my neighbors who were each giving me their two centimes on where I should go for gynecological care. This was going to be especially helpful since, a year and a half after we arrived in Versailles, we were thrilled to be pregnant with number four.

"We," I write. By then we were apparently speaking in the royal plural, which happens, I suppose, if you're learning the French of Versailles. I now felt comfortable in the language, which for me was an essential prerequisite to entering into the most intimate world of a culture, the world of giving birth. No way had I been willing to *føde* (give birth) in Norway unless I was able to manage start to finish in that language. And no way was I going to *accoucher* (give birth) in France unless I could muddle through in French. It was this curious little deal I'd brokered between my tongue and my ovaries.

I had been reading as many articles as I could on French obstetrics and gynecology, and was concerned but somehow not surprised to find out that France ranks among the top ten countries in the world for the highest number of *césarienne programmées*, or scheduled cesarean sections. This concern I took to my friend Eleanore, who was as narrow as a baguette and always smelled of lavender. She'd grown up in *le Midi*, or the south of France, so certainly she, I thought, a girl from Aix-en-Provence, would be a naturalite and would not prefer scheduled C-sections or anesthetics like epidurals, or episiotomies or intravenous drips, if avoidable. I figured her perpetual scent of lavender meant she'd given birth to her two children in a field of it. But no. She explained the same thing my other neighborhood and church friends told me. *On ne fait pas ça en France.* Meaning, we don't do that "natural thing" in France.

The *ça*, the "that," was always spoken as if in secret and with a wince. My friends, their friends, and their doctor friends refused to believe my talk of meditation instead of medication, of concentration instead of caesarean sections, of walking and rocking and singing and water births, and when I told them about the simply beautiful (and natural) birth of burly Dalton, it invariably left them with a look in their eyes that was a mélange of panic, pain, embarrassment, and bemusement. My fulsome praise of Ellen my Norwegian earth mother, who essentially left Randall and me alone in our private birthing room requesting only that we ring a little cow bell when everything was ready and I knew it was time to give birth, made my full grown adult French friends slap their foreheads and drag their hand over their eyes in disbelief.

"Oh yes, we've heard of those primitive tribal practices in Lago-Lago," Rita told me.

And, "Those poor Nordic women are too naïve to know they have modern options. Right?" from Mathilde.

But what else could I say? I had had a really pleasant birth experience with a child that had weighed in at nearly five kilos, and yes, I was still walking. To me, it seemed unremarkable. But my women friends made me step back and turn around twice, all while looking me up and down and sideways, like I was Connie the Barbarian.

"There is a center I once read of," another friend Caroline whispered to me, "in Paris in the bottom of the fifteenth arrondissement." She lowered her voice even more. I had to cup my hand around my ear to hear her. "There, you might be able to convince a clinician to assist you in such a birth." Caroline was glancing both ways, too, as if this place were where a branch of illegal immigrant Wiccans shared a practice with a voodoo soothsayer, a tarot card reader, and a psychic named Esmeraldino.

Aeh. The fifteenth meant Paris, a fifteen-minute drive in predictable traffic. Too far, too risky.

The French preliminary gynecological visits themselves were nothing like what I'd experienced in Norway. There, my family doctor, Doktor Ø-N (his actual initials), had been the designated "attending physician," but in Norway a doctor *in* the delivery room was looked upon kind of like a strand of puka shells or maybe a tiara: one accessory too many. Hence, the presence of a highly skilled team of earth mothers assisting the woman in labor, and across the hall an operating room with a squad of emergency physicians who were always on hand in the hospital itself.

Doktor Ø-N was thoroughly Norwegian. This means he was ruggedly handsome, matter-of-fact, and dealt with his patients like he probably dealt with all living organisms from moose to mushrooms: with respect, equanimity, and a certain androgyny. There was never a thing in his manner that could have been interpreted as flirtatious or even drolly suggestive. On a scale of one to ten, one being acrimonious and ten being fawning, he was a solid 5.3, courteous on all counts but never chummy or chatty about anything personal. His job was to monitor my growing baby, which was only incidentally, it seemed, housed within my uterus.

There was one exception to Doktor Ø-N's professional distance. On a below-freezing January morning I arrived at his office with three-week-old baby Dalton bundled snugly in the car seat for his first new baby check-up. I got out of my Subaru and stepped into the eyeball-freezing cold, closed the driver's door, and through glacial winds scuttled very carefully over the blue-gray ice to the other car door where I would take out my baby bundle. There, on the other side of the car, I discovered that the car door had either frozen shut or was jammed. I yanked and pounded on that door then shuffled quickly back to the driver's door— also jammed or frozen—then pounded and shook all the others, even the hatchback, but nothing opened. In that short time, everything had frozen shut. My newborn was sitting inside this meat locker. Panicked, I ran, slipping and falling on ice all the way, to the building then up the stairs to my doctor's office. "My baby's locked inside my car!" I panted loudly to the woman at the reception desk, "My baby's freezing! I'm locked out!" Hearing me, Doktor Ø-N stepped out of his room, already pulling on his coat, a spray can in one hand and a metal rod of sorts in the other.

Without exchanging more than four words, he and I raced down the stairs and out into the gale and to the car, then, deftly wielding the magic spray and wedging this metal rod tool under the lip of the Subaru's hatchback, the doctor pried the back open. Then all six-foot-four of him climbed into the back and over the second seat, and he got right next to the car seat of my now-crying baby. He unlatched the car seat and handed it back through the hatch to me, but not before checking on Dalton, who was wailing his husky self into all shades of mulberry, but who (was this even possible?) went completely silent when my doctor, still crouched and contorted in the back seat with his knees up to his nostrils, blew one light puff of air into the baby's face then covered the baby and the whole car seat with the thick thermal blanket I'd tucked in there for warmth and lining. With one nod of the head and "*Sakte, sakte*" (slowly, slowly), my doctor sent me back inside the building carrying the car seat with my baby boy.

While I stood, infant in arms, watching from the window of his practice, this man stayed out there checking every door of my Subaru, coating the edges and lock mechanisms of each door with the spray, checking and rechecking. After ten minutes or so, his reddish brown hair looked like a flocked wig and the back and shoulders of his coat appeared to have been dipped in glass. Only now did I see he hadn't even put on gloves.

When he did come back inside, frost rings for nostrils, frost awnings for eyebrows, there was not a conversation, not even a word about what he'd just done for me and for my child. He just stamped off his shoes, hung his coat, shook off his hair, and returned to his other waiting patient. Just like that. Your everyday, no-frills superhero MD.

"In bad weather like this," he explained to me during our appointment, "You can just phone a day ahead and we can organize a house call." At any time and for any reason, in fact, I could call him and he'd visit my baby in the comfort of our home.

Well, then. "As long as you might be stopping by," I added, "could you check the oil? And there's this weird clicking sound in the steering column."

(I got him to smile with that one.)

As for medical advice, throughout my pregnancy my doctor told me to keep eating heartily, rest if I got tired, to not go slalom skiing after, oh, maybe the seventh month (it was a minor balance issue, he said) and to drink something called *tran* and another thing called *Vørter øl*, if I could gag them down. All the Norwegian mothers swore by them, he told me, but they might be an acquired taste, he warned. And so with typical zeal, I of course gagged down double doses every single day.

That I was putting on weight at a steady rate of two kilos (five pounds) or more a month was neither surprising nor troubling to Doktor Ø-N. "We want you to be well-nourished and your baby to be strong," he told me. "You also need a good layer of fat to produce good milk for your child. Don't worry, you'll ski it off by the next year."

He was unfazed when I tested him about actual birthing options. What if I wanted to birth, say, in a tub? Or on all fours? Or while practicing arias? He said it was my birth and my body, and given this was my third child, I should know what worked best for me.

So Norway had set the standard for giving birth. It had proven to me how lovely—how exquisite—the experience could be, how powerful in some respects, physical as well as spiritual. And now all France had to do was follow that act.

With the help of my next-door neighbor, Florence, who had heard about my unconventional wishes, I was led to *Monsieur le Docteur*. His *cabinet*, or practice, was in the center of Versailles, and he assisted births in various facilities in town, including the clinic closest to our home, Le Clinique du Château de la Maye.

Monsieur le Docteur had a slightly different approach from his Norwegian counterpart. This Frenchman was a balding, fatherly intellectual with spectacles on the tip of his nose, and his cabinet was a converted *maison parictuliére* with a grand stone entrance through which horses and buggies would have once passed. Once through the main portal on the street, there was stained glass at the end of a shadowy corridor and wrought iron fixtures indicating a one-man elevator installed, probably in the early nineteenth century. There was a huge walnut door on the right with the brass plaque giving Le Docteur's name. The door had a burnished brass knob which was, as is the case with these old world door knobs, right in the middle. The door weighed even more than I always managed to weigh at full term, which means I had to lean in on that brass knob with all my force just to enter. As you walked into the practice, you stepped from the seventeenth into the twentieth century, but still a twentieth century of the old France that was cramped and randomly geometric, and narrowed into what felt like what might have once been servants' quarters. A receptionist behind a modern desk set at an angle sat straight ahead under a framed Picasso sketch of Mother and Child. Le Docteur's office itself, once I was invited to enter it, had a massive leather-topped walnut desk, deep embossed carpets in rich hues, surrounding bookshelves, gilt-framed paintings of *La Chasse* and *Les Aborigines*, and low mood lighting. I was in Sherlock Holmes' library, not a medical facility.

"Please, Madame . . . Madame *Braaaaaaaaadford*, tell me first about yourself." The Docteur smiled from his side of the desk toward where I sat in a nineteenth century curve-backed chair with burgundy and gold *petit point* upholstery. His grin had something of the Cheshire Cat to it, which caused me to feel something like Alice: teenaged, blonde, perched on a mound of ruffles and scratchy petticoats, shrinking and slipping into a hole.

So I played the expert. I was prim but relaxed, The Mother in Control, dotting my French *i*'s and crossing my legs tightly.

"*Alors*, Monsieur," I said, motioning to the stack of papers I'd handed him, "This you should immediately note is my fourth child, as I have explained in the papers there. I'm no *debutante*." I smiled coolly and straightened my spine, trying not to hold my handbag too tightly on my lap, as if I needed a shield or a prop or a weapon or anything.

"*Ah! Une mere d'un certain âge! Charmante, charmante*," he was scanning my papers, but kept grinning and staring up at me, as if awaiting something. A mother of a certain age? And this was charming? I'd written in bold black Bic that I was thirty-seven, still very young in my book, hardly worth a comment. For heaven's sake, coltish, right?

The doctor raised one brow and smiled at me, leaning back in his leather chair, hands crossed over his middle. Something about the setting made me feel as if the next thing that was supposed to happen was I was to jump up and sing my eight bars from "Oklahoma!" Or was I supposed to start listing my GPA and extracurricular activities for this administrator interviewing me for a college scholarship? I kept my school bag—I mean handbag—on my knees. I heard myself swallow.

"And you are . . . " he ruffled through the big stack of forms I had spent more than an hour filling out in the small red and peacock blue waiting room with four chairs and five patients, "You are . . . an American citizen, *vraiment charmante*, and will deliver in April and, oh! I see you are the woman I've heard of, the one who wants to deliver *à la scandinave. Charmante, charmante*."

"Yes, I would like to deliver as naturally—"

"Now, tell me, Madame, where did you learn to speak your lovely French?"

"In the streets, frankly. Now, to the birth: I hope to deliver with as little—"

"In the streets? *Charmante! Vraiment tellement charmante*."

And so on.

Throughout the exam that required what all prenatal gynecological exams require, there was no privacy screen, no paper gown, no nurse in the room, no professional distance. No Geisha fan. No fig leaf. No strategically placed standing fern, even. Just your typically invasive examination performed on a *vraiment charmante* pregnant woman by a gentleman in a burgundy wool cardigan and a perpetually sleepy grin.

I'd called a whole list of French girlfriends as soon as I got home. Could what I just experienced have possibly been standard practice? Every last one of them was surprised by my concern:

"Ah, Mélissa, it's nothing to worry about. I know you Americans tend to be a bit touchy about your bodies. But really, wouldn't you rather get random compliments from your doctor than insults?"

And:

"So, you're telling me that even in Norway, they give you a gown for the exam? But . . but *why*?"

And:

"You could do *what*? File a lawsuit if some nurse is not in the room with you? But . . . I don't see why she's even necessary."

And:

"A little room behind a screen? To change clothes? Never heard of it. Charming concept, though."

And:

"Listen, I'd be flattered if my doctor told me I was beautiful when pregnant. My husband doesn't."

I had to conclude that this was a cultural oddity, evidence of the deeply calcified gender roles and the ever-present tension between the male and the female that is more a part of French culture than any other place I have ever lived or spent significant time. Yet, in spite of that sometimes edgy Alice-and-the-Cheshire-Cat feeling, and even when he told me at six months gestation that I now had to go on a strict diet because I had reached the official twelve kilo weight gain limit, I kept *le Docteur*.

Why? Because he was a fabulous physician, had saved not only the uterus but the life of my girlfriend in what was supposed to have been a complete hysterectomy, was an invigorating discussion partner about everything besides just obstetrics: Soviet politics, Sub-Saharan water initiatives, Patagonian turtles, art, music, literature, cuisine, world religions including (or especially) mine. I almost—almost—looked forward to our visits if only because I knew I'd be able to enjoin him in some sort of debate. He could not hear enough about my Mormonism, not just because of my personal commitment to abstaining from coffee, alcohol, and nicotine (which he said he admired and wished his other patients would do) but chiefly because of my full-hearted belief in chastity before marriage and total fidelity afterwards. This was a concept I just could not emphasize enough or with sufficient fervor in my chats with this Frenchman.

More than for his sterling medical reputation and the lively conversation, I stuck with *le Docteur* because, all corporeal concerns aside, he was gentle, worked right in this town, and frankly, he was the one and the only doctor I could find after months of searching daily, who vowed to let me deliver my baby as *I* wished. Which meant, incidentally, without much of his help.

Under a full moon, Randall and I arrived at the looming doors of the Clinique du Château de la Maye, just a couple of blocks from our home. We drew up the heavy cast iron doorknocker, and let it drop four times, announcing our arrival. Christine, our *sage femme* (or, literally, "wise woman" or earth mother or midwife), answered. She was, as fate would gift us, a native German, and the one sage femme we had already met on a previous tour of the facilities. During that tour, we'd all spoken German together, Randall, Christine, and I. We'd spoken and laughed and mused about how unlikely but wonderful it would be were she to happen to be on call the very hour we would come in for the birth.

And there she stood. White frock and stethoscope and a warm hand extended, she swung wide the door, "*Einen recht schönen guten Abend, die Familie Bradford! Treten Sie herein!*" I knew right then it would indeed be what she said: a "really beautiful and good evening," and I did as she asked. I wobbled right in on Randall's arm.

True to her role as a sage femme, Christine wisely escorted us through the quiet modus operandi leading up to birth. With only one exception to what I'd done in Norway, where I birthed kneeling on the floor next to my big bed, I birthed in Versailles exactly as I'd requested.

Granted, French law said I *had* to have an IV drip. So I rolled my eyes and let Christine poke it in and tape it down. And according to French law I *had* to be *on top of* the birthing bed. So Christine, the resourceful German, hiked up the one end to a full sitting position, I knelt on the bed facing that upright part, grabbed the back with both arms, closed my eyes and began humming. My wise woman let me do as I wished—sing, chant, rock back and forth, crochet little booties—No, I didn't. I don't know how to crochet—and afterwards, she asked me for a copy of the French lullaby I'd sung as Luc, our luminous one, was entering the world.

Only after Luc's arrival into this world did Monsieur le Docteur arrive at the château. Early into the process of labor, while I was still on my feet and moving around to help gravity pull things along, when Randall and I were still joking about how he should have been forward-thinking and brought a better selection of flannel night shirts for me to wear besides this one—in other words before I assumed the kneeling-on-top-of-the-bed-singing-like-a-large-mermaid posture, I had conspired with Christine about the delivery itself.

We couple of wise women had plotted that, if everything proceeded as smoothly as it had to this point, we could skip calling my doctor at all. At least she wouldn't make that call until the absolutely last moment, the moment we would hear our baby squeal. And so it happened. Le Docteur made his obligatory surveillance of things, congratulated Randall, signed his name, smiled for our photos, and returned to his home and to his slumber. Ah, that familiar welling up of maternal satisfaction and breast milk.

For just an instant I was feeling competent—*I'm now a mother of four?*—until the nurse responsible for our baby's care (weighing, cleaning, swabbing yellow disinfectant into his eyes) entered the room and turned to me, asking, "Do you have your baby's layette? Diapers? Body bath? Cotton swabs? Lotion? Head cap? Mittens?"

Non. I had none of the above.

"Ah . . . and for yourself? Your peignoir? Makeup? Jewelry? Fresh clothing to greet your visitors?"

Uh. *Non.* I acted as if I were patting my pockets, searching. No, that's right. *Non. Encore: non.* I had none. I had an overnight bag with a toothbrush and soap and had this fetching number, a man's oversized checkered flannel nightshirt she'd certainly taken note of, and I'd planned on sleeping most of the day in those very clothes. If no one minded.

"Was I supposed to have brought a . . . a *peignoir?*" I snickered. She stared at my nightshirt. Did I even have a peignoir? Do women in this century for that matter, reputable women, that is, honestly *have* peignors? What else had I forgotten to bring so that I had to sit there slouched like some stinky Insta-hillbilly? *Fluffy high heeled slippers? A powdered wig?* I was sponging up sweat as it now pooled in every possible ravine of my physique while the yokel in me bloomed into full blush.

"Well, most women do, Madame. It's customary. You might want to note that the photographer makes his rounds in the early hours, when the natural light is best. Maybe you will want to be presentable. You will receive today."

Recevoir? Présentable? Photographe? In the flurry and quiet thrill of being part of the incomparable wonder of welcoming new life into this world, somehow I'd forgotten: in Versailles I couldn't just deliver and then hunker down in a milky-mothery-baby blob for a blissful week as I had in Norway.

Non. Here I had *delivered.* So here I would *receive.*

The pattern had been set at least as early as Marie Antoinette, who had given birth in her château with the entire royal family and the whole court as audience. The birth as well as the product of the birth, I suppose, had to be demonstrated, authenticated, and celebrated by a stadium full of witnesses and well-wishers, a one-stop package deal. And because in Versailles what *was* still *is*, the delivered mother needed to present herself and her baby to the visiting entourage and the planned paparazzi.

I had Randall run home to grab lipstick, pearls, and something in silk.

15

ENCORE!

Luc we called the Luminous One. Or Lucky Luc, from a French comic strip. Or, most often, The Luc Factor because this luminous, funny boy was also a force of nature. And this factor didn't make the several serial moves that followed in quick succession any easier.

Sooner than we'd planned, the Versailles landlord returned to his home and we were out house-hunting again. We found a place being built in a village called Croissy-sur-Seine. The fact that the day the moving van pulled up to the house the house was yet unfinished (that is, if you consider a house with no glass in the spaces intended for windows to be "unfinished") was the first concern. But in Versailles I'd weathered fire ants and bats and no parking for our two cars and four basement floods and the destruction of the *Tempête de 1999*, which uprooted much of Versailles and her magnificent gardens and landed a 200-year-old tree squat across the front seat of our next door neighbor's car. Optimist that I am, I figured lack of windows just meant better ventilation. Glass half full. House half finished.

But then the rains came. By that point, luckily, we did have windows, but we also had a basement and in France, as they say, when it rains . . .

it floods your basement. I bailed for hours and hours. That was the first week of September. The next week the entire world changed.

Cidalia, my Portuguese girlfriend, was breathless and crying on the phone, "*Faut regarder la télé, Mélissa. Faut regarder maintenant!*" I had to turn on the TV, she said. Had to turn it on right now.

There were images of smoke and imploding tall buildings I recognized instantly. This was New York. It was an earthquake or a detonation. But the French news said it was an *attaque terroriste*. Within twelve hours, all families associated with the American School of Paris were notified by the US Embassy to go underground, to not visit any typical American haunts (certain restaurants, bars, shops, theaters), to not even step out on the streets if possible, and if that was unavoidable, then at least to not do anything that would advertise oneself as American. The children were brought home where they stayed in quasi house arrest. Our American missionary friends came and hid out at our home. We folded away any clothing that might look American: logos, brands, an embroidered eagle. We waited for word on the next move.

Within an hour, my French friends flooded my phone line asking if Randall was safe, if my whole family was safe, if I had any more information, that they were *horrifié, terrifié, bouleversé,* that they were praying for us, for the victims, for our country.

That this was *un temps pour faire du deuil.* A time to grieve.

A chapel full of both French and American church members gathered the next day, visibly heavy-hearted and many in tears. There, I stood and sang the American national anthem, which was challenging enough. But when I reached, "and the rockets' red glare, the bombs bursting in air," I was unable to make a sound.

The children did eventually return to school, but when they did, they passed by security guards with submachine guns and black fighter dogs in muzzles. The campus was in profound hyper security and palpable mourning.

Randall canceled his September 12 business trip to Islamabad. His work in the Middle East changed permanently, the events of September 11 leaving hot tremors across Paris and across our remaining lives.

By November, still keeping a low American profile, and still getting settled into this home which meant still sorting through boxes to find Christmas decorations I'd barely restacked in a now-dry basement, Randall got a call. It was word that he had been selected for an advancement that would put him at corporation headquarters. In New Jersey. Could he move immediately?

Let me pause. Let me allow that to sink in a spell.

This scene is not all that atypical in expatriate life. You move to a place—to Moscow from Minneapolis or to Mumbai from Moscow, let's say—and you just begin figuring things out when a call comes. The call might ask you to repack your boxes and head back to where you just came from (to the home you just sold, to the school you just forfeited your children's slots in, to your spouse's practice/studies/firm/office he or she just closed or sold off), or repack your boxes because to head to another place entirely (where you must find a new home, schools, a new life track for everyone), or to repack your boxes because the company is sorry, there is no job anywhere for you in the brand new corporate structure. Imagine the scenario where you have uprooted because you've accepted an assignment in Cairo or Stockholm or Bangalore, where you in good faith are digging in your roots and drinking from a new soil . . . only to be Rubik's Cubed back or away or out of a job, full stop. Most of the time employees are given the option to keep their job, but sometimes that means the job is in one country and the family stays in another.

It is a less-known and less-appealing side of the international life. But given the backdrop of 9/11 and a subsequent military invasion in Iraq, such professional dramas are, we certainly must agree, mini-dramas, petty. Still, they aren't easy.

Besides, I was writing about Randall's new job.

"No," he said, "We can't move right now. We're just moving *in* right now. But," he eyed me for the go-ahead nod from across our bedroom where he was receiving this phone call from headquarters, "*I* can move in the new quarter. I'll move. Melissa and the kids will finish out the school year here and follow in the summer."

We did this for many months, Randall in the US, the rest of us in France, which time it took for us to get our heads around the prospect of reentering The Homeland.

Homeland. We were moving to a Heartland Homeland and, in many ways, the American Dream Land. A thirty-minute drive south from Randall's company's headquarters, it is a bucolic, historic swath of Americana with two-hundred-year-old farmhouses and snaking stone walls surrounding horse farms and apple orchards, a place known, as my new neighbor dressed in a Phillies t-shirt told me, for its Blue Ribbon schools and Blue Ribbon beer.

Despite that appealing description, there were early indications the adjustment was not going to be so easy. Parker was immediately called "Frenchie" at a middle school that had a two percent rotation rate, meaning that people were born there and schooled there and never moved away. Next to zero international influx. Our children were mortified when everyone but them knew to stand in perfect unison at the beginning of the school day and recite, "*Verbatim*, Mom," Claire said through gritted teeth later, an "Allegiance chant," Parker cut in, all gluey and glum. "I had to *lip sync*, Mom," he went on. They had never heard it. Never knew it existed. And how would they? But they knew the Norwegian and French national anthems by heart, and I suggested they teach them to their classes as compensation.

Then the girls on the elementary school playground were tittering in a tight clump about someone named Lizzy; her clothes, her hair, the way she talked, what she did this week and the week before, and what she might do next week. And Claire, a month into this new world, interrupted to ask, "So . . . who's Lizzy? Is she new here at school like me?" To which all the girls stared. And laughed.

"Lizzy *McGuire*, Mom," Claire told me later, not crying, but looking stern, like an anthropologist who's just spotted a member of an endangered species. "Lizzy M-C-G-U-I-R-E. We have *got* to get American TV."

And Dalton was having his own adjustment issues, not spitting at children this time around, thank heavens, but doing other things his teacher was trying to manage. "Twenty-two years as a teacher, Mrs. Bradford, and I have to tell you I've never seen anything quite like your dear Dalton."

At thirteen, Parker would have probably been riding the plate tectonics of an identity crisis anywhere, but here he was trying wardrobes and body postures and accents in order to fit in. When asked were he was from, he never mentioned a word about his real upbringing, would no longer speak anything but English with us although we'd always hopped from Norwegian to French to English in our home, in our private conversations, to keep secrets as a family when on the streets. It seemed he'd made an overnight decision to be a new person.

"*Where*, Parker? Where'd you just tell that guy at the gas station you were from?"

"Fully" he tipped his head, on which he now wore a flat-rimmed cap tilted strategically off to one side. "Fullydelphia."

My son—maybe you remember him from barnepark and the Versailles Club du Basket?—had morphed in the course of exactly 0.6 minutes into a boy from the hood. From the *Fully* hood.

After having written an essay for entrance into an honors English course for his school, Parker reported to me later how it had gone.

"So, *ça va, mon cœur*? How'd it go?"

"'Salright, I guess. I finished the thing. Wrote a good full three pages."
"Sounds good! What did you write on?"
"Eve."
"Eve? As in Eve . . . *Adam and Eve*—Eve?"
"Yuh. Eve." He was adjusting the hat and letting his oversized pants bunch sufficiently around his untied basketball shoes. My boy from Fully. Where'd this kid materialize from?

"As in, you wrote about the Bible story? Or, uh, what?" I kept smiling, taking it easy, knowing that I was now in a country where the separation of church and state is at times maybe a bit smudgy. But . . . *Eve?*

"They gave me three choices to write on," he said, "And I picked, 'Describe the life and accomplishments of your favorite First Lady.'"

"And Eve . . . She was the—"
"The First Lady."

And the only one he knew of. So clearly, we hadn't taught our children well. Or maybe we *had*. They were doing what they'd done elsewhere: watching, observing, mimicking the locals to blend in, picking up the language (or accent), and figuring out the jumble of norms and nuances as they went along.

It went on like this for months and for all of us. Misreading cultural cues, not knowing language signals, not knowing TV lingo or TV personages or TV jokes, feeling alien, foreign, and making up for it each in our individual way. Parker became a gangsta. Dalton got frustrated with himself and too easily with others. Claire buckled down and took the lead in the school musical. Randall buried himself at headquarters. Luc gave me another round of debilitating back spasms.

To be fair, it was not Luc alone but the house renovations that gave me the back spasms. You see, with everything pointing to the probability of our staying in this place forever, we decided to dig in deeply as if this was it. *This* is where we will belong. This meant buying a home, which became the project into which I invested my energies, that is when I wasn't sitting in conferences with teachers trying to help ease along whichever child was struggling with the adjustment that week. I invested myself into making this home just right for our family, invested myself the way I threw myself into just about everything else. Like a windtunnel full of pepper spray.

This meant a total overhaul from replaced floors to painted walls to added closets and woodwork. It meant a split rail fence around the entire property, a Hansel-and-Gretel cottage on the back of the property. A copper weather vane. It also meant jack-hammering out the whole kitchen and putting in a new one. It was eight months of consuming work that spanned the dead of winter when we had to heat up pizza in a microwave rigged in the garage. And, yes, it was expensive work, work for which we'd been saving up parsimoniously for over nine years assuming that one day we would, with a mortgage and window boxes, pin ourselves permanently on a map somewhere.

We had vowed, Randall and I, to pass no judgments on this new life until these renovations had run their course. In the meantime, I found myself hunting in grocery store lines and around the edges of the local soccer pitch for a hint—any hint anywhere—of a foreign accent. Otherwise, we felt strangely alien, unable to share a great part of ourselves with others. One can expect to feel alien in a new or foreign country. But this? Feeling alien in what's supposed to be your home country? I knew less about being a soccer mom than I did about buying fresh produce from local vendors in an open market, less about American sports teams than about Norwegian arctic explorers, less about the goings-on of my native country than I did about Norwegian, in the end, no one seemed to want to hear much about.

This no-man's-land feeling we tried to counteract by accepting volunteer positions in our church, Randall in the three-member leadership of our 450-member congregation, I in the regional presidency of the organization for all the teenaged girls. We connected with kind, enterprising, talented, and patriotic fellow-Americans, whose friendship would accompany us into the years ahead.

But first came March. For ten days we'd been functioning in our new kitchen. I stood in the middle of it and took it all in: hammered copper farm sink and mustardy-sepia granite counter tops and our few select pieces of Provençal and Italian pottery. Norwegian touches. French touches. An antique Swiss cow bell holding back the traditional Scandinavian linen drapes. Modest but tasteful, but most important, it bore our international imprint.

And the beautiful room made me ache. Relentlessly and acutely, I longed in my bones for France, for Europe in general, for my friends from the world over, for my children's friends who understood them. What's more, I was sniffing for the musty smell of a tiny corner market run by a Moroccan, for pungent cheeses sold by someone I knew by name in a shop that closed every day at noon for lunch and every Sunday. But beyond that, I ached for a place where we could be who we all had been individually and as a family, for that special roughness and refinement of a vibrantly textured international setting, and I missed—till-my-throat-constricted, *missed*—hearing and speaking French.

But that was all over and out. So I was trying to focus on all that *was*, over what was *not*; the great ease and comfort that homogeneity offers, the undeniable traction that a societal system has when there are ample funds and loads of optimism. America's abundant pluses, including her tremendous energy and enterprising people, the head-spinning convenience and collective casualness, they were not lost on me. That, in spite of my anxiety attack the first time I visited a Costco, or the first time I saw a $5.99 burger the size and weight of a French subcompact, which sight gave me heart palpitations and sent me running for cover. Otherwise, I was calmly, steadily fighting to come to terms.

So what do you do when you're fighting to come to terms? You suit up in chocolate, of course. I was making chocolate brownies (the first brownies I'd ever made, I had to borrow a recipe) for a school function, as I remember. And Randall called.

"Hon, can you meet me at the bottom of the hill? I'm almost home. Come alone."

From my journal:

> *The hardest moment was in our bedroom tonight. We'd already told P by himself, which was a good move. We knew he'd be ecstatic. But C just finished doing Marian the Librarian in* Music Man *and just last week we promised her a dog. Finally, the dog she's waited a decade for. For D and L, we would just announce the choice when we'd make it, not discuss it, so we didn't involve them at first.*
>
> *P and C were sitting on our sofa. We told them we had big news but wanted to discuss it. This isn't final, kids, we said. Want to get your reactions. And when we told C, she immediately glazed over then her eyes welled up. P put his arm around her, and she just started crying, crying. "I don't want to go back to that hard life. This is easy, good, perfect. I want to be here. I want to STAY HERE!" And she fell into P's arms, bawling. I think I gave R an evil look, and I know I lipped to him, "This means No Go."*
>
> *We kept trying to reassure her. We haven't said yes to a thing, we said. We've just been asked if we could and we are free to say no, we said. We'll never do something that makes all of us miserable and that Heavenly Father does not encourage us to do. We walked around and around the backyard, C between us, our arms wrapped*

*around her shoulders, listening as she cried out all the reasons why
this was all bad, all wrong. "All bad, all wrong," she kept crying,
stopping to catch her breath, to bend over and then shake herself
upright. It broke my heart. I wanted to weep, too, but held it in. I
was believing her. I felt how selfish it would be to pluck them out
of such bounty and ease, and I had just hung red geraniums on the
wrap-around porch, gorgeous! Why would we ever head to where
things were, as Claire knew, much harder. The edges, harder. The
expectations, harder. The language, harder. The traffic and school
and rules and sky and air and everything, she said, HARDER.*

What happened when Claire went alone into her room is something
Randall and I didn't ask or hope for. We sat, nauseated and sweaty, conflicted and brokenhearted, hands between knees, rocking back and forth
on the edge of our bed. *So what?* we said to each other, if the company has
an "acute" and "special" need? *So what* if that need is, as they assert, "tailor-
made" to be filled with Randall's expertise? *So what* if this would only be
"a couple of years" and then we could come right back to the home and
the huge yard and the cul-de-sac on the hill and corporate headquarters
where Randall, having done this, overseeing his function in the company's largest subsidiary outside the US, would be "very well-positioned," as
he was told, to take on the job that his whole career had been grooming
him for, the top and final level.

So what? I said.

So what? he said.

So what?

And Claire knocked on our door. She wanted to talk. She came with
news that became a turning point and a landmark to which our whole
family would refer for years to come. She sat with us on the bed and told
us she'd run while holding back tears to her girlfriend down the road.
That friend, whose parents were in the middle of a horrible divorce,
reassured and comforted Claire, and listened as her new friend cried.
Claire had then come back home to kneel at her bed and pray. Not for an
answer—to move or not to move, that was not the question—but simple
comfort in this hurting moment. It was then that she felt warmth and
heat wrap around her twelve-year-old shoulders and a voice (she felt it,
she didn't hear it) told her clearly that though this would be really hard at
the beginning, over the long run it would be the best thing for the family.

Yes, she should, we should, move to Paris.

The head of the moving team, a burly guy you'll remember from earlier, a man I call *Le Chef*, stood in the middle of Rue du Colonel Combes in Paris' seventh arrondissement brandishing a huge pair of industrial clippers in his hand ready to perform the ceremonial Cutting of the Lock. In theory, our forty-foot moving container had not been opened between locking in the US and lock-cutting in France, so I wasn't paying too much attention as I leaned out of the second story window, eager to just get this move moving.

Le Chef cut the lock. One door creaked open a couple of centimeters, and with it, a quick swish of water spilled out of the bed of the container and onto the street. All the moving crew threw quick glances up at me. I was cool. Imperturbable. Blithe-lite.

The second door creaked open a bit, held back by a man who watched me, not the door. More water. Then two men swung both doors wide open, their eyes squeezed shut, and as those doors swung, a veritable waterfall gushed out onto the road. These men, former fishermen from Brittany, actually hopped out of the way as one mattress after the other, eight in total, slumped out of the back of the trailer. Like enormous slices of pound cake soaked in an ocean of coffee, every bed we owned was moldy and saturated with brine, and fell limply one after the other onto the street. I remained immobile. Blithe-less.

Then someone down on the road cleared his throat. "Madame," Le Chef called up to me, in French with a Breton accent, "Uh, it's maybe best you get something to write with."

And after several hours of unloading a container that had not only been somehow partially submerged in water, but had been tampered with somewhere during its thousands of miles in transit, after those patient hours of watching these men fish out our waterlogged belongings from deep in this container, I filled seven full pages of legal pad note paper. Line upon line of damage, disappearance, and loss.

All eight beds and bed frames including headboards and bunk beds, trashed. Two vintage leather chairs from the Marché aux Puces, wedding anniversary gifts to each other, rotten from prolonged exposure to moisture and punctured with . . . bicycle handlebars? Lamps, crushed and bent around . . . a basketball? A couch, gored through with . . . fireplace pokers? Clothing, boxes of what we had planned on wearing the next week, rank and fuzzy with mildew. And in the end, a personal visit and apology from the global moving company's owner and namesake. Our Norwegian long table, shipped in a separate and smaller container, made it to France (and as you know from having read this far, also made it into the apartment by being lassoed and dragged through an upper-story window), unscathed.

An email to a friend:

> *Unpacked 17 days straight. All the damaged stuff has to stay here so insurance folks can come by (when?) and verify damage. Moldy mattresses, broken bed frames, incinerated treadmill, everything, stacked against walls in an apartment one-third the size of US home. Only clothes are what we had for summer vacation, we're trying to clear a path through piles by taking stuff down into the communal cave beneath the building, the greasiest, dustiest dungeon in Paris. Borrowing towels, inflatable mattresses, essentials from church friends who schlep them here by Metro. Incredible folks! Haven't had a chance to stock up on food which takes forever here, so I've been eating mini yogurts from the grocer's down the street and handfuls of pretzels. R is "floundering," he claims, totally consumed because his job is 100 percent in French every day. Works councils, labyrinth-like French legalese; he had to appear in court and testify in French last week, ooh-la-la. P and C have long school days with a forty-five-minute bus ride both ways. D adjusting, which means, yes, I'm losing lots of sleep over him. (Can you lose "lots of sleep" from four hours of sleep? Do that math for me, will you dear? :-)) Luc in sweet bilingual Montessori preschool across the street: saves my sanity. Living in the middle of Paris is a decidedly different experience from Versailles, and of course a universe apart from where we've just been. Intoxicating, energizing, really. At least . . . I hear it is, because I can't get to it for all the piles and the work of replacing the piles and all the details of just getting settled, like finally getting working Internet, voilà! When I die and have that Life Review, the whole film's going to be a vast landscape of moving boxes. Come visit when I have a few square inches for you to stand in.*

I've asked this question once before, but it bears repeating: How does one recover from a stress-induced depression? I'd been like this five years earlier, and knew that this, like last time, was legitimate depression, serious enough to send me to bed not for a week of debilitating back spasms like Versailles, but for a week of spirit spasms, too, down ten pounds again, but this time the self-incrimination didn't stay locked inside my cranial Hi-Fi system, but leaked in mumbles out of my own mouth: Inept. Not up to this. Exhausted. Ruining everyone's life. Claire gave up her cozy American existence and her dream of a possible dog for a rubber mattress and dog poop land mines on every sidewalk? Had I been nuts to drag us all into this? And by the way, what kind of worthless whiner is in a fetal heap in bed at 2:45 on a sunny afternoon? In Paris?

Another mother, a new acquaintance from Luc's school, saw my bagging pants, the olive circles under my eyes, and the splotches of rouge scrubbed on to cover the ashenness. She took me aside.

"*Ça va, Mélissa?*" she inquired delicately, putting an accent on the first syllable of my name and her hand between my shoulder blades.

"*Oui, oui, ça va, ça va,*" I answered, smiling too brightly. Her handwritten note and little card of teeny blue pills suggested to me that I hadn't hidden much from her.

"These are a sample of my antidepressant," she wrote. "Ask the psy [French shorthand for psychiatrist] whose name and coordinates are at the bottom of my note, to prescribe the right dosage for you. When I have moved internationally" (I later learned she'd lived, among other places, in Buenos Aires, Brussels, Mexico City, Abu Dhabi, Toronto, Prague, if I recall these all correctly, and now Paris over her twenty years of expatriate living), "every single time," she wrote, "my whole system gets overworked. Then it shuts down. It just crashes and shuts down."

Mr. Psy had wavy salt and pepper hair and a softly lit office at the Hôpital Americain in Neuilly. Feeling oddly Kept-Womanish, I almost canceled the appointment. Then, when I forced myself to drive there, I nearly chose to wait out the whole extremely pricey nonrefundable hour in the parking lot. I was conflicted, questioning what my problem was, wondering if I was not really depressed but simply self-pitying. Pitiful. An expatriate Stepford Wife *and* maudlin. Triple scoop of loathsome.

"But this is easy," Mr. Psy said, removing his glasses and folding his manicured hands while leaning forward on his frosted glass desk top. "You're an *artiste*. You have the *tempérament d'une artiste*. You feel things *profondément*. This is a *qualité*. This *tristesse* is simply the price you pay *pour l'art*."

My problem now resolved to his liking, he wanted to discuss music and painting and favorite sopranos and Glenn Gould's Bach recordings.

I thanked my artsy Psy, left with a prescription for little blue pills, and never saw him again.

What I had not succeeded in helping him understand was what I scarcely understood myself. It was gnawing my soul out, though, that sharp-toothed conviction that I was utterly and fully a failure, I was a dithering fool, my life a waste. Clearly I was profoundly spent, my body was screaming that much, but my mind kept responding, *Spent? But spent for what?* I'd been working hard for so many years, it seemed, but couldn't show anything substantial for it. Every time I built something—established myself and our family in Norway, penetrated Versailles with my children in local activities, or renovated our first home ever and buttressed and held up my children—in the very instant I'd gotten to that spot, this international job track leveled what I'd built. Any time I felt I got an inch of grip, I'd be back at zero, starting all over again, knowing that whatever grip I got *this* time around would be ripped out and disposed of again.

Disposable. Like the rotted mattresses and moldy clothing which slumped against my hallway walls, sneering at me. Useless. A wasted life. This was the voice of the mattresses and the clothing. It spoke loudly and incessantly in my head. I could hear little else.

The seventh day after beginning the blue pills—"Take one a day, Madame," Mr. Psy had said, "until you feel things start to uncoil"—I awoke feeling like a cello whose strings had been muted. Or a big bell with a four-inch-thick felt lining. Or like a mother moved to the heart of Paris, and someone had turned the city to one of those sidewalk chalk drawings done by Dick Van Dyke's character Bert in *Mary Poppins*, the drawing that washes to a swamp in the rain. Indistinct and dissolved. A mirage.

I tossed the remaining fifty-three pills in my bathroom wastebasket.

That I never took another pill does not in any way mean I judge anyone else for taking theirs. Nor do I judge my benevolent Montessori mother friend who'd suggested them in the first place. It just means I could not function so well for my family as a muted cello or dulled bell living in a chalky mirage. I preferred, believe it or not, functioning like the wrung out metallic wad of last year's tube of Colgate, because even if it was curled, pressed flat, emptied-out, and pasty, well, at least I could feel it.

So I tried another approach. I took a hold of the bar I'd rigged (again) too high above my head. I lifted it out of its slot and lowered it down. A notch. Or four. I closed my eyes—shut them tight—to the complete disarray I'd been trying to dig through and work around. And I walked out. At 6:00 a.m. five days a week, in fact, I walked out and ran several kilometers along the Seine with my husband.

Then I lowered the bar another notch. I stopped tidying and list-making and got to bed by 10 p.m. Every single night.

I figured out ways to simplify some basics, like I ordered groceries online and had them delivered to my kitchen floor. I relinquished control over that part and other parts of my existence. I let things go, lowering the bar another notch.

I ate carefully and regularly. (I have never since eaten lapsed yogurts with pretzel shavings.)

I slowed down to read, very slowly, sacred scripture without fail every day and for at least thirty minutes at a time. I prayed in a steady stream. I let God pour His love into my open tank.

I did not immediately take on any major volunteer positions at school or at church, as had always been my tendency. I let other people volunteer for a while since they obviously wanted to. That meant I lowered the notch seven-times-seventy notches.

And my beautiful family, including my good parents, who came to stay for a couple of weeks over the holidays, rallied around me. We rallied around *us*.

Finally, I'd let enough things go so that the bar was ground level. I could step over it in heels. And okay, okay. I took off the heels. (I needed them to dig a hole and bury the bar.)

With the bar buried, and with the self-proclaimed permission to not achieve or work hard or do things perfectly, with *carte blanche* to be flat-out broken and slobbery and hobbling and thread-bare tired and low-to-the-ground, devolved-to-the-point-of-being-amphibious—and with the pronouncement that *that was absolutely smashingly fabulous*, well, guess what, I grew better quickly.

In a matter of about a month, actually.

I realized I was even whistling (who whistles in Paris?) and smiling involuntarily (and who smiles?), skipping, as I recall, on a Thursday right past this century's grouchiest old soul, the man who stood guard at the entrance of our parking box two blocks away from Rue du Colonel Combes. I skipped, he snarled and hucked a cigarette butt in my path, and I think I might have kicked my heels together just as I winked at him. *Wink-wink, Monsieur.*

Someone might conclude that it was one week of blue pills that pulled me out of the death spiral. I have no hard evidence to the contrary. Could be. And someone else might think, well, duh, it was *Paris*. Of *course* she was happy.

But tell me, has that someone actually *lived* in Paris in January? This is *not* Happy Land.

No, I believe something else happened, and I thank my terrestrial and celestial partners for that something, because that something tugged, shook, and Swedish-massaged my contorted double helix into fresh and hale alignment.

And having such things straightened out would be needful indeed. Because we were galloping right into Camelot.

Top left: Blakstad barnepark;

Middle left: Vigeland monoliths, Frognerpark, Oslo, Norway;

Middle right: Russ- and Barnatog, Karl Johans Gate, Oslo, Norway;

Bottom: Barnatog, on the island of Nesøya

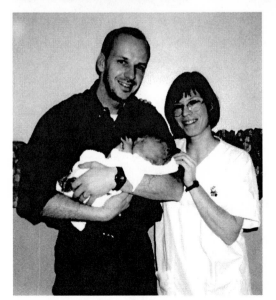

Top: Russ and their Russ buses;

Middle left: Deep, half-nursing slumber with our Viking baby;

Middle right: Bradford family, 1996, Frognerpark, Oslo, Norway;

Bottom: Randall and midwife, Ellen, minutes after Dalton's birth

Top: Our Nordic island, winter;

Middle left: View over Geirangerfjord, Norway;

Middle right: Arrival at Prekestolen, or the Preacher's Pulpit, Norway;

Bottom: Lofoten islands, Norway

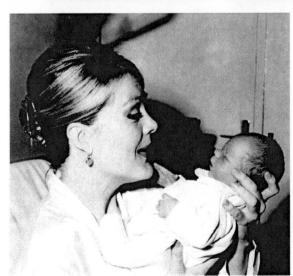

Top left: Parker, Claire, and Dalton Haakon, in bunad;

Top right: Luc's birthday party *pique-nique* under the Eiffel Tower;

Middle: Dalton entering the *maternelle* of Richard Mique, Versailles, France;

Bottom: Luc's day of birth, Château de la Maye, Versailles, France

Top: Luc at Montmartre, Paris;

Middle left: Dalton and Luc at Chartres cathedral;

Middle right: Parker, the percussionist;

Bottom: Sunday shot, Notre Dame, Paris

Top: Visiting the Papal Palace, Avignon, France;

Middle left: Parker, high school talent show;

Middle right: Claire and Parker, American School of Paris high school graduation, June 2007;

Bottom: Brothers, loving Provence, end of June, 2007

Top: Memorial bench, English
Garden, Munich, Germany;

Middle left: Bench overlooking a
tributary of the Isar river, English
Garden, Munich;

Middle right: Revisiting Oktoberfest;

Bottom: Singapore's Little India with
friends from Shanghai and Beijing

Top: Tanzania, Maasai village, visiting Claire in Arusha;

Middle left: Zwischenland;

Middle right: The *langbord* finds its place in our village home in Prangins near Geneva, Switzerland;

Bottom: The Bradford family, 2010

16

VILLAGE EN VILLE

The Quai d'Orsay runs right along the left bank of the Seine and is roughly the French political equivalent of America's Pennsylvania Avenue. It's where one finds France's primary governing body, *l'Assemblée Nationale*, housed in a grand neoclassical building that stands right at the mouth of the Pont de la Concorde, close to where the seventh arrondissement, or district, eases into the sixth. By partial accident and tremendous providence, we'd landed one street south of Quai D'Orsay. We were in a political hot seat.

To our left was the Eiffel Tower, icon of audacious French inventiveness and sturdy pride. Surrounding us were the Senegalese, Austrian, Romanian, Finnish, South African, Swedish, and Georgian embassies. Our apartment shared a wall with the central offices of the American University of Paris, two streets away in one direction was the American Library of Paris, and farther in the other direction, Napoleon's tomb and the Musée d'Orsay. Immediately to our right was the American Church of Paris, seat of the *Societé Franco-Américane*, and that just about sums up our Parisian corner.

In spite of Jacques Chirac's touching expressions of support after the World Trade Center attacks (*"Nous sommes tous les Américains,"* "We are all Americans") Franco-American relations were tense following the US invasion of Iraq, a move the French found unsubstantiated and rash. I tell you all this to underline how we'd landed not only in the center of a politically stimulating neighborhood, but had done so in a moment in history when being an American in Paris was loaded with consequence.

As had always been the case everywhere we moved, we eventually eased into serving and worshipping in our church community. The congregation we attended met in a small rented meetinghouse in the narrow Rue St. Merri between Notre Dame and the Pompidou Center, and proved to be a cultural mix like we'd never known before and have never known since. There were as many non-French members as there were native French. Once I took count: among the 150 members, there were seventeen native tongues. French with every accent you can think of or make up.

Our bishop, or pastor, who was married to a German, was born in former Serbo-Croatia to a French mother. His Italian, Russian, and English were as solid as his German, Serbian, Croatian, and French. His assistants were two men from Madagascar and the US. The presidencies of the women's and youth organizations were composed of a Malagasy, an Ethiopian, a Romanian, an Iranian who'd converted from Islam, members from the Ivory Coast, Cameroon, the Congo, Angola, South Africa, Ghana, and California. Working in the nursery with the youngest children were a Finn who spoke French, Swedish, and English; a Swede who spoke Croatian, German, French, and English; and myself, an American, who spoke French, German, and Norwegian. We were overseeing children who spoke Spanish, French, English, and Croatian. And the missionaries, young men and women from America, mostly, but also from France or other Western countries, were bringing more and more Mandarin-speaking investigators of the church, students from mainland China and Taiwan, to meetings. When, on top of all these visitors, tourists also flooded our congregation (which was a regular thing from April to October) everyone fought over the earphones through which we would give simultaneous translation from French, the lingua franca of our organization, into whatever language was required. That was primarily English but sometimes another European tongue. French to German. French to Russian. French to Spanish. When enough Chinese members began attending, special rites like the sacrament, were performed in French as well as in Mandarin.

The effect of all these cultures crowding into one cramped place made the overflowing facilities look like a general meeting of the UN. Or, given the microphone headsets, a rehearsal for a Madonna concert tour.

At home, Claire's flute teacher spoke French with a Mexican accent. Our temporary live-in student spoke French with a Colombian accent. And Parker's *petite amie* (or crush) was native Peruvian, but had lived most of her life in Paris and thus spoke French with no accent whatsoever and spoke no English at all. Reformed-gangsta Parker, like the rest of us, was at home in all this, as comfortable as you've ever seen a teenager, back in his circle at the ASP playing the drums in three ensembles (jazz, rock, and orchestra) and on the weekends with his friends at impromptu percussion gatherings at le Trocadéro overlooking the Eiffel Tower, or on le Pont des Arts overlooking the Seine. He also played basketball in the pick-up basketball games with the local guys (Algerian, Moroccan, Tunisian, Egyptian, and Lebanese) who gathered on Saturday mornings at the Champs de Mars, and with one of his best friends from school he set up a volleyball sand pit near the Eiffel Tower. He was our resident PPE, or Paris Public Expert, who could shepherd brothers, sisters, friends, and strangers like your normal befuddled tourist to whatever place they needed to reach via public transportation. Paris quickly became *his* town, the place to which he swore he'd one day return as an adult to live out the rest of his life.

Randall bought a Vespa. Creamy lacquer paint job, classic lines, toffee colored leather seat deep enough to take a passenger on the back. With it, he could whip out to Versailles to pick up Parker late at night when weekly scripture study classes called "seminary" were moved from Paris to the Mormon chapel there. And the two also sliced through the common knots of Parisian traffic to visit and help young families and widows from our congregation. At every opportunity, Randall was out scooting and scouting the roads, weaving through stalled traffic, sailing past the honking horns and fists flying out windows.

When he didn't take the Vespa, he could easily walk to work, either over the Pont de l'Alma past the golden torch that stands as an unofficial memorial to the car accident that took Princess Diana's life, and up Avenue George V. Or around l'Étoile of the Arc de Triomphe and down Avenue Hoche. Or over the Pont Alexandre III, across the Champs Élysées, and then winding his way to the office. These streets became our morning jogging routes. We'd leave before morning traffic at 6:00 a.m. from our place near Pont de l'Alma and run along the Seine, passing drunks stumbling out of the Metro but also centuries of architecture, political intrigue, artistic ingenuity, religious devotion, and as much variety as one can get in an hour. We chugged past ancient citadel prisons and Gothic chapels and the hidden apartments of international legends. Past the Louvre at minute eleven. Past the Hôtel de Ville at minute nineteen. Over the Pont d'Austerlitz at minute twenty-nine. And so on for another half hour past the Institut du Monde Arabe, Notre Dame, Musee d'Orsay, trotting at stop lights where guillotines once stood, where revolutions began and ended, over stones where American soldiers and German tanks and English carriages and Italian horses and white-coated monks and destitute writers and hailed composers and defected ballerinas and ermine-cloaked despots passed.

You can understand why sometimes I had to stop to catch my breath, not for all the running, but for all the significance. That's some dense history to cut a 15k through.

Sometimes, Randall took the Vespa to the office because his work was just across the street from Dalton's school. The two would head off together, helmeted and wearing biking gear, Dalton holding around his dad from the back. They could drive right up to the gilded gates of the Parc Monceau, where inside was the splendid converted mansion that housed *l'École Active Bilingue*. Here Dalton spent his days and earned his French stripes.

The Parc Monceau is about as far from Norwegian barnepark as you can get. In fact, it's much closer to a Japanese Zen garden, only without bonsai trees, a stone replica of Mount Fuji, and bamboo rakes for everyone to comb the sand. And because it's French, it is sumptuous but just about as ornamental. Here is where Dalton, and then Luc when he joined the same school a year later, spent their *recré*, or recess periods every day. Dressed in navy and white uniforms, they stood in packs, boys here, girls there, for their thimble-full of outdoor time. Half an hour of a nine-hour day.

Under the shade of huge old sycamores, the children huddled to play a rousing set of *billes*, marbles. They sometimes drummed up a modest round of tag or ran after one another's Yu-Gi-Oh! cards, very popular that year. But that was the extent of their movement for the day. "Your boys should participate in one or two sports outside of class," the *diréctrice* of the school had advised me in our first private consultation. "Swimming, soccer, tennis, anything you can find to use up their energy and help them metabolize all they're learning." She was a small-boned woman with a strong brow and imposing presence, flawless Parisian French, and always a gold insignia ring on her left pinkie finger. For someone so no-nonsense, she sure wore delicious perfume.

"This is why we have the open Wednesday afternoons," she continued. "The children are encouraged to do all their sporting activities then. I suggest you sign them up. *Vite, vite!*"

After the requisite bureaucracy for which I was braced this time around, we did sign them up: swimming, chess, choir, tae kwon do, and because we were in France, we of course signed up both boys for *l'escrime*.

That's pronounced *eh-scream*, which should have made me nervous, but didn't. That is until I saw that the boys' fencing instructor had no right ear. It was a detail that inspired in me both confidence (*hey, this guy really fences!*) and worry (*hey, but, uh . . . ?*). The gymnasium full of twenty young fencers in tight white unitards and mesh-fronted helmets looked like an audition hall for *Star Wars* Stormtroopers wielding swords instead of lasers. For months and months they swung fearlessly, my two youngest did, while mincing and shuffling back and forth, arms raised just so, feet poised just so, an exhausting and beautiful discipline *cum* sport *cum* art. Fully French.

At least as French, but more exquisite to me than sword fighting, was our Wednesday afternoon ritual. In fewer than ten minutes, even with traffic, we could drive from Parc Monceau to the Louvre, park, dart right in, take our lunch at one of the cafés near the glass pyramid (wherever there were the fewest tour groups), wipe our mouths, and, sketchbooks and pencils in hand, make our way to the Richelieu wing. That is where we found our private sanctuary, the Cour Puget.

The Cour Puget is a three-story hall flooded with natural light. Its ceiling is a variation on the famous I. M. Pei pyramid, its walls and statues nearly all bone-colored marble. Entering, you might feel you're walking into the reception hall of heaven. At least we did. At nine and five years old, our two youngest were normally kinetic experiments gone awry, but when we entered heaven, we all settled into a new rhythm that stirred our creative juices into a mellow foam. This is the setting that made the three of us feel we were artists. More important than becoming artists, though, we went beyond the familial relationship and became each other's intimates.

Once—and only once—we thought we'd wander over to the Cour Marly just across the corridor, check out what the Renaissance statues there were up to, but it didn't feel right, didn't feel like our place. "Our place" was the Cour Puget, up on the top tier on a marble bench against the wall. After a few minutes, one of us would be sprawled or curled up at the foot of the statue we were sketching. The guards who rotated daily came to expect the three of us there at about the same hour every

Wednesday afternoon. A nod, a reciprocated *"Bonjour les enfants,"* and we knew we were in our element.

"So, who do you think this guy is?" I asked, Dalton on one side, Luc on the left. We were staring up into the piercing eyes of Caton d'Utique. "And check out that serpent," Dalton said, turning to see a Mr. Universe Spartacus wrestling the beast to the ground. "But why've they got a bust of John Kerry?" Luc asked, walking over to a bust of the French scientist, Cuvier.

We would go home and google the background of our favorite statues, then go back the next Wednesday to make up stories, stories we wove into a screenplay, we three floor-squatters. Ours was an elaborate screenplay about the Louvre and its statues and all the lives embedded in stone. Dalton cast his imagined movie, role-for-role as we three sat with our sketchpads on our laps, capturing a young Joan of Arc or a dying marathon runner in the gentle brilliance of the Cour Puget.

In every way, those Wednesdays were a delight to me. The light, no matter what the weather outside, was always brighter during those hours than anywhere else in the world. I was with my children, we had baguette crumbs on our sweaters, the sky was warm, we were surrounded by history and beauty and tourists, tourists we realized we were not. We basked in great art and created mediocre art ourselves, but more importantly, we created a moment that defined the three of us as part of this place, part of each other. I saw to it that a woman in a Louvre children's bookstore hung my boys' two best completed works on the official corkboard. We laughed in the van that their artwork now hung in the Louvre.

We were loaded in that same van in late December. "Just a few minutes more and we'll be there, guys." The ruse was that we were on our way to pick up an English exchange student stranded in a village. She was, I told the family, homesick over Christmas. I'd gotten the call just yesterday. We had room. We could invite her to our place and make her feel at home. Not exactly what the boys had had in mind for the holidays, but they were used to having houseguests and were actually curious since Claire was especially excited.

"She's sharing your room, right Claire?" Dalton asked, since he and Luc already shared and sharing with Parker wasn't an option.

"Yeah, that's the plan." Claire threw me a glance in my rearview mirror.

"She's adorable, I think, from what Claire and I could tell in the pictures I got online."

Parker perked up from the half-doze his earphones were lulling him into. "Cute?"

"Really petite. Curly reddish hair. Her name is . . . What was her name again, Claire?"

"Josephine. I'm sure you'll love having her for the holidays."

The skies were that typical *grisailles* gray of Parisian winters when we pulled up to a farm, its old stone wall crumbling in large chunks, its pastures muddy. Claire and I said we'd run inside to get Josephine, no problem, you guys just wait here and we'll be right back out.

"Wait! Where's she even going to *sit*?" Luc was worried.

"Don't worry!" Claire called back over her shoulder, hopping from dry spot to dry spot on the stone walkway leading her way to the front door of the old dog breeder's home. "I'll have her sit on my lap!"

That was the way we introduced Josephine the English Cocker Spaniel to our family. She was the size and color of an unfrosted cinnamon roll when Claire, cupping the ball of fur in her two hands, brought her promised puppy out to where she held her up to show her brothers through the van window. Only a few weeks old, she could have been wrapped in a crêpe.

And that was the way we were introduced to *le monde du chien à Paris*, a world that rivals the world of Parisian fashion, politics, or gastronomy. Josephine was Joey to the kids. On the paper to register her for the French authorities, however, she was Velvet Josephine Dalton Bradford, "Velvet" because this was dog year "V" in France (the last year was "U," the next would be "W," and so on), so any dog born, named and implanted with a state-prescribed chip in that year had to be given, by law, a name beginning with "V."

(There was a moment when I wondered if Norway's Names-Laws office had alerted France to the arrival of a certain Bradford family, a bunch of name renegades, who might try to slip in an unacceptable first letter. A holdover vowel from last year, or worse, a preemptive consonant from the next year.)

Puppy Josephine waddling the sidewalks on her leash incited more conversations than had Luc William Bradford as an infant in his mammoth Norwegian perambulator cruising the ancient Marché in the heart of Versailles.

"But Madame," the lady at the produce line in Rue Cler leaned over her artichokes, "Has she had her second round of vaccines yet?"

"Madame, you must dress your dog properly for this cold weather." I listened patiently to the woman I'd crossed as she walked her well-dressed Shih Tzu around the Esplanade des Invalides. "Here, the business card for my own designer. All natural fabrics, no polyester, colors to flatter your little one's eye coloring."

The lady at the bus stop with a nervous Yorkshire Terrier on her lap had been watching me with Joey for a few minutes. "I must give you the name," she whispered, "of our therapist who treats our Goliath with massage, lymphatic drainage, and reflexology."

And to think: no one had proposed cranial manipulation to help newborn Luc potty train.

"Oh-la-la-la-la, Madame Bradford," my veterinarian said, his bushy brows twitching. I had brought Joey to this practice in the Avenue de la Bourdonnais adjacent to an entrance to the Champs de Mars, which spreads its sixty lovely acres from the Eiffel Tower to the École Militaire. "*This*," the doctor said, "is a hunting dog." He struck both his hands on his boney knees for emphasis. "And *this*," he stretched his arms in a wide arc above and behind his head, "is a city. A hunting dog and a city are not an easy combination. But you are in the seventh arrondissement. This is your *village en ville*. So run her, Madame," he said, pointing toward the window that looked out onto the Champs de Mars. "*Run* her here as often as you possibly can."

Every other morning, Claire and I ran (or stumbled all over the leash) with Joey through our village in the city, just like the doc said. This meant jogging from our apartment, up Cognac Jay, across the top of Avenues Rapp and Bourdonnais, down Rue de L'Univérsité behind the Musée du Quai Branly and around the circumference of the Champs.

This Monsieur le Docteur R. was someone straight out of a movie. I wanted to visit him not only for my dog, but to take notes on his hand gestures, his swift gait, his flamboyant bedside manner. Take the eyes, hair, and enthusiasm of Christopher Lloyd from *Back to the Future*, mix that with the height, lankiness, and intensity of Jeff Goldblum from *Jurassic Park*, and swirl in Einstein. You have our dog's doc.

"*Alors, ma p'tite*," le Docteur spoke to our hound in a disciplined French, bending low to look her straight in the eyes, "I do not know what you are eating, but you must now keep a close eye on your *ligne*." I had to check right and left to make sure he wasn't talking to me, since there was this certain history of French doctors patrolling my waistline. But no, he was off-siding to me only because I was my pet's food-dispenser, and Joey was going to be spayed, which operation would change her metabolism.

A chubby Cocker, I was advised, is (gulp) an ugly Cocker. "If she puts on weight," he whispered so as to not upset Joey, "her mental health will suffer more than her physical health does." A week later he performed the operation, and as if to make sure she wouldn't suffer post-op spread, he put Joey in a turn-of-the-century canine corset for a month.

After her bandages were removed, we tried our best to run her and keep her out of the cookie jar. But Joey was domestic. She spread. And she became, as domesticated dogs can, quasi-human, sleeping right where Claire felt any purebred hunting dog would be most useful, most at home—in Claire's arms, where both got used to their element.

It's no exaggeration to say that we were *all* in our element. Our mini solar system's orbit was aligned; everyone was whirring in his or her deep groove, with life unfolding in a peaceful, predictable pace, although the universe itself showed intermittent signs of mounting devastation. There were louder and louder anti-American and anti-French sentiments being lobbed back and forth, acts of terrorism, and escalating tensions between races and religions in Paris herself, which led to acts of arson and threats of a worse kind in the periphery of the city. We were reminded every day in the papers that life, as the planet itself, is a fragile and tenuous place. But in the immediate cycle of our family's life, in its rhythms and patterns, things were briskly routinized, colorfully calm. Camelot.

Each new day in our *village en ville* broke when Monsieur B. slapped open his metal shutters beneath us in his ground floor apartment. Our friend and neighbor lived the life of a well-mannered metronome. At 8:00 a.m., the ten shutters of his five windows clanked and clapped. At 9:00 p.m. a repeat of the same percussion, closing out the day's pulsating hum of traffic, high heeled clip-clipping on concrete and staccato street conversations. For almost fifty years he'd lived here on the corner of Jean Nicot and Colonel Combes—enough time, I imagine, to have watched things evolve and to have gotten the shutter habit down to a reflex.

We, the American family of six, lived directly above him, and so he heard, no doubt, the muffled soundtrack of every detail, mundane or intimate, of the life of *la famille* Bradford. I begged him to forgive us for the bass pedal thumping of Parker's electric drum set. I apologized for Luc's night terrors and shrieking around 4:00 a.m. I'd thought of explaining why the toilet above his bedroom flushed thirty-three times during the night, but stopped short of describing the flavorful details of a whole family whopped by the flu bug. We just hoped he was a deep sleeper. I clasped his hand, pumping his arm in mortification while explaining why there had been a girl's chorus howling "You Ain't Nothin' but a Hound

Dog" with a Cocker Spaniel yelping in syncopation, directly above his
dining room table at what must have been aperitif time.

That was the hour when on Thursdays I always saw Monsieur B.
sitting at a small square table next to his window there at street level,
Monsiuer B. and three friends sitting in their suits and ties, one always
with a cigar in his lips, another always with a cigarette, all sitting at their
respective (and I noted, fixed) corners of that table, lit by two old brass
standing lamps pulled up just for the occasion, playing a soundless game
of cards. Models for a Cézanne painting.

But Monsieur B. never once complained of the percussion and re-
percussions of our herd above his head. In fact, he never once hinted at
irritation. When we greeted each other, he was consistently radiant and
gracious. At one of my fits of self-deprecation, he once smiled, saying
in unmistakably elegant French, "We live in a community, Madame. We
must value each other in such a community," his sincere blue eyes reflect-
ing the color of his trademark azure shirt. I'd only seen him once without
one of those brilliant blue shirts when, earlier than usual, I was leaving
the building. He was at his door receiving a small wicker basket from
the Portuguese gardienne who took in a little laundry money from this
widower. That morning, he was wearing his camel robe and a bright blue
ascot, which, even at 7:00 a.m., made his eyes shine and his thick shock
of silky white hair glow like a million watts. My own private Maurice
Chevalier.

What I knew of Monsieur B. I learned by close observation and by
stitching together scraps he volunteered during our neighborly encounters. Twenty years earlier, after forty years of marriage and four children
(all raised on this corner in the apartment less than half the size of ours),
his wife passed away. The four children went on to have their own children (totaling well over a dozen in number), and on the evening of the
highly charged US presidential election between George W. Bush and Al
Gore, his long-awaited first great-grandchild came into the world a week
overdue.

This man, like our family, was sleep-deprived after the string of nights
awaiting what was momentous news: Monsieur B.'s new generation and
what we were convinced was our nation's new generation.

When I took him congratulatory flowers late one evening, he and I
chatted briefly, comparing notes on paternity and politics and what kind
of future world would greet his newest offshoot. "Capucine," Monsieur B.
confided, "will be the little cabbage's Christian name." (Calling an infant
a cabbage and a cabbage a Christian might strike one as odd, but the

French logic works well from many angles. *Capucine*. Very crisp. Very Catholic.)

Proud of his baby's first snapshot, the Monsieur was all gleam and beam while I was all gloom and doom, disoriented in a stupor from an election process that appeared to have been slippery, questionable, un-American. Maybe I might have seemed, in the face of his measured manner, too oozing of pessimism, too panicky and reactionary. And maybe he was simply pleased about Capucine, this fresh validation of life, to take my anxiety too seriously. Whatever the case, he didn't grouse with me. Instead, he heaved a sigh and then, stretching upward his five knobby fingers, twinkled those blue eyes: "I've lived through this many wars, an occupation, my bride's death, changes I could have never imagined would have happened in my lifetime. Capucine will survive, too." And he smiled that smile.

Moments later, we returned to our apartments, Monsieur B. and Madame B., those parallel universes split by a sliver of flooring. Against a backdrop of the Monsieur's serenity, my native country's vibrating map of red and blue "moral values" throbbed a garish neon nuisance across my mind—a mind already fuzzy from weeks of breath-holding over teetering politics, months of being on the global political alert.

That night in the Bradford's cosmos, life felt so slightly perilous and slap-dash, with our six jostling bodies whirring like asteroids, weaving and whipping through what should have been a bedtime routine—our night time orbit—but which felt to me, at least, more like an enactment of chaos theory. Certainly the galaxy was off kilter, the Milky Way curdling, I thought, with our earth stuck in a hiccup rather than expelling her usual steady breaths. How could Monsieur B. just shrug off the recent events as "mere politics" when, as I was convinced, the whole globe was convulsing and reeling toward ruin?

Then, at nine on the dot, the Monsieur's street shutters rattled their regular racket, our grandfather clock incarnate chimed. A wad of laundry in my arms, I stopped for an instant to absorb the ritual beneath my feet, that common constancy like so many other quotidian patterns, which, when noted anew, pin infinity in place and set fretting aright. In his cozy retreat from the world, Monsieur must have at least believed he was invulnerable to it, I reflected. *And at his age*, I thought, *what else?* Lining the level above his, all our shutters were agape as they always were, allowing our garrulous glow to flood the streets, whatever part of our private lives was not under wraps.

He'd watched foreigners come and go, Monsieur B. He'd seen the old open market that was once supplied by the boatmen delivering goods on the banks of the Seine one block northward razed to make way for the Senegalese Embassy and the Erik Satie Music Conservatory. He'd watched an adjacent villa converted into the bland headquarters of the American University in Paris and had heard the choir rehearsals, aerobic classes, and karaoke nights through the wide-open stained glass windows of the American Church across the street. He'd heard more and more English-speakers just outside his windows asking for directions to the Eiffel Tower (two blocks that way), or Napoleons' tomb (two blocks the other way). He'd witnessed the high-pitched spectacle of four sweat-slippery men cursing in chorus at each other and at their weave of pulleys and cables holding our dangling long table which was to be hoisted through our windows. He'd quietly tolerated restrained ruckus, my occasional high-heeled prancing and Parker's gym-shoed thudding overhead, and had graciously avoided even the most subtly judgmental political commentary as Franco-American tensions simmered and at times passed the boiling-over point. And he didn't grow the least bit hysterical when his own French presidential elections kicked up dust in our own neighborhood, where camera crews interviewed candidates, pundits, the local political in-crowd. There I was, practically salivating with curiosity at the whole scene, and there was Monsieur B. watching silently from his window, his ascot tucked in his camel blazer, a cup of coffee held in the right hand, the saucer in his left.

Stalking our flat that late autumn night, tidying room after room, I was ashamed that our comparatively super-sized portion of dwelling space was super-imposed, squat, right over the head of this frugal Frenchman. I cringed, feeling personally responsible for the astronomical US deficit. Then I also thought of the thriving terrorist cell, which French intelligence had allegedly exposed in a northeastern sector of Paris, eight Metro stops from our door.

To what end, shutters? To what end, self-imposed blinds? Was this gracious neighbor, this truly gentle man, what US Secretary of Defense Donald Rumsfeld had in mind with his pejorative, "Old Europe"? And did French foreign minister Michel Barnier have a chance at realizing a "New Day" in Franco-American relations, where an alliance wasn't always tantamount to absolute allegiance, but where mutual respect reigns, and where, as Monsieur B. once said, "we value one another in a community"?

To be sure, in a few hours some version of the next day would break, and I'd be counting on the 8:00 a.m. downbeat from Monsieur B.

17

Toot-a-loo!

I t is late April. The whole world descends on Paris in April. Throngs walk the wrong way up the wrong roads on the banks of the Seine, missing the Musée d'Orsay entirely. They walk with maps flapping out of their back pockets or unfolded and held so high they miss steps and fall over poles or into potholes and get injured. They maneuver through the Louvre's Grand Gallery, dodging other visitors who, on tippy toe and with upstretched arms, point their camera periscopes over the shuffling masses. They get pushed in the crowd past the Winged Victory and practically into the Mona Lisa and always seem to lean a foot too close to the Delacroix or the Ingres or the Corot so the guards, hot and bothered with swollen ankles, have to lunge from their seats and bark a reprimand.

And who can blame a single soul for wanting to be a tourist? Paris, from April through September, is magnificent beyond what you'd ever imagine. It is because it *is* magnificent and because everyone (including me) is telling you it is, that everyone comes to Paris right then. And all of this can make this magnificent town miserable.

You can count on Paris being like this except in August (again, a forewarning) when the residents of Paris go on vacation. Restaurants are closed, the cousin from Basel has stepped in to man the carousel in the

Luxembourg gardens, the only good meal is at a tired fast food chain with lethargic-eyed, part-time fill-ins and napkins made of recycled mothballs. Streets are almost quiet compared to their September crush, which is called *la rentrée*—the school re-entry—and that school restart means the business restart which means the traffic restart which means the stress restart.

The sogginess of early April has evaporated, leaving the trees in front of the Église Americaine fluffy and bright, with splotches of sunlight dancing on the cobblestones upon which I am strolling. I'm strolling in head-to-toe seafoam green—heels and a linen suit—as an exception to my normal errand-running and dog-walking attire (jeans and ballet flats or black Converses), because I've just come home from an important appointment. It is barely chilly enough to wear a silk scarf. I'm in this linen outfit with its matching shoes and matching scarf, and I am strolling. Strolling our doggy Josephine, strolling la-dee-dah-dee-dahing *je ne sais quoi-ing* in full sun-speckled springtime ease along the Parisian sidewalks of my neighborhood. This is one of those harmonious moments when I ache to grab those few people who hate Paris (or hate the French or French politics or what those folks claim is "snooty" politeness or "snotty" elegance or "pungent" crudeness) and, with my arms stretched wide above my head, say, "*See?* This is what we mean! *Enraptured.* Don't tell me you're not."

Next thing, I hear voices. Loud voices. Voices speaking English. Foghorning English.

The voices belong to two grown women. I see them approaching me. As I hear them and watch them, I keep walking my pooch and prancing delicately in my green heels, if you remember. And oh, did I forget to mention the large black sunglasses? While I promenade keeping a low sunglassed profile, I hear the amplified ladies coming closer. My breathing quickens. I zoom in on a particular cobblestone and whisper to Joey, "C'mon girl, do your business and let's split." Joey, though, has leisurely bowels. I turn my back to them as their voices approach. And when I do, I feel an essential part of me start to shift. But before things shift completely, I listen.

"Chill out! You never *did* get to reading maps right. Now look right here. *Look!* You listening? Look: this right here says Ei. Fel. Tow. Er. *Eiffel Tower.* Now I'm telling you, it's somewhere close. Real close." This woman yanks the map from the other woman, muttering just loudly enough for me to hear, "Should've *never* let you hold this thing in the first place."

I focus on Joey, my canine distraction, twirling her leash around one hand, and put my cell phone to my ear pretending to be engrossed in the most important call of my life. They come closer. I'm lipping a fake conversation, trying to avoid that uncomfortable moment of being witness to sororal street violence. I'm just not dressed for breaking up an assault.

"What do you mean, should've never let *me* hold this thing? *You're* the one who got us all lost up in those streets by Noter *Damn*. Think I'm gonna leave it up to *you* this time to get us to the Eiffel Tower? No way. *No. Way.*"

They are acting like sisters. Or at least they're dressed as such: both in tennis shorts in a pale color, and both in t-shirts with capped sleeves. Neon colored fanny packs. White, terry-cloth lined visors. The last three items listed, all with American flags that glittered. One of the sisters, the one who has spoken first, has nails I can see from this distance. A huge part of me wants to swoop in and strut with them arm-in-arm right down the street and to the Champs de Mars. But their anger at Paris seems beyond repair. Anything I might say will be rebuffed, useless.

I'd like to write that I considered a few approaches; "Hiya. You two look lost. Can I help?" or, "Hey, ladies, if you're looking for the Eiffel Tower, I'd be happy—"

Those don't enter my mind.

I straighten my shoulders, adjust my scarf, loosen my clench on Joey's leash, drop my fake phone call into my handbag.

"'Ello?" I make my voice small and perfumy.

The two stop bickering into their map and look up.

"I am zo zorree," I sing, "but I am zeeing you are een . . . trubbéll? I may 'elp you, *non*?"

"You . . . you from here? You French?" one woman asks, quieted.

"But *oui!*", answers la Parisienne, who, smiling, extends her hand, stepping lightly in heels and pulling her Cockér with her. "Juste ovair zair! Zees ees my, 'ow you say?, neigh-bor-'ood? I zink? We are veree, veree luckee, are we not? We find each uzair?"

I smile.

One of them smiles.

Joey tilts her head. *Seriously?*

You see, I had this French thing down pat. I'd practiced this accent every time I'd found myself at a dinner table where language acquisition came up in the conversation (which happened in every single multicultural gathering), and friends occasionally gave their light jabs at the typical, broad, American accent with its cardboard corners and vowels as vast as the prairie. I just loved it when, at about the moment things got sufficiently mockful with people mimicking the wrooower-ly broahwerly American accent, I could slip into the conversation in an English with *the* thickest Inspector Clouseau accent. Hardly comprehensible for all its curlicues deep in the throat, the impossible "th" sound, zee veree, veree, veree tight, uh, 'ow you say? *wowel* sounds, *non*? And I would then explain that I had yet to come across a Frenchman, even among my friends who are ridiculously gifted linguists, who spoke English absolutely *sans trace*—without a trace—of a French accent.

So I am perfectly rehearsed for this street performer moment. In less time than it takes to spread a crêpe, I've made the fatal shift, consciously positioning myself to do one thing and one thing only: make these two fellow Americans fall desperately in love with this city, this country, with all things French. Even, if necessary, with moi.

"And-uh," la Parisienne asks, escorting them to a bench, "Where-uh eez eet zat you bose leev? Amaireeca, *I 'ope?*"

We sit down together. I 'elp zem fold zeir map.

Joey whimpers.

"We're from Detroit. Michigan. Know it? Here just a couple of days, you know, doing all of Europe in three—"

"Meecheegan? *Detwah?* But zees eez a veree, veree wondairful place. But, zut!, I do not know eet. I 'ave only been to, oh, 'ow you call eet? Zee *Floreed*? To Miameeee." I slap both hands on my lap hoping they love Florida.

They nod, looking me a bit up and down. "We go to Lauderdale, Fort Lauderdale, mostly."

"Ah, yes, zee Floreed. I love your countree, love zee peepel. Zo wondairful, zo friendlee."

The woman closest to me has fingernails, I can now see, with miniature frescoes painted on them, each an emblem of the USA: the Statute of Liberty; the Liberty Bell; the Flag; The first line of the constitution, "We the People . . . "

"Hiya, poochie," she says, "you only speak French huh, girl?" and she reaches down to Joey, petting her head, which makes my heart trill a bit. The other woman is retying her Reeboks.

"Oh, yes, yes, *oui*, *oui*, I weel show you zee Tour Eefell. Eet eez veree close," and I walk them to the corner, right under the windows of our apartment, down to the intersection of Rue de l'Universtié, then point. Joey drags her hind legs.

"You go-uh, 'ow you say een Eengleesh? *straight on* an zen, at zee end of zees road, you turn zee right. Voilà! You weel zee your Tour Eefell."

By now both women are cooing at Joey while barraging me with questions about what the French think of America, *Do they all hate us*, they ask, *is French food really so good, have I tasted snails, where can one get a good milkshake?* Which questioning is just as well with me, since I am trying to keep my side of the conversation really low, knowing that at any moment a neighbor, Monsieur B. for instance, might walk out on the street for his afternoon promenade and bump right into me, la Poseur Parisienne.

Sweating under my scarf, feeling duplicitous and conniving on one level, I am also feeling patriotic and conniving on another. I know, as I walk these two endearing women to the corner, that I am doing my two countries, the US of A and la France, a magnanimous service.

"Ladeez, wen you come to zee end of zee road, I weel teach you zum-zeeng I learned in Miamee. You know zees zeeng you zay een Engleesh, 'toot-a-loo'?"

They nod, "Toot-a-loo, yeah."

"*Eet eez from zee Frensh!* Een Frensh wee zay 'À tout à l'heure,' weech eez to zay, 'Zee you een zee 'our.'"

"No kidding! Ha! Toot-a-loo comes from France?"

"Now. Leesen: Wen you are to turn zee right-uh, you weel zay to me, '*A tout à l'heure*'. An zen I weel zay to you, 'toot-a-loo.' Good?"

I watch, nauseated with glee-guilt, as the two women saunter down Jean Nicot. There they go: fanny packs, Reeboks, visors, right past our boulangerie, past Luc's best friend's apartment across the street, all the way down to Rue St. Dominique.

All anyone can hear as they walk down the street bumping each other and laughing is the two of them hollering, "À tout à l'heure! À tout à l'heure!"

When they turn the corner, I am still standing there as I promised, my Josephine on the leash, my scarf draped just so, my heels nipped neatly together, my arm waving and waving. "Toot-a-loo!" I sing to the women of Detroit. "Tooooooot-a-looooooo!"

18

MADAME, VOS TRÉSORS!

Out of 365 days on our family's kitchen calendar, 281 were marked with visitors who stayed in our apartment. That's not bragging. That's fessing up. Our place turned into *la Grande Gare Centrale*, with its constant stream of bodies, roll-on suitcases, extra mattresses, and fat stacks of Paris maps. Despite what that kind of traffic meant for predictable bed times and bathroom rights, the children learned to share their space, we made delightful connections with people from all over the world, and others got to experience Paris.

As is typical in many Parisian apartment buildings, ours was outfitted with rooftop garrets, or, in French, *chambres de bonnes*, or maids' quarters. Our apartment was allocated two such rooms, hardly bigger than a walk-in closet each, but enough room for bunk beds, a chair and a sink. In them we kept our frequent houseguests or visiting missionaries from our church. We grew especially close with some of these missionaries who missed their families and homes and often ate around our long Norwegian table, hung out with and became like siblings to our teenagers, spent holidays with us, even went Christmas caroling with us to the homeless sleeping in tents along the Seine.

When missionaries were using the garrets, then other visitors were necessarily crammed into a back room with pink walls, a red futon, and access to a bathroom the size of a Parisian elevator, which sort of elevator is suited only for solo trips, not some convention of *two*.

If someone was abruptly left homeless, as happened to a newly arrived family of five from Boston, we took them in. The Sorensens had been jerked around, as is often the case, by Parisian real estate capriciousness. Translated, that means they'd found one apartment, signed a contract, and were geared to move in, then the owner changed his mind. So they found another apartment, signed a contract, were geared to move in, then *this* owner changed *his* mind. A cosmic joke? To the Sorensens it felt like one. But when I told the story to my dry cleaner down Rue Malar, he hardly blinked. "I know," he shrugged, "slippery as eels, these apart-ments," and went on to ka-ching-ka-ching up my bill.

So the Sorensens (Greg, Kristiina, Rachel, Caroline, and Sam) were understandably less than charmed by Paris, and were repacking their bags to head back to Stockholm where they'd previously tried living Scandinavianly in a peaceful yellow country house on a quiet lake with a green rowboat and a family of ducks. They rowed to the other shore to pick up fresh eggs, fresh milk, fresh gooseberries. They opened up their shutters to the sight of field flowers and climbing roses. They sun bathed on their quiet balcony.

This Parisian apartment yanking thing felt, well, yanky, if not uncon-genial. But we convinced them to stick it out a bit longer—"Paris isn't *really* hostile; she's just playing hard to get. It's a tactic." And to help them stick it out, we took them in for a few weeks. *This* was a legitimate tactic, actually, to get them to move into our neighborhood, across our itsy bitsy street. When that actually happened, it was as improbable as it was magical. Our children conveniently matched in ages, and Kristiina and I discovered that we were suited to be more than friends; we were more like long, lost sisters.

As for real siblings, my brother Aaron also paid a visit. Homelessness or cramped quarters never as much as fazed this seasoned traveler, who, over the thousands of miles he'd wrapped around the planet, had slept in igloos, yurts, luggage compartments, train station photo booths. He and I were of the same cloth: we were able to suck the marrow out of life, out of Paris.

One night on a visit to see us, and while sitting and chatting with me at our kitchen table, Aaron glanced at his watch, went white, and yelled, "Chaudun!" knocking his chair to the floor and racing out the door and down to the street. I was trailing him, quickly putting two and two together as I took the stairs two at a time, seeing it was 7:08 p.m. which meant that the *chocolatier*, Michel Chaudun, whose hidden treasure of a shop was just around the corner, had closed eight minutes ago. This was Aaron's last night in town. He had to get some boxes of what were our (and Catherine Deneuve's, reportedly) favorite treats, Chadun's signature *pavés*, to take with him back to the States.

Rounding the corner in a scramble, Aaron spotted a dark Chaudun delivery van inching quietly away from the curb. He bounded across the intersection, my tall blonde brother, waving his long arms, and then began whacking, flat-palmed, on the window, begging the deliveryman behind the wheel to "*Arrêtez! S'il vous plaît, Arrêtez! Votre chocolat, votre chocolaaaaat!!*"

The driver stepped on his brakes in the middle of the intersection of Rue de l'Université and Rue Malar where I rushed up to try to explain that this rabid stranger pounding on the window was not a felon. And he wasn't a drunk. He was my brother, a mostly sane and normally upstanding citizen. It was dark by this hour, and so it wasn't until I'd pushed my head inside the now rolled-down window that I realized this "delivery guy" was Michel Chaudun himself. He is a finely built man with a broad smile; his whole portrait is soft and lightly wrinkled, as much physics professor as chocolate artist.

Chocolate artist? Chaudun is a legend in the world of the cocoa bean, and there I was, behaving (no, my baby brother was behaving) like a strung-out cocoa junkie. *Just one hit, man*, was the look in Aaron's wild eyes. *Just one last hit, man, I swear.*

You might be able to accost strangers in other big cities, and you might be able in other neighborhoods to fling yourself and your wadded fistful of money across the hood of any random delivery truck, but this was all so wrong right here, so indelicate. I wanted to melt into a puddle of waxy Nestlé right on the pavement.

But I didn't have time to, because Chaudun was already reversing his van and pulling it against the curb. He stepped out, smiling and laughing to himself, motioning to gather all three of us under the lamplight, dear Monsieur Chaudun, the kindest and smallest konfection king you could ever imagine in your life, asking us in his soft voice how he could be of service. He then recognized me as a regular customer and also a member of this little neighborhood we shared and, understanding the situation, started sorting through his key chain while walking back to the shop door, which he then opened and waved us through. "*Entrez,*

entrez," he smiled like a sane and pint-sized Willy Wonka. "This must be why I had not been able to start my van," he explained in French. "I needed to wait here for you! No problem, please do come in."

I rolled my eyes at my little brother and whispered something about "never living this down," and being "the personification of all that scares the world about Americans," but forgot all that embarrassment while Chaudun walked us on a full tour of the kitchen, letting Aaron sample things from the shelves at will. Aaron took pictures, asked questions about the fabrication process, Chaudun's childhood, about the enormous solid chocolate Statue of Liberty and Sphinx and Fabergé eggs in the window, all questions (and then responses) I had to translate while the *chocolatier* himself packaged in their signature brown box the delectable *pavés* Aaron had come for in the first place. Chaudun signed the lid with a black felt tip, and wrapped the box with the recognizable grosgrain ribbon. He embossed the wax stamp, gave Aaron change from his own pockets, and took his time before turning off the shop lights one by one, locking the door, and then gently shaking our hands. He smiled so deeply his eyes disappeared into the wrinkles. We backed away from the curb nodding our thanks, chocolates in hand, sweat evaporating off our necks in a cool evening breeze.

From that curb in that tight corner of Paris and for what would be over four full years we lived there, we ventured broadly across and deeply into the town. The children found their favorite places to buy crêpes and gallettes (in Montmartre at the foot of the hill of Sacre Cœur and at the same crêperie every single time), where to grab the best ice cream cone, where to buy toys and CDs and shoes. I knew where to get great art supplies, kitchenware, second-hand French books, fresh-cut hortensias, a decent hair trim, and where I could meet a friend for rose petal tea. I knew, above all, where to let myself get lost looking, for instance, for Gertrude Stein's, Hemingway's, Cole Porter's, F. Scott Fitzgerald's, or Rudolf Nureyev's apartments.

Randall found the ideal tennis partner, who rode a Vespa, too. They met at a court early Saturday mornings. When the season came, Randall enjoyed taking the boys to the French Open at Roland Garros, the courtside tickets gifts from a generous friend. The boys knew every corner of the Jardin d'Acclimitation, Palais de Tokyo, the Esplanade des Invalides where they roller bladed and walked Joey. The man who ran the peddled race car track tucked in a corner of the Champs de Mars knew the boys by sight. We'd found the best comic book store in the Latin Quarter, the best art movie theaters at the Reflet des Medicis or the Balzac, and knew what new releases in their VO or *version originale* were showing at the big Gaumont houses on the Champs Élysées. We knew how many steps it was to walk past Harry Winston's windows to Fendi, or from Dior and Chanel, all on our walks to school up the Avenue Montaigne. That we did when weather was just the right shade of warm and Paris at her most ebullient.

At the bottom of that Avenue Montaigne, right next to what had been Marlene Dietrich's apartment, was the clean white façade of *le Theâtre du Champs Élysées*, where Randall and I went every so often with or without the children to concerts. René Fleming. Cecilia Bartoli. Kurt Masur conducting. Sylvie Guillaume dancing. Or we went to the Salles Gaveau or Pleyel to hear Jessie Norman, J. J. Milteau and his jazz harmonica, The King's Singers, or African percussion.

Not only were we delving into the city, but we were crisscrossing the country. With visiting relatives and sometimes friends, we made our way to the castles and beaches of Normandy. Then we discovered Brittany, with its seaside fishing villages and ramparts. With my parents as enthused travel partners trailing us in a rented green Punto, we penetrated the Charentes, Perigord, Dordogne, Bordeaux, the Pyrenées, and the Loire. We lodged, as you can in France, in troglodyte hotels, working farms, renovated monasteries, erstwhile castles, and some bring-your-own-toilet-paper youth hostels. There was almost no region of France we didn't visit, and yet we always felt we'd scarcely scratched the surface.

All of this was an investment in our children who, at eighteen, sixteen, eleven, and seven, could appreciate the things they were seeing and experiencing. They loved, of all the places we traveled, the late springs and early summers of Provence. That was a relaxed existence, slow and warm like the landscape and the light, unlike Paris, where our teenagers had to learn to be alert and capable of managing the complexities of the big city on their own. Parker was especially fearless when it came to physically navigating the buses and rail systems in the city. He and Claire stuck together mostly if they went out on a Friday or Saturday evening, but if the occasion ever presented itself when Claire was somewhere in town alone, the two had a habit of texting each other non-stop.

Like my teenagers, I was also navigating a convoluted and intoxicating city. I'd long since conquered parallel parking in a spot which by all physical measures was too small for my vehicle, and I knew exactly which underground parking lots in town would accommodate my Renault van. I also knew which ones would leave me wedged inextricably in a corner, nine other motorists stacked up behind me, unable to turn in any direction at all, so I finally had to exit my car and walk from driver's window to driver's window, asking if, one-by-one, they could reverse into the street so I finally could, too.

I relished, at this point, swirling several times around the Étoile, or the traffic circle around the Arc de Triomphe that is an enormous vehicular vortex of twelve converging roads like spokes on a wheel, or rays from a star. It was my favorite place to drive in all the city. Why? Because it embodied the French concept, the "Système D," "D" being short for *débrouiller*, which means *to manage*, or better, to slug one's way through. I was debrouilling well, so to speak, and was so grateful to see my family was, too. Given the learning curve we'd ascended, this was plain gratifying.

"There's a place to buy in the 16th if we're serious." Randall's voice came from where he was lying next to me in the darkness of midnight. In between his slow breathing, I heard a couple murmuring, walking on the sidewalk beneath our window.

"And what about the smaller apartment in the 17th? Three bedrooms? Fifth floor? Not far from John and Renée? Should I make an appointment and see it? We ready for that?" That was me speaking from where I lay, covers tucked up under my arms, hands crossed thoughtfully on my abdomen, staring at the lights filtering through our drapes. This dialogue was happening nearly every night. It was Ceiling Talk as you know, and this was September 2006, and this was Randall and Melissa considering, as we had done in Norway, *to just stay*. To settle, to buy, to go native.

Randall was thriving at work and he could call this the end of his career and "coast on out," as he put it. I was busy volunteering at our children's two schools, singing in various venues, and seeing to the needs of the teenage girls and their teachers of our church in the greater Parisian area. This meant I was regularly going to Normandy, Chartres, and the small congregations throughout the city. In addition, I was writing pieces for an international journal and compiling chapters of my own book. I had the application forms on my desk for taking courses at the Sorbonne. We were looking ahead to having Parker graduate and head off to college that June, and Claire was cruising along beautifully at ASP, too, with her locker right under her brother's, a spatial closeness that symbolized nicely their unusually strong relationship. Dalton and Luc were gathering friends at EAB, fencing, singing in French choirs, collecting marbles, writing screen plays based on the Louvre. And Joey—may my crazy vet be praised—was finally, *finally* house trained.

So why move?

Unless the company, in October, approached with a reorganization that would bump Randall from his position overseeing the French subsidiary to another post in the regional offices based in Munich from where he would oversee his function for all of Europe, the Middle East, Africa, and Canada. Could he move immediately?

"No," Randall said into the receiver. "We can't move right now. The school year has just begun, our oldest child is a senior in high school; he has to finish out in this program. But," he eyed me for the go-ahead nod from across our bedroom where he was receiving the phone call from headquarters, "*I* can move. I'll move. Melissa and the kids will finish out the school year and follow to Munich in the summer. That is, if the family follows at all."

Despite the fact that Munich as a location was in many ways an ideal spot to drop us (we had roots there, as I've mentioned before, and were both German speakers), no one, including myself, could imagine leaving Paris. We had *dug some serious grooves*, as Kristiina Sorensen put it when I told her the news, and what place on earth could ever suit us as well as this place now did? So from that point in the early fall until the end of the school year, we conducted a test to see if living in one country—France—and working in another—Germany—would be not merely feasible, but preferable in terms of stability and consistency for the children. Randall lived during the weeks in a small hotel room outside of Munich, and I managed during the weeks with our four children and their four worlds of needs. We texted and called and emailed, stitching together our family with fiber optics, dangled in a world wide web.

Living in two different countries. One country for the employed person, another for the family, weekends together, if we were so lucky. More often, it turns into monthly or quarterly visits. Writing that today sounds so ludicrous it makes my fingers go rigid. But many families deliberately choose to do exactly what we were considering doing, and for the long haul. As I already knew from my circle of expatriate friends, more and more companies seemed to tacitly encourage such a thing. After all, with no family around to go home to, their employee could be counted on to work until or after midnight, could take international conference calls throughout the night, and be back at the office at 6:00 a.m., on Saturdays, on Sunday, on holidays.

Friends like the Sorensens and others from church and school and the neighborhood helped fill in some of the gaps when one has an absent father, and Parker, now an inch taller than Randall, became my right-hand man; a trusted, loving, fun and easy-going friend. Not a surrogate spouse, but my man-on-site who took care, literally, of some of the heavy lifting. He picked up brothers from their Parc Monceau school, carted heavy things up from the dusty cave, hauled the Christmas tree across town and up our building's entry steps, and hauled it out again in January.

With the volleyball and basketball teams at school, Parker had to make his way by train or plane to sports trips all around Europe, the Mediterranean, and northern Africa, and at the same time he was pushing his way through the college application process. We saw Dad nearly every weekend for twenty-four or forty-eight hours, connected daily by every technological means known at the time, and kept extremely busy. Life was spinning as quickly as I had ever experienced it, the hum was rising, the date, June 2007, drawing us ahead.

It was February, Parker's eighteenth birthday, when Randall and I announced our formal decision to keep the family physically together at all costs and make the move from Paris to Munich. It felt right, healthy, and it appeared to be falling at the most opportune moment possible, when our oldest would be leaving our home and his Paris *home*, anyway.

How could the rest of us stay in this city without Parker? We would move immediately after all the festivities leading up to graduation: Parker's many concert engagements as a solo drummer, his sports trips including the international championship for basketball; last trips (we returned, for instance, to Norway as we had been doing nearly every year since moving from there; Randall took the children one last time to our favorite place in Provence, our friends Liz and Zaki's home near St. Rémy, while I packed for the move), and many, many gatherings at our apartment and outings around town. We lapped up, as a family, the very last delicious droplets of Paris.

After being accepted and receiving a scholarship to a small liberal arts college, after dancing all night at Senior Prom, after graduation ceremonies and packing up his room and drums and sports equipment, and after having said his final goodbyes to the Greek and Lebanese and Tunisian and French restaurant owners around town who knew him well and always gave him extra large portions although he had a running tab, and after emotional goodbyes to school faculty as well as his dozens of friends also heading off to universities in many different countries, Parker was ready to leave Paris.

But not before one last night. It was the night of the *Fête de la Musique*. Throughout that June night, Paris vibrates with its annual citywide festival of music, when musicians of every sort—madrigal choirs, rap artists, reggae bands, orchestras, flamenco guitarists, string chamber ensembles—are free to make their music any place they want in the streets or in concert venues and for as long as they can hold out. As the name Fête de la Musique says, it's a music party; but fête is pronounced just like *faites*, the imperative form of *to do*, making of the title a typically French *jeu des mots* or play on words: "Do music!"

Nothing could have suited our firstborn better. Parker, who as I've written was part of a circle of local percussionists, met with them on the Pont des Arts for many hours of pure drumming explosion.

Walking toward that bridge, you could feel the electricity thrumming in surging beats already in the ground and through the air. Crowds had already packed the bridge, so the children couldn't see over all the heads, and Randall and I couldn't see around all the bodies to find Parker. But we knew he was there somewhere. Maybe listening. Maybe hanging out with friends one last time.

As we moved closer, Dalton and Luc, who could see under people's arms and between their knees, spotted their big brother. "Hey, Parker!" Luc yelled. But the drum beating was so thick, you couldn't hear your own voice as it left your own mouth, let alone hear the voice of a waify seven-year-old.

Luc pulled me by my hand toward the crowd, then motioned to Randall to hoist him on his shoulders. "The crowd!" I yelled over the din, "there must be hundreds!" At least four or five hundred people on that one bridge alone, and they split apart just enough so we could edge our way toward the source. And there he sat, djembe between his knees, the white boy with blue-gray eyes, his hair cropped very short to his well-shaped skull, the American boy (but who would have ever known?) named "Par Cœur" by the likes of Shafik, his closest Tunisian drumming buddy, and five others all of African descent. There they all were, swaying and pulsing to the pounding of their own djembes and large tub drums, or rocking, eyes closed, as they pummeled their instruments together.

The energy could just about lift you off your feet. It made the bridge tremble and sway. And standing there in the push of all these people, I sensed I had to hold myself together, had to keep myself from throwing my arms in the air and spinning for sheer delirium. This was a Paris I understood, a place where millions of people sing their songs and beat their rhythms but do it all at once. Somehow, it's not cacophonic but something beyond it, a grand intimacy and intimate grandiosity strung along the river and its several bridges.

Over those bridges, under those bridges, behind the museums, in front of the Metro stops. Children, old people, all colors, all persuasions, tourists, policemen, the homeless, the political elite. Everyone on one night crowding the skies with their music. In the center of this—really in the physical center—sat my boy, the one who'd banged into pieces my big Tupperware bowls on linoleum in New Jersey and broken to splinters my mixing spoons on the wooden kitchen floor in Norway. Who'd gotten his first drum set from a retiring musician down the street on our island and had beaten the sticks to a pulp. Who every Thursday late afternoon and in the fifteenth arrondissement of this city, had shown up for his drum lessons from a French percussionist with a long gray beard tied neatly with a red macramé bow. There was this son, shoulder to shoulder with the world, whamming and jamming with his people—all people, everyone and anyone who would stamp and clap and catch the hem of his rhythm.

"Dad?" I heard Dalton trying to raise his voice to get Randall's attention through the noise. "Dad?" our blonde and reticent eleven-year-old was standing, a bit self-conscious, awed, visibly, by his brother. Not as comfortable yet in his skin as this muscular drummer was, but every bit as thoughtful as your average fifty-year-old.

"Yes, Dalton?" Randall crouched down to hear better.

"Dad," Dalton was watching the movement ripple through crowd encircling the place where the seven drummers sat, feeling the surge of the drums' cadence. "Dad, do you think . . . heaven's anything like this?"

Randall and I laughed a bit then smiled. But Dalton was sober, stone cold serious.

I've held those words as if in plaster in my mind. And I have had to wonder.

Dear Mom and Dad,

I write from a hotel where I'm staying as of today until Monday when I fly to Munich. Packed the house all week. Sent off Kristiina and her kids Thursday morning. Hard goodbye for me. R will flee with the kids to Zaki's in Provence while I finish up all the messy boring moving details here. Cleaned and spackled today, walked around an echoing apartment and remembered 4 years ago arriving alone to an echoing apartment, the ordeal of getting our Norwegian table through the windows, the crazy and hilarious moving team, the growth in our family, the depths of my friendships here, and I realized all the things I have learned during these critical 4 years, the gifts of wisdom I hardly deserve. Before they left, R and the children and I knelt in the middle of our empty living room, so strange, to offer a prayer of thanks for the gift of that home, of the years we were blessed to spend there. All the miracles.

You know some of them. I'm giving the main sermon in church tomorrow (on seeking for wisdom and not for riches), then will do the official apartment walk-through on Monday morning. I'll ship Parker's big African drum to you after that, please be watching for it; he'll want it at university if he can play it and not get in trouble for the disturbance. That thing is loud! After that, I'm thinking I'll probably walk the streets feeling wistful, so wistful I can hardly formulate words. Then I'll fly to Munich late afternoon because goods arrive Tuesday morning and we unpack all week . . . and so forth and so forth until I fly to meet up with all of you and the kids in Utah on July 14th. Have been overwhelmed with work for so many weeks (months?) now, that I haven't really allowed myself to feel very much about this departure. Now I'm so completely clotted with warm fluid feelings. I think my earlobes are waterlogged.

Love you both always and see you very soon!

And so that late Parisian June evening of the Fête de la Musique, I had been standing with my family on a bridge. A day later, I found myself alone, standing at a crossroads. It was a literal crossroads, the moment I am describing now, since I was standing in front of our building, which stands at an intersection, and the extra-large moving truck with its forty-cubic-meter container was parked there, too. We were leaving an epoch, a densely blessed whirring Camelot of a time; we all knew it, and I was balancing all that emotion with the practical necessity of overseeing the countless details of clearing out our apartment and making sure every last gram of our material lives was packed into a box that would roll out the very next morning heading for Munich, Germany.

I'd sent Randall and the children off in the car to say neighborhood goodbyes and pick up baguettes still hot and crusty from Secco, our local boulangerie. They timed it so they would show up to see off our moving crew, a spicy mix from the *banlieue* of Paris, headed by a great, burly fellow whose charm and salt-and-pepper eyebrows were equally luxuriant.

As that leader clamped shut the massive lock on our container parked in teeny Rue du Colonel Combes, he raised his voice and arms in a dramatic flourish, smacked the hind end of the trailer, and pronounced to the skies, "*Madame, vos trésors!!*" Madame, your treasures. In that very same instant, Randall rounded the corner in the Renault, kids hanging out windows wielding baguettes, waving, whooping, "*Bonjour, Maman!!*" like a chorus of French schoolchildren.

"*Non, Monsieur,*" I responded, an eye on the family van, "*Voici mes trésors.*" No, sir. *These* are my treasures.

In that serendipitously choreographed moment, I truly felt what I was saying as it caught in my throat, and I thought I knew just how completely those gangling arms and hoarse voices were my true treasures. I knew that if my forty-cubic-foot, padlocked trunk of treasures drowned in the blue black of some ocean, I'd survive it well because I knew what was most precious. And what's more, I had it. Precious and irreplaceable. My treasure. My treasured family. I had every last one of them.

19

PORTNEUF

Seven. I count them.

But I can't lift my hand to touch them. Seven. Seven, number of perfection. Seven gashes. Big-big-big-small-small-big-big, like a Morse code across his forehead. A blood red message. I try to decipher it in the insulated silence of the ICU. I scoot my metal-legged chair closer to the gurney.

Morse code. Morte code. Portneuf Regional Medical Center. Port. Neuf. French. But we're in Pocatello. Idaho. What is this place?

There under greenish lights lies Parker. He is facedown on a gurney, draped from his ankles to his waist with a crisp white sheet. On his ample shoulders there is no blue t-shirt like there had been just a day earlier when I had hugged him, chirping something into the hot summer air like, "See you in a couple of days."

Was that yesterday? Was that us? Was that this boy? Is this me? Is this happening? What is real?

Except for the deep streaked abrasions on one shoulder blade, these shoulders are just as perfectly formed as before, but now they're nearly motionless.

I have never seen him this still, not even in his sleep. Is he sleeping? What is this machine?

Enabled by a ventilator, his smooth muscular torso is rising and falling, if only barely. I see the large, white machine with its steel wheels and tubes, and its presence is disturbing, unwelcome.

A nurse with brown hair and glasses avoids eye contact with me as she checks the machine on the opposite side of this gurney, but she answers what must be my questioning look: "They've laid your son like this to give his lungs a chance to drain fluids, Mrs. Bradford." She's making an effort to act neutral, I sense this. She continues in a whisper, "This helps them contract and expand." There is a long thick space of heavy silence. "He is so handsome," she says. I nod. I know this. He is beautiful. *And he is going to be just fine. You're going to be just fine, Parker. Can you hear me? Where are you?*

I ask something about the life support or about the need to be face-down. *Honey, I know you, how can you be comfortable like this?* A question like a schoolgirl asks questions, afraid to not know the obvious. But the nurse just says, "He's in God's hands, now. It's all in God's hands."

The machine rattles in-and-out as if clogged with mucus, and I sit without speaking outwardly, but carrying on a steady dialogue with God and with Parker. *This boy must live. This boy will live. Make this boy live. Do you see, honey, how my hands are so cold and shaking?* My body and my world are buried in a stunning, boldfaced cold I've been feeling since the flash-fire receded, the fire that took flame at 11:00 p.m. when the phone rang and the unidentified male voice told me about a serious accident.

Mrs. Bradford, can you come right away? Don't speed, now.

I did not speed during the four and a half hours I drove north from Utah to Idaho, crossing from one state to another, from one state of being into another, arriving at 3:30 a.m., my body stiffened against the unknown, the unthinkable. But it felt like a frenzied rush that brought me to this ICU room where I am deposited, curled forward in this chair, stroking steadily the arm of my comatose child.

"There has been a serious water accident, Mrs. Bradford." The male voice on the other end of the line had not identified himself, or at least I couldn't remember who he was, as my brain had waved off that detail. But somehow he'd reached me in Utah. How had he found my parents' number? We were spread across six locations, all six of us, during those two odd weeks in transit—Paris, Munich, Parker's first student apartment in Idaho, my childhood home in Provo where Dalton and Luc were in sleeping bags on deep pile carpet, Claire with Caroline Sorensen at a youth camp at the local university—and I'd just arrived from Munich a couple of days earlier. Randall was still back there, surrounded by boxes marked *Paris → Munich.*

Who was this man on the phone? And what information did he have that he was not telling me? I listened carefully to the voice in the receiver and began, mentally, trying to repair this thing that had happened and that I was barely starting to understand.

"Seems there was a hidden whirlpool in that darned irrigation canal; no one could have seen it," the man's voice continued blandly, almost glibly, "and that other boy was pinned under. Know how that happens? How people just get pinned? Those darned canals, always making trouble. Your boy went in, Mrs. Bradford, to get the kid out, looks like. Now that's something. Thing is, the other boy got flushed out early and someone managed to do CPR right off. But your son . . . "

"My son . . . ?"

"Well, it was a real long time before he came out, Mrs. Bradford."

"Long time?"

"Ten, maybe twenty minutes . . . or more . . . Maybe."

Silence.

"Now, uh, we'll connect you with the desk, Mrs. Bradford, so they can get your insurance details. You'll want to get your card ready. Then you'll want to be making your way up here as fast as you can. But not *too* fast, all right? Don't need two accidents in the trauma center tonight."

This is not happening. This cannot be happening. With a new phone purchased in Munich a week earlier, and while reconfiguring the universe, I'd begun making calls. The first was to Randall: "Honey, come to Idaho. Come right now," which set him on a track running and running, kneeling and praying and weeping in airports and airplane bathrooms, rushing and begging for his luggage to be taken off this flight and put on another, no, onto yet another one, then a certain flight attendant mapping out on a napkin a short cut through one airport to a domestic desk that could possibly get him in Pocatello by midnight on Friday at the absolute earliest. Miraculously, within twenty hours from my call, he came. That long, excruciating journey skimmed closer to heaven and to hell than he had ever traveled.

Claire we'd reached in a dorm room she was sharing with Caroline, who had accidentally left her phone turned on through the night. Greg and Kristiina in Boston, conferenced us all in—Randall in Munich, Claire in Provo, Melissa on the road to Idaho—all of us trying to explain the inexplicable, and weeping and reassuring and weeping still, trying also to arrange Claire's release from the youth camp so she could ride with relatives to this Idaho trauma center.

Friends vacationing in Utah gathered up Dalton and Luc and brought them five hours northward so that if and when Randall would finally arrive, we—friends, extended family, and our own family of six—could be together.

Our family of six. Together.

My parents, on vacation in Colorado, received all the voicemails I'd left between 1:00 a.m. and 2:00 a.m. from behind the steering wheel of a rented Durango while crossing the haunting moonscape of the Utah-Idaho border. "Mom, Dad, it's Melissa. Please, please pick up. *Please.* There's been a terrible accident. *Please, please pick up* or call me back. This is a Munich number, so first you have to dial zero-zero and . . . "

Praying all the way, my seventy-year-old parents drove eleven hours without a single stop on back roads and while reading a tattered map by flashlight. They arrived at the ICU to find their middle daughter ashen and wrapped in a hospital blanket, praying at the side of their oldest and stone-still grandchild.

Aaron, Parker's body double, brought our sister, and held her from around the shoulders as she nearly drooped into a heap on the floor as soon as the two entered the room. My brother's body, when I held it and we wept together openly, almost filled in for my son's. One body was standing and shuddering in a wail-turned-inward, while the other lay flat and static under spotlights.

Kristiina had caught the first flight from Boston. Maja, the first flight from San Francisco. Bonnie Jean and Elaine and Sharon and others drove through the night from wherever they were on the nation's map. And Melanie came from the next city with a train of rolling thermoses filled with food and drink for all the support people quickly filling up the waiting area. Calls were coming in to my phone, which I had to give to someone else for monitoring, calls from Paris, Oslo, Salt Lake City, Philadelphia, Rome, Munich, Paris again. And Paris again and again. Around the globe and around the gurney, our friends and family held vigil.

Without Randall at my side, I felt I was breathing with one lung the cement air of dread, which made me have to sit and bend forward, my folded hands propping up my head as I softly, rhythmically rocked back and forth, crying and talking to God and trying to take this all in. Many times, as often as I was left alone, I read aloud from my open set of scriptures, the first thing I'd dropped into an overnight bag. As I read, I leaned close enough to smell Parker's skin. That familiar musk. That left ear. I whispered into it for long stretches, pulling back only to study its curves. What a miracle it had been at his birth, that perfect, furry whorl. That same ear had somehow transfixed me only a few weeks earlier at his high school graduation when I had been seated a few rows behind him and he sat so proudly in his shiny royal blue cap and gown. He'd looked so poised that afternoon in Paris, even dignified. But I knew better: he was absolutely crackling as he sat there waiting for his diploma. This I knew because his whole life long his nervous reflex had been to reach up and pinch, lightly tug, on one ear lobe reddened with adrenalin. There had been a single, sleight-of-hand earlobe tug that graduation day. But there was nothing now. Only the sight of that left ear and the whole symphony of meaning it conveyed to me, and then his hand impossibly stiff, unresponsive as I traced it and stroked its creases. I put my mouth next to that ear. *Parker, listen to me my love. I will tug for you.*

Somewhere in this vast and eviscerating moment, a thought flicked its tail: *Here is when I can just let go.* Come unglued. I could lose my mind, the thought told me, collapse into craziness, never come back. No one would blame me; there would be an explanation to my insanity, my bitterness, my apostasy, negligence, rage, whatever. There would be a sort of subtitle beneath the pictures of me losing it, curling up in a corner, or unraveling into stark raving uselessness. "Oh . . . Melissa? Yeah, it's kind of a sad story. I mean, her oldest had that accident, you know . . . and then she kinda . . . well . . . unplugged. Guess you can't really blame her."

It teased me for maybe thirty seconds, that thought.

It never returned.

At 7:00 that Friday evening, pale and breathless, Randall burst through the ICU doors. I watched every frame as it passed without soundtrack, feeling torn to pieces like a melting hulk of upheaval, as my beloved husband steadied himself against the scene that met his eyes. From one step to the next, he aged fifty years. "*Parker,* oh, sweet son. Sweet, *sweet* son."

Silence and awe. There are moments that cannot and should not be rendered in words.

Together, Randall, Claire, and I wrapped our arms around each other in an unlit spot while others left us to grapple with the description of the medical reports the attending doctor shared with us in a low murmur. It was Claire who said the words we dared not think, let alone say: "If he cannot live in his normal body, he doesn't want to live." I squeezed her hand to stop my tears. I was startled by her frankness, pierced through by her intimate understanding of her brother, a boy who had taken excellent care of his body, a young man who was wholly flesh and blood, a creature so of this earth, so rooted in this world, the most physically *alive* person I had ever known. And now: "Mr. and Mrs. Bradford, *survival,* any kind of survival? Percentage-wise, less than ten percent. Meaningful survival? Less than five percent."

It took that whole holy night, that long labyrinth-like passage we spent wandering together through our minds and hearts, to come to terms with what this meant. And though "come to terms" would take not just one night but months and months into years of long nights of the soul, we did in fact feel a gradual enveloping. *Enveloping.* That is the best word I can find to describe it. Slowly, coming from all around us, Randall and I noted a sturdy-ing, something that stabilized us, that settled us down into deep assurance, like when you dig holes in a beach to stand in, hip deep. You step in and the sand, packed wet and heavy around your flesh holds you firmly, buttresses you, and you know you cannot be knocked over. That was something of that sensation: the packed sand sensation. We would neither fall over nor be washed completely out to sea.

After walking outside of Portneuf past the landing pad where the very helicopter stood that had brought our son there only hours earlier, under the stars and the moon that seemed to hold their breath with us in terror, and after speaking aloud to God and to Parker, we made that walk back into the ICU room. There, we waited out the morning while the final, definitive tests were run.

From somewhere, I already knew this setting. It seemed distantly familiar: father, mother, my handsome mother in a corner, a hospital room. Fluorescent lights. Medical personnel. Machines making polite, melodic bleeps. A pervasive antiseptic smell. White sheets. And a helpless child moving from one world to another. At the births of all our children, Randall and I felt joined by the hopeful surge of life coming at us. The process for me as a life-giver hadn't felt Herculean, but Zen, and had rendered me hardly cognizant of much but the child being drawn by gravity and pushed by powerful muscular pressure out of my womb. I'd visualized during labor the dilation of my body, the infinitesimal fissure that was expanding and stretching to allow passage into this life. I'd ridden the waves of accelerating pressure, that splitting-expanding-welcoming feeling, the wrenching of the physical self, the giving up of my body for another's body.

Now, at Portneuf, we were joined by the ominous sensation of life being torn *from us*, reducing things to their most particulate, bare-nerve-endings essentials. We felt ripped wide open, skinned alive, scraped down to the marrow of our bones. That skinless, reduced state can make one receptive to much that never penetrates one's awareness when one is wrapped in the normally thick skin of mundane living, poised in the armor of self-composure. What ensued were hours lined with divine instruction and encased in such holiness, I choose not to speak or write much about them.

It is perhaps like the experience our friends, Cory and Amy, had, who sat alone with the body of their young adult son, Ethan, in the moments right after he quietly passed away from a lifetime of suffering with muscular dystrophy. These devoted parents felt, as they talked openly to Ethan's lingering presence in that sacred hour, that they were communicating with a truly huge spirit. "Like the disciples must have felt on the road to Emmaus," Cory told us later. "Which makes me wonder," he added, "if we ever really have any idea the kind of majestic spirits we are walking our roads with right now."

We brought all the waiting family and friends into Parker's small room and gathered around the edge of his bed. There was such a weight of reverence in that room that the space itself felt denser and more illuminated than the hallway. Walking through the doorway was like moving through a plasma membrane. As Parker's body had by that time been turned over onto its back, we could freely study and memorize his face during these, our last minutes of private communion with him. As heads bowed, I looked around. I felt that reverence or that illuminating presence, that vibration, only greatly heightened, and realized in an uncanny way for which I cannot account, that everything was exactly as it was supposed to be: the shape and placement of the windows; the slant of late morning light on the floor; my own hands so ice cold their nails were blue-gray; Randall's soulful expression like a late Rembrandt self-portrait; Dalton, whose bearing and depth was of a forty-five-year-old; Claire with her open, light-filled stare; my parents, so vulnerable and shaken; the soft faces of friends and family; the sense that others, unseen but real, were there, filling in all the blank spaces. And Parker's Adonis form under a perfect sheet of white.

Then, through a ton of ruins that was my soul, my voice broke through. It shocked me. It pushed through without plan or my permission. In the shimmering stillness I began singing, "I know that my Redeemer lives . . . " And by the end of that phrase, the whole room joined in. Heaven floated down, encompassing us like a great, weightless, sky-blue silk curtain. I added a verse each of a children's church song, "I Am a Child of God" in the two languages Parker himself had sung them in, Norwegian and French. The room kept singing. We barely warbled through tears streaming down our cheeks, scarcely squeaking through emotion that locked our vocal cords. We stood there, encircling Parker's form, and we sang. Souls sliced open. We sang to him, we sang to heaven.

With "Amazing Grace," I'd sung my Dalton out. And with "Souviens-toi," a French lullaby, I'd sung Luc out. Now, we gathered to sing hymns at the foot of this makeshift altar and our first child. We sang and sang. We sang our Parker out.

Then that sky-blue silk curtain wrapped us in silence.

And we listened.

There, I heard God speak to me in a two-syllable epiphany. *Port. Neuf.* It's French, of course, the name of that Regional Medical Center hidden in the corner of rural Idaho. Of all places, of all names, to be associated with the last hours of our French-speaking boy's life. *Port. Neuf. New haven.* God's communication to us was transparent. He was navigating our son, His son, into a new and safe port. He was taking him home. We bowed under the weight of the unthinkable: we were being asked to give Parker back.

On the morning of Saturday, July 21, sixty-five hours after I'd made a quick trip north to see my boy fresh at college and deposit his big African djembe at his first student apartment, after a mid-afternoon goodbye in a parking lot where I'd felt his heart beating against my own in a hug under the summer sun as bright and vital as he was, Parker Fairbourne Bradford was pronounced brain dead. Life support was removed. His lungs released a final sigh of this earth's air. And as his head tipped gracefully to one side, the earth fell off its axis and began spinning strangely, drunkenly, into unchartable and inaccessible regions out of which only a God can escape, or from which only a God can rescue.

"Mr. Bradford? Here, they're on the line."

The ICU nurse hands the telephone to Randall and I listen, sitting next to him on a chair I've pulled over from the wall. She's very thin, the nurse behind the reception counter, Diet Coke lean with a tan and silvery highlights. Her wrists are sinewy and she wears no wedding ring though I remember she'd mentioned having a son. In those last minutes around the gurney she had mentioned, this nurse trying to be casual and conversant in the thickness of sacred silence, how handsome our son was. *Almost the same age as mine*, she'd said, smiling brightly.

Working ICU in Pocatello to put the kids through school, I thought. A loyal girlfriend to many and street smart, her face told me. There to witness the last assisted breaths of the son of this woman wrapped in a blue hospital blanket that an earlier nurse had brought from room seven. There to stand at the foot of the son of this woman who had been singing church songs in different languages and had been reading from her scriptures into the left ear of her firstborn.

And now the parents from room two sit in front of that same lightly speckled Formica reception desk. And the thin nurse who is a single mom, I've decided, with the son my son's age is handing us the phone, and my husband is going to do the talking as my legs and hands and even my shoulders and ribs begin to shake. My teeth chatter. My nails are the color of grief. I wrap the blue blanket more snugly around my thighs, pull it higher over my shoulders and push it up around my neck. My husband's voice is paced, warm, and the nurse steps away, eyes following the top of my husband's head as he nods and agrees to the voice on the line. He is, even in this ice block of time, an impeccable—though decimated— professional.

He will take the questions from Organ Donation. He will repeat to me in fragments the impossible litany of queries this interview requires. This Organ Donation interview scheduled out of necessity within two minutes of when room two turned off life support.

"Has your son ever used recreational drugs?" the voice asks my husband through the receiver.

"Never."

"Pot? Meth? Ever abused prescription drugs?"

"No, never."

"Has he abused alcohol or even drunk socially?"

"Never."

"Sexual activity, Mr. Bradford. Was your son sexually active?"

"No. He has never engaged in sexual activity."

"Mr. Bradford? Um, can you be sure of that? This is to rule out any chances of STDs or AIDS, you know. We can't use his organs if there is any chance of those in his system. Any activity? With women, Mr. Bradford? Or with men?"

"No. None. I know this for sure."

"Okay then. Ah . . . yeah, okay, next question, Mr. Bradford. We still have quite a list here . . . "

While the voice from Organ Donation asks for a detailed profile, I watch another nurse walk toward my son's room. From where I sit, watching Randall, watching my body quietly convulse, I cannot see what this other woman is doing. But there she goes. Into that room. With *my* son. I have no strength to follow either her or this thought any farther.

And part of me is trying to be here in this plastic chair so I can love my husband through this disorienting phone call.

"Where has your son lived during his life, Mr. Bradford? Idaho, right?"

"For nine days, if that counts," Randall answers. "And Utah. And Hong Kong. And Pennsylvania and New Jersey and Versailles then Paris, France."

"Whoah, okay," the voice laughs lightly, "Moved, I see."

"And Norway."

"Norway?"

"Oslo, Norway."

"What year would that have been, Mr. Bradford?"

"*Years*. From 1994 to 1999. We lived five years in Norway."

"Ok. Mr. Bradford, can you just please hold on for a sec?"

Randall looks at me and tucks the blue blanket up under my chin, up behind the nape of my neck. Through a steady stream of stinging tears I smile at him—smile, oddly enough—but certainly not out of mere courtesy.

"Mr. Bradford. Seems there's a problem. Government records show that there were three cases of mad cow disease in Norway during those five years you lived there. This means your son's organs are unfortunately unsuitable for donation. But we do thank you for your time, Mr. Bradford."

I am in a gummy state, all senses on hyperdrive but my soul tuned to submission. All my joints, though chilled through, are limp, my will utterly pliable. *So we can't even give his organs*, I think. *He'll be unhappy about that.* Unable to move myself from this hospital chair with its aluminum legs, I stare at my hands. Randall's hand reaches over to mine.

A nurse walks into room two, wearing her scrubs, her brown hair in a pony tail, prepared to do what she is trained to do. She walks to my son. To the body of my son. My handsome, my gorgeous, my sweet, my son on the gurney. Those are his feet whose toenails I'd taught him to trim. His hands I'd marveled at in the delivery room the minute he was laid on my chest, hands he'd pushed up against my breast when I nursed him all those eleven months. He'd pushed and pushed with those miraculous mitts, routinely kneading my flesh as he suckled life from me. They were the same hands whose calluses and blisters he'd shown me proudly after all those hours spent pummeling his djembe with his buddies on the steps of the Trocadéro.

Now, this stranger, this woman with white support hose and an aluminum rolling trolley is walking toward those hands, hands with calluses she cannot read, toward an entire geography of flesh and blood she cannot know. Nothing but foreign soil to her. And then, with everyday grace softening her movements, she proceeds with the speechless routine of turning and lifting, wrapping and bending, of dipping a cloth in cool water and tracing a limb with it. Wringing it out, that hospital rag, in a utilitarian metal dish. This unnamed woman, cradling my son, following the curve of his mortal landscape, sharing with him his final sacrament.

Dearest friends and work colleagues,

It is with profound sadness and heavy, heavy hearts that Melissa and I confirm the passing of our sweet son, Parker Bradford, following a tragic water accident that took his life. He died at 11:19 a.m. on Saturday morning, July 21, 2007 at the tender age of 18. It will be impossible for me to convey in any words the utter depth of our sorrow. He is the oldest of our marvelous four children, but more than my son, he was my closest, dearest, and most cherished friend. He graduated in June from high school in Paris, France, and two weeks ago joined 350 other students in a Freshman Academy at university in Idaho. Last Thursday evening, he and a group of twenty fellow freshmen students were swimming in a familiar local irrigation canal, when Parker and a classmate were suddenly dragged upstream by a hidden undercurrent and pinned in a whirlpool beneath a small bridge. Parker somehow freed himself and was hanging by his fingertips onto a small concrete ledge under the bridge from where he yelled for help. Two passing students heard his cries and summoned others to come help. But before those others could arrive, Parker dove into the whirlpool after the first student. Parker was then out of the canal and standing on the bank, yelling to form a human chain, for which he assumed the lead. Four students went in, hands linked, but the chain broke and Parker and the original victim were still pinned and drowning. Soon thereafter, the first student's body washed out of the vortex and he was revived through CPR. Parker, however, remained pinned underwater. Many minutes later, his body washed out, then floated farther downriver and fell over a waterfall marked by jagged lava rock. He was dragged to shore unconscious, not breathing, and badly pummeled. Friends performed CPR for

30 minutes, until paramedics arrived and managed to establish a faint heartbeat, then evacuated him by helicopter to the Portneuf Medical Center in Pocatello, Idaho. His doctors worked through the night, but he could only be sustained by life support and never regained brain activity, his body having been deprived of oxygen for too long.

I would like to tell you how deeply moved I have been by the support we've received from you, our friends, family, and my professional family. The outpouring of encouragement, well-wishes, and help that have come from you have been nothing short of astonishing. And although I still find myself helplessly sad, lying awake for hours through each night, and longing to hold my son again in my arms, your tremendous kindnesses, gestures of genuine love, and prayers have helped so much to soothe the searing pain we feel since he left us. He was such a beautiful person, and I feel an unsurpassed sense of pride for the life he lived and the choices he made, including his final one. It has been and continues to be such an honor to be the father of a son like Parker.

With deep gratitude to all of you,

Randall Bradford

20

MONASTERY

"Good Lord, Mitch, I'm going to *kill* you!" The mom hisses, smacking her seat where she sits behind me in Row 34. "You're hogging my space! Agh, these legs of yours, they're on my side again. Shi–!" and the boy grunts something indistinguishable, kneeing soundly the back of my airplane seat. Then he shifts, I'm guessing, away from his mother. I stiffen and look out the window then close my eyes, burrowing into my thoughts.

> *I'm standing in a cloud of steam that dapples with beads of sweat the small, wooden-framed window at eye level above the clothes dryer. I lower my eyes to my hands planted flat on warm t-shirts. We arrived in Norway eleven days ago. Eleven days of non-stop snow—trees bending, cars engulfed, and roofs groaning under the weight of all that white.*

Midflight, somewhere over Canada, I'm guessing, on our way from Salt Lake City to Munich. The mother and her teenage son sitting behind us keep at it, and Claire, who's seated next to me staring straight ahead into nothingness, touches my knee with her pinkie finger and turns her glance to meet my eyes. I look at her long and hard for several seconds. Then I close my eyes. I lean my head back.

In my mind I see my hands pull limp limbs from the heap of en-twined fabric, children's pajamas sizes four and two, and I flatten and fold them just so, then place them on the counter to my right. They're for Parker and Claire, who've knotted themselves into one fleshy double pretzel where I left them in an easy chair waiting for 5:30 p.m., the magical hour. Theme music, Norwegian lyrics, and in that far corner of the living room I hear my two hop out onto the pine floor and start dancing. Barne TV.

Randall is seated right ahead of me. He's aged ten years in these few days since July 21. Gaunt, hollow, his eyes the color of fresh abrasions, always crying. Always crying. He's hearing the mother, too, I think, the one behind me, and knowing him, he's pinching his eyes shut.

"Look, bud, now you're really getting on my nerves. Honestly, put your elbow on my elbow rest one more time, so help me, I'll wring your neck. Got it?" She flings a high-pitched laugh. Mitch grunts again, "Well, if your bag weren't so—oh forget it," then he kicks the back of my seat again and moans. I like to imagine he's pulling a blanket over his head. Things are quiet for a little while.

I stare at my children. Claire seems made of wax, all soft contours and extraordinarily still. Dalton and Luc are sitting across the aisle from her, arms linked. All three children are staring—no movies, no books, just staring—which makes them look punished or sworn to silence, as if they have the secret of the whole universe hidden under the airplane blankets they've drawn up over their chests.

August, but the whole world feels cold, so inescapably cold.

It's late August and I'm with my two in a New Jersey park. In truth, though, I'm in the spongy dome of my brain batting around to-morrow's lecture on Carl Sandburg I'll give to my students at the community college. I push two children—one-year-old Claire with the right hand, three-year-old Parker with the left—who squeal as I stoop and run back to front under one swing then front to back under the other, tickling their feet.

"Honey?" Randall's eyes are still closed as he whispers back to me, stirring me from my thoughts. I stretch my hand between the seats. The place next to him has been vacated, and I lift myself over Claire, who now has her eyes closed. "Hm?" I ask, sitting down, entwining my arm around his, leaning my head to his shoulder, my eyes closed. Like Randall, though, I'm widely, wildly awake, praying Mitch's mother is asleep.

"The funeral," Randall whispers, "It was . . . just . . . I can't believe they all came." I don't want the children to notice our tears; weeping is almost all they've seen and heard and done for two weeks straight.

"They flew across the world, all those people," I look down at our hands, gripping one another's. He shakes his head. "How could they . . . ? I'm just . . . And the *music* . . . " We tilt our heads to where our crowns meet. I feel him shaking.

The day of your own child's funeral is the day you should never live to see. It is, in the imagination of those anticipating it in the abstract or in the minds of those observing it from afar, the hardest possible day of any parent's life. It is the day when the father should collapse with a heart attack, one thinks, or the morning the mother should do something dangerous in her bathroom. The day you should never ever live to see. The day you would of course never want to relive.

Yet here we are, The Father and The Mother, bent together in Row 34, aching to relive it frame-by-frame. The day was brilliant—brilliantly excruciating and brilliantly exquisite—like the sun affixed stubbornly at its peak, a sun that wouldn't be dismissed from early morning until early evening, perched there on the topmost rung of sky, like the high sounds of a bugle's call, punchy, relentlessly scorching, and brassily happy. All those things at once. That was the day.

We five had held the principal sermons or offered the prayers in the service, so we'd sat facing the congregation from up on the podium of my childhood church building. It hadn't been only a full church, but it had been a church full of the world. Students, parents, and administrators flew in from the American School of Paris. The Sorensens, Renée, and Natalie (Parker's first girlfriend) all came from our church in Rue St. Merri. Zaki, whose house we always rented in Provence, came. Johanne's children and Christian Karlsson and his family were there from Norway. Missionaries we ourselves had served with in Austria and Germany and others who'd eaten at our Norwegian table or lodged under our Parisian roof sat in the pews. Friends and family and work colleagues from Germany, Italy, Canada, Singapore, Pennsylvania, and all corners of the United States, they were there. It seemed we were part of a community, a whole chapel full of people who'd been victims of the same air raid, bombed straight through and ready to rebuild from this rubble. That sense was so strong that when the crystalline moment of the funeral was over, devastation wasn't the aftertaste, reconstruction was. No wonder photos show Randall and Melissa smiling through tears.

Smiling? How? It was the presence of our people alongside another much more powerful presence that Randall and I and many on hand that day had recognized. Author and bereaved mother Anne Morrow Lindbergh calls it the "condensed presence"[1] of those newly departed, a *véritable ami mort*, as she calls it, the familiar and knowable presence of the one whose death you mourn, the literal attendance of the beloved. It was everywhere, Parker's spiritual presence, and nowhere more conspicuously than when we stood to sing the closing number.

"Could you believe . . . ?" Randall lifts his head from the airline headrest and clears his throat to raise his voice only a bit. "And when the organ opened up and . . . ?" The plane is very quiet at this hour. His eyes are alive, looking upward.

"And all those people toward the back kept turning around?" I can still hardly believe what we'd heard, "Looking to see where the hidden speakers were for the extra choir?"

Tears are coming fast, now, "It felt like a tidal wave . . . "

"Of fire . . . " I weep but smile lightly, too, keeping an eye on the passing flight attendant. She nods once. Randall holds my arm and squeezes tight.

Tears. I would've never believed a body could lose as much fluid as we did and not turn to a big heap of powder in the process. And I'd had no clue, no clue in the least, of how enormous the physical pain of psychic trauma could be. Our bodies ached like we'd had multiple, simultaneous, major invasive surgeries, so much so that Randall walked hunched over, wincing like a ninety-year-old, holding his arms around his middle.

For weeks, we couldn't get more than ten or fifteen minutes of sleep at a stretch no matter how much we longed for it. Finally, we took prescription medication, but even with medication, half the time when my throbbing head drifted into blackness, I was dragged by the suction of ice-cold water underneath a bridge, and I had knees and elbows and feet jabbing into my face, someone's body weight heaped on my struggling back, stones and knees and concrete slamming my head, water filling my lungs. I'd shoot straight up in bed, gagging for breath.

That was half the time when I tried to sleep. The other half, sleep held luxurious promise. It was in sleep, or more in moments of half-slumber in those hours right before dawn, where I met and talked with Parker. I touched his arms, smelled his skin, stroked his forehead, looked into his eyes, asked him questions, felt the vibrations and moisture of his voice next to my ear, and listened to his wise, measured answers. I saw he was lustrous and self-contained, unhurt, occupied, yet at peace. He was surrounded, as I saw him in those dream visions, by caring family and friends in a glistening, borderless place of beauty, music, and learning. Whenever I arose from a dream experience like this, I wrote it down as quickly as I could, a pattern that, after many months, built a substantial dream journal. When Randall had an experience like this, he told me and we wrote it down. When Claire or Dalton or Luc did, we told them to write it down, too.

> It's early September and I'm at the neighborhood swing set, new-born Claire in the Baby Bjørn, the top of her flawless head tucked up near my chin. The smell of her skin is sweet and muggy. The clean curve of her tiny, translucent fingernail a masterpiece, her heart beats like a swaddled sparrow pressed against the thunking behind my chest wall. Parker, my blonde-bobbed two-and-a-half-year-old Titan is rambunctious, squirming and bucking on the far end of the teeter-totter that I'm pumping with my right leg. He demands I pump him higher and faster. His voice is hoarse and his diction crisp. His hair reflects the sun . . .

> It's September again and I'm scrubbing grass stains from trouser seats at the kitchen sink while rehearsing lines into kids' eyes that are shimmering like mirages. I'm playing the narrator in Joseph and the Amazing Technicolor Dreamcoat in a few weeks, so three-and-a-half-year-old Parker's correcting me, because he's already learned the entire script by heart . . .

> It's October and I'm sifting through a pile of yet-ungraded research papers after going through another show's dance steps with toddler Claire barefoot on the linoleum I'd scoured on my knees only that same morning. Parker is whacking with wooden spoons and un-canny rhythm on all my upturned mixing bowls . . .

> It's November and I'm cutting and saving coupons for diapers, Cheerios, and Stove Top Stuffing, marking a script for an audi-tion, tabulating semester grades, and making construction paper pilgrim and Indian headgear. Parker's made his own cotton ball beard and is reciting his lines as Governor William Bradford for a church spectacle on the first Thanksgiving . . .

Why didn't I take him away that Wednesday afternoon when I drove up to see him in his first college apartment? Or why didn't I just take him away right then when he was in my arms as we hugged goodbye in the parking lot, before I drove away, watching in my rear-view mirror as the blue of his t-shirt darkened then disappeared in the shadows of a doorway? Why didn't I take him far away with me, back to a place that knew and cherished and understood him? Or visit him again on Thursday? Or call him when I felt that omen about some water accident, call him and say, hi darling, this is radar mom, don't go to the canal? Why did I raise him to help strangers, to dive into things? Why was I sitting, just sitting, writing some meaningless email while my boy, my boy, my child, my son, oh Parker, while you were in that evil water, in that dangerous unmarked lethal canal all those locals call The Meat Grinder but you'd been told was fun, why was I sitting and typing calmly while you were screaming for help, while you were being spun and crushed and while someone else was climbing on your bruised back to get his gulp of air, to get air you couldn't get, to get that one gulp of air so he could go on living while your head would get smashed and you would—

"Mel? Hon?" Randall's fingers are touching those of my left hand, which, as I open my eyes, I now see is gripping one of the airplane armrests. My jaw is clenched, my fist grips, and I am quickly aware that my back is tight as a metal girder. I look toward my husband, toward my children, each one inert (or just exhausted) as our plane descends for its predictably smooth landing.

But I'm bracing against an entirely different descent. I'm trying to halt this tumbling, vertiginous plummet through a gravity-less universe, a universe where anything at any moment can happen. Where boys get sucked into vortexes and never emerge again. Where a big life is blipped out in less than half a breath. I'm trying to plant a foot somewhere on a stable point in this new reality, trying to grab a branch, dig a fingernail into the air, get my bearings against the suction of a gripless, spinning free fall.

At the Munich airport, we all stand silently at the luggage carousel where we collect our two suitcases each except for Dad, who'd come with only one carry-on. And just then as we heave from the conveyer belt all of Parker's two large cases, one red, one black, and his backpack, I spot Mitch and his mom on the other side of the carousel. They aren't looking at me or at each other. I stare, unafraid. They seem farther apart from each other than I am from them, a world apart. So much wasted space between their two bodies. And right then, I want to yell it and I might have, I'm not sure, it felt as if I did, but I'm almost certain I kept this all in my head: *You! Lady over there? You with the son? Listen to me! You're a fool, lady, a blind ignorant fool, and you don't deserve this boy. You do not deserve to keep your boy!!*

My hand is over my mouth.

God forgive me if sometimes I think in megaphone, and if for the rest of my life every mother with a son will be the focus of my scrutiny, and every son with a mother the object of my protectiveness.

Parker's two big cases are on my trolley, the ones I'd bought with him and packed together with him, Samsonites that are full of all those things I'd picked out and bought with him. *"Oh, my gosh, honey, okay, this shirt has 'Babe Magnet' written all over it." "Yeah?" "Seriously, yeah. Great color. Look what it does to your eyes!" "You're serious?" "Trust me. Wear it to the first dance, promise?"* I spread my fingers out on the ribbed fabric surface of the red suitcase. My hands look ancient; I feel ancient. Then I happen to meet eyes with Mitch, who manages to smile, if just with half his mouth. His hair is matted but soft and touchable, his shoulders boney but huggable, and he has a sixteen-year-old's case of pimples, but features that are beautiful, the eyes so painfully alive. His mom walks several steps ahead looking away from her boy, snarling at someone inside her cell phone, "Never again, got that? Never again a seat *right next to him.*" Mitch turns, barely smiling at me, half-dragging his sweatshirt on the floor.

A nice woman in Idaho had gone to Parker's apartment and packed all he'd had in his room. Late one night, we'd sat on someone's living room floor, Randall and I, sifting through those things: his journals and class notes (his handwriting), his wallet, a Post-It with "remember to call Kevin"—simple, chest-crushing tidbits. A bitter, obliterating treasure hunt. His laminated student ID with its unwitting, wide-open smile. I'd clasped it ferociously to my heart.

Now we're in a taxi van driving from the airport over Bavarian farm-land into downtown Munich. Holding Dalton's hand on one side and Luc's on the other, and seeing Randall holding Claire's, I submerse my head again in the velvet world of thought.

> *I'm done with laundry. The dryer stops. I push the window wide open, drawing one long gulp—stunning, enlivening—into my lungs. A few flakes, defectors, flutter through my window, bending gently toward me, landing intact on my sleeves like iced insects. For a moment they quiver before turning to crystalline droplets. And with the next, deep breath, I open up, singing Gershwin's "Summertime."*

Now it's uncomfortably hot and I'm standing on the banks of an Idaho irrigation canal. It's Monday mid-afternoon, July 23, but more than hot, this place feels on fire, spitting and spluttering in the flames of my mind. I'm speechless, staring at a simple, scrub-oak lined canal maybe fifteen feet wide with its sleepy current, another canal feeding into this one, narrower, with a brown and white speckled cow dipping her muzzle into the smooth green glassiness of water. And between the two canals, a narrow single-lane bridge just the length of one car, with old dented metal guardrails on each side. University officials are here with the Bradford family, trying to help us piece together what happened the Thursday evening before, since they know the local news got it wrong, but no one's tried yet to contact the twenty or so students who were eyewitnesses, who were there to watch my son's struggle for life. So we're all pacing aimlessly. Here, I'm being told, is maybe where they first went in. And here, where they probably stood in waist-deep water. Here is where we're pretty sure they got pulled into the vortex under the bridge. And Melissa, right here by this bush and these pebbles, here's where the paramedics couldn't get a heartbeat.

The men are patient and solicitous, and I am politely grateful to them, but they have no idea on earth what kind of inferno rages in my head, how loudly I am conversing with heaven. The heat pounds on my back and shoulders, I'm hiding my whole face with both hands, hiding my head from distractions, from what human voices are saying, from anything that keeps me from hearing Parker's voice which is responding to my questions matter-of-factly. In sound scraps that drop in my mind like a trail of bread crumbs, but which expand, explaining volumes . . .

Norway, and now four-year-old Parker is calling for me from the next room. I know my son's voice. My head is low over this pile of laundry as is my own singing to myself. It is on the final note that an entire slab of ice dislodges itself from our roof, pitching itself head-first past my window and into the white netherworld.

Someone slams the van hatch.

We've arrived at our Munich apartment building and make our jet-lagged, funereal way up the hulking black and burgundy entry staircase to our place on the second floor. Hibernation is all I crave, long, silent, 20,000 leagues-under-anything hibernation. But before we round the corner, we hear the shrill sounds of power tools, the whacking of hammers, men's laughter. It's the workmen there already at 8:00 a.m. I've forgotten that three months ago when the universe was intact, when we'd found this apartment with its empty room intended as a kitchen (a typical feature in Europe), I'd scheduled them to begin installing a kitchen on this very day. This day was supposed to be a joy-suffused day, when I'd looked forward to it out of that life from before. The first day of all of our new lives, of Our New Life.

Behind us lie our people, those who'd gathered to grieve with us, the folks who'd made that funeral happen, who know Parker and aren't afraid to speak his name or to keep speaking of him. Behind is all that is solid and smooth, like the fresh dark soil over a grave surrounded with brilliant flowers only then beginning to wilt. Further behind us lies the Paris life—intact and innocent—that included Parker, a life that was so far from a tragic irrigation canal in Idaho. Behind us is *Before*.

Before us now lie, in tall stacks in this old Munich apartment building entryway, the makings of a kitchen. Inside these unfamiliar front doors, a Bavarian installation crew hammers, drills, and bolts us to this new planet. We fidget with the key, and open the double doors to a place the children, weary from the terrible emotional voyage, have never seen before. In one step, we will enter the sharply disconnected world of *After*.

Speechless, we drag our suitcases across the threshold of Widenmayerstrasse 44, an address we will later come to refer to as "The Monastery." This is fitting, given that Munich itself was founded by monks, or *Mönchen*, as they say in German. Entering that old apartment is as close to entering the stark world of monasticism as most non-monks ever get.

"I think I see an element of grace in this," my mother had whispered that Saturday morning of July 21 as she and others had watched us shuffle back into the room to take our final farewells from Parker before life support was to be turned off. "This is all happening just as they leave Paris for a new life in Munich," she'd added. "No haunting reminders of Parker everywhere they turn. None of those painful memories that point to his absence. They can start all over."

My mom, normally so on-the-money, was just that once understandably and utterly off-the-mark.

As are we.

Having never moved to this particular land—not Germany, but the strange and barren continent of grief—we had no idea that it's post-funeral when grief really, truly, exponentially sinks its teeth in. And it was going to sink its teeth in just as we were heading for a world of polite but oblivious strangers. After the blow torch gush of spirit and of communal mourning, after all that dynamite funeral comfort, friends disperse and their lives resume their routines, everyone else's universe trundles right back on the old usual tracks. At that same moment is when the reality of the permanence of loss settles down on the survivor's quiet household, and with that, a leaden emptiness threatens to fill up the world.

Munich, to clarify, is far from *leaden* and worlds from *empty*. Indeed, it's a postcard, without question a lovely, livable town. The people, too, are lovely, lovable. On top of that, we'd been optimistic about moving there, even after our long and ardent love affair with Paris. Before life split into Before and After, Randall and I in many ways felt like Germans at heart. Even with all that language and cultural background, though, we hadn't overtly lobbied for a job in Munich; Munich was plopped in our laps. Thus plopped, we agreed God's fingerprints were all over it.

Then in the very split second of moving, disaster struck, and what we hadn't known then is that disaster calls for regrouping, reorienting, and rebuilding. It calls for people, *your people*, and even a small handful of them will do. You need people with eyes that look into, not merely *at* or *past*, you; eyes that see your present stillness not as aloofness or faithlessness or bitterness, but as what it is: shock, disbelief, loneliness, and maybe a swelling understanding, even reverence. You need people who require neither small talk nor big talk, nor any kind of talk at all for that matter, to understand when you can't talk at all or when you crave talking all night. You need people who know and recite the old stories of who you were, who will help you make sense of the story that has gashed wide your soul, people who will stay with you while you agonize over whatever story must fill the blank pages ahead. All of this hushed storytelling or this speaking silence you need to be able to share while you shed tears and stack stones, rebuilding.

Munich, though neither leaden nor empty, was, by no fault of its own, only full of strangers. It was full of people who had not known us all those years when we were buoyant, energetic, singing at farm weddings, or biking around our Nordic island, horseback-riding with little French school friends in Versailles, globetrotting for work, negotiating *barnehage* or *maternelle* or bureaucracy or house renovations, faking accents to lost tourists, dancing with drummers at the Fête de la Musique. And no one knew us from two weeks earlier when we stood broken at the side of a grave of a beautiful boy named Parker.

Strangers, in their effort to no longer be strangers, ask questions. Harmless people, mothers at bus stops, shop owners behind cash registers, old couples walking dogs, jaunty mail deliverers, genteel neighbors, they all ask typical and supposedly harmless questions. "Are these *all* your children?" and "Do anything special during *your* summer vacation?" were such hurtful questions, they cut off blood flow to my head and ripped off my wits and emotional armor right there in front of the Bäckerei. So I grew anti-social, panicky, felt geriatric and at the same time jittery with fear at the mere thought of doing something as simple as walking one block to the local grocer to buy a dozen eggs. Or taking my two youngest to the local park . . .

A young German mother is pushing her toddler in a swing next to the play structure where Dalton and Luc are letting off steam after school. Offhandedly, she asks if I have other children.

"Yes," I say, "Two."

"Younger? Older? Where are they?" she asks, pushing her blonde son by the soles of his shoes, squealing as she tickles his stomach each time the arch of the swing rushes him, laughing, to her arms. I am silently tallying how many hours and days and even months on end I had done the same with my tow-headed toddler Parker.

"One is sixteen, a daughter," I say, "And—" my blood heats up, "nine weeks ago I buried my firstborn, a gorgeous son, who was exactly eighteen years and five months old to the day."

A fraction of a second passes as I look right into this stranger's eyes. I am searching, holding my breath, hoping. She keeps pushing her little boy, then shakes her head, as if to rattle its contents, blowing a puff of air to lift the bangs off her forehead. Not missing a beat, she sighs lightly, "Well, thank heavens you have three others."

I could never return to that park.

The next month I'm sitting in a pediatrician's examination room.

Eleven-year-old Dalton has contracted a bad chest cold he just can't shake, and a starched-smock doctor I've known for twelve minutes takes notes as I recite Dalton's medical profile. I would like antibiotics. Frau Doktor would like a complete history. Dalton would like to get out of there. Sitting stripped to his underwear on the gray examination table, he appears disconnected from our conversation, which is in German, a language I incorrectly presume Dalton cannot yet understand.

"You know, Frau Bradford," she places her pen flat on her clipboard, "this boy seems depressed."

"Depressed?" I feign nonchalance. "Hmmm. You think? Well, maybe he *looks* sad." I act like I'm studying him. He does indeed look very sad. Mournful, even.

Weakly pulling at a string dangling from the leg of his underwear, he coughs that foamy, upholstered kind of cough, wiping his nose with the back of his hand. Frau Doktor's Kleenex reflex is snappy.

"And the reasons your son would be sad . . . ?" she asks, extending him a tissue. She then poises her pen to make the list: "I suppose your recent move from France? The new school? Losing friends?"

"Actually . . . those aren't the reasons," I say. "Well . . . except maybe the last one."

I sense where this is going, and I'm hoping I can escape without entering the holiest of all my holies and maybe breaking down. That would be bad, breaking down in front of my sad, stripped-down son, in front of this woman who peers at us like lab rats, clipboard and pen in hand.

I search for Dalton's eyes. They are the same eyes, peeled wide open with pain, during those very last minutes—just three and a half months earlier—in an Idaho ICU. Under this long, hot moment boils up in me a visceral craving to go back. I want to flee from this moment, to escape this language with its pointy hospital corners, devoid of condolence, barren. Childless.

Oh dearest Lord, I want to be back where we were all together. Take me back.

"Frau Bradford . . . ?" She clicks her pen and raises her eyebrows.

I adjust myself in my chair, fold my hands in my lap, breathe deeply. Then, like some reporter from the nightly news, I orate: "On July 19, in a canal on farmland in the western United States, there was a water activity organized by a group of university students, among whom was our oldest, our eighteen-year-old son. That night, he and another student were sucked up stream and pinned in a hidden undertow. Twice, my son got out. Twice he went back in trying to save the other boy. The other boy survived. But my son . . . "

I finish. The woman tucks her pen in her breast pocket. And with all the tenderness of a tongue depressor, says: "Ach, such strokes of fate. You had best not think about it. Best get on with your life."

She needn't offer me any tissue since I am drier than the cinders I feel reduced to.

We're at church. This new, tiny congregation of well-meaning strangers is struggling to know what to do with us. I know this because from where our family sits in a sodden clump in the back pew I watch as eyes flit from looking into ours. Smiles strain. Shoulders turn away to some sudden, nervous preoccupation. And behind my stock-still façade echo all the words I crave hearing—honest ones, simple ones like, "I know what happened, and I'm sorry." Sunday after Sunday, silence swells.

My gut winds itself into a knot as thick and bristly as ocean-liner rope. Is wanting someone to ache with me presumptuous? Is quietly weeping through the sacrament hymn ill-placed? Is my grief selfish? Self-indulgent? Self-pitying?

The knot groans.

And then one day in late autumn, a member of our church who hadn't spoken to us until that moment strides up to me, plants one hand on my shoulder, and with the other hand pumps mine, exclaiming, "Smile! It's such a *great day* to be alive!"

My scripture pages, the Book of Job, to be exact, still bear the little warped pockmarks from the tears I shed as I took refuge in our car.

Lars is straight from the cast of *The Sound of Music*: blonde, blue-eyed, with a bank of snow white teeth, as quick and light on his feet as a Bavarian leprechaun, perfectly proportioned, and perhaps thirty-one. Or nineteen. Ageless. He's murmuring along with Celine Dion (his German accent does wonders for her English), who's piped into the salon where I've arrived for a long-overdue trim. Lars tries to make small talk while admiring our mirrored reflection: me stiff and old in the chair, him elfin and nimble on his toes. I sense under my lips a polite smile trying to emerge from hibernation—I've not been able to smile since July, months ago—but I just don't have that kind of strength.

Lars hums and sections off hair, cooing, crooning, and combing. But I'm so clogged with anguish I sit frozen, fearing what will come out of my mouth if I open it. My mind scampers ahead, frenzied, trying to plot escape routes around the inevitable question about family and children. At the rate Lars is talking, we'll hit that question head on before he takes his first snip.

"Life's short," he says, stretching smooth a swath of my hair, scissors held at attention. "There's never enough time to love the people who matter the most to us."

My scampering panic stops like I've pinned its tail under my boot. My throat constricts.

"You're right, Lars,"—and where this came from, I'll never know—"I buried my oldest son four months ago today."

Scissors in his right hand frozen, length of my hair held taut in the left hand, neck craned forward and eyes narrowing, he asks,

"Wha-what . . . ?!"

I repeat myself, whispering. But it costs me my composure.

Lars drops hair, scissors, and both his arms, hangs his head in a slow side-to-side shake, turns from the mirror to me, tears welling up in his eyes, and with a scarcely audible groan, bends toward me to wrap my shoulders in a hug. "Oh, no, no. I am so sorry, *so sorry* . . . "

Not everyone can be a Lars. And because he was just so unusual and I was so vulnerable, I went back to him again and again, even when my hair didn't need a trim.

One day late in the spring, I found myself reclining in his salon chair, my hair a wad of suds, Lars working the scalp, when he asked me something truly bizarre, even inconceivable. "So, if you're a singer," he said, "why have you never sung anything for me?"

"Sung anything?" I hadn't been able to sing for anyone since Parker's funeral. "Like . . . *a song?*"

"A song, yes. Why not? You love to sing." He finished sudsing. "I want you to sing for me."

I closed my eyes and let Lars rinse warm water through my hair. As was always the case when I allowed myself to go a quarter inch beneath the surface in my thoughts, my mind went first to a dry, hot July and an ominous canal in Idaho. Behind my eyelids I felt the swift seep of tears.

"And . . . where should I sing? For you?" I held my eyes closed while salty memories drizzled down my temples and into the water spraying my hair. The soothing gush of Lars's rinse melted every taut, anxious, self-protective, and throbbing boundary of my spirit, and I was taken back to a warm laundry room where I was watching my own hands folding my children's clothing. Those small empty limbs of cotton tights. Those flattened undershirts. My hands stroking their fibers. Their feathery voices in the next room. And then my mind's eye looked out a window on the soft soundproofing of tumbling, eternal, harmless and unharmed Norwegian snow.

"Where you should sing? Well, where else?" Lars laughed once. "*Here,* of course. And now."

I sputtered lightly, a tactic that should have deflected his request. But he didn't let this one go. He kept rinsing, now more slowly, tenderly, and gently stroked the last suds from my hairline. In my mind, I opened the small window, the one that looked out onto the gorge padded with a white comforter bolted in place with quiet, wise pines. I watched my hand open up that window. I felt my mouth open slowly, taking in the brisk Norwegian air, as warm water flushed a world of anguish out of my head and down the salon drain.

ENDNOTES

1. "Anne Morrow Lindbergh: The First Days of Grief Are not the Worst," *Conso-loatio*, last modified May 1, 2005, http://www.consolatio.com/2005/05/the_first_days_.html

21

OKTOBERFEST

Trumpets squeal and blare through the flat blue autumn sky above Marienplatz. Tubas honk and boom in between the raucous amusement park rides on Maria Theresien Wiese. Accordions wail and wheeze on every corner of Viktualienmarkt, where men dressed in lederhosen, loden hats, and woolen knee stockings are hugging two-liter steins in their portly arms.

Beside them are the bearded cross-dressers wearing wigs of yellow yarn braids, lipsticked circles on their cheeks, their chest hair prickling out of the plunging necklines of their embroidered dirndls. Women dodge around them, their cleavages climbing to clavicles, doughy décoltés sloshing out of white lacy blouses, frilly anklets spilling out of hiking boots. Aprons cinch in corseted waistlines, petticoats pouf under gathered skirts, and everyone parades with pretzels the size of life rafts, beers the size of birdbaths, and taut pink or gray sausages the size of airline neck pillows. Yodeling, hollering, swaying, and puking, broad oom-pah-pah-ing. And over there, a man in a hunter's hat with an enormous feather, his knickers bunched awkwardly, is relieving himself in the shrubbery.

Welcome to Brueghel meets Hieronymus Bosch, only earthier than the first and more surreal than the second. *Willkommen zum Oktoberfest.*

The assault made us shrink shortly after the first time it met us upon our arrival in Munich, our spirits draped as they were then with death.

By retreating, I was able to enter right into grief, heart first. Grief, its own country and more foreign to me than was Munich, became my primary place of residence. This land of major loss was uncharted terrain, a land with its own language of silence. It was something more than a country, it was its own planet with its own air pressure and gravitational pull. In fact, and this is odd, for many months I had the sensation of being dressed in a spacesuit—present in this world, but insulated, inaccessible, breathing another consistency of air, hearing things through a filter, my voice muffled within the helmet of my thoughts, never comprehended by outsiders.

For this new moon of loss I found my beloved family and myself living on, I did instinctively what I had done in other unfamiliar geographies—Austria, Hong Kong, Norway, France—I pulled out the maps and guidebooks, went to the resident experts and scholars, and did serious research. Throughout that first year and well into the second year living in Munich, I followed a daily ritual. Highly functional and engaged throughout our morning routine, I got Randall and the children out the door for work and for school. Then I retreated into my cave of written words for most of the day. I sat in total quiet, my "maps and guidebooks" to the land of grief surrounding me on my bare wooden living room floor. Cross-legged, encircled by a ring of sometimes twenty books laid open at once, I took copious notes. I read the entire Bible cover to cover, a big stack of professional journals on parental grief, the entire *Book of Mormon* and ancillary scripture, a couple of French novels, numerous German lyrics, a Norwegian memoir. I collected discourses from the greatest spiritual leaders past and present. I scoured my Riverside Shakespeare. I delved into several accounts of Mormon pioneers, Holocaust survivors, 9/11 survivors, tsunami survivors, avalanche survivors, POW survivors, cancer survivors. And I laid out on the old parquet all of Parker's own words captured in the many journals he'd kept his whole life, plus his poetry, school essays, lyrics, and letters, all downloaded from his laptop.

Why research grief in response to grief? There were several reasons, but the most compelling for me was community. The nomadic lifestyle, with all of its pluses has one glaring lacuna: continuity. You are again and again ripped up, ripped out, and replanted amid strangers. There is little if any continuous community. Now, as never before in our life, our family needed people who had more than a vague inkling of our *story* ("We heard they just lost their son") and more than a cursory sense of our *history* ("They are a really close family who's moved a lot and has just lost their son").

What we needed were people who *were* our history. We needed those whose common narrative included Parker.

That wasn't going to be possible in Germany. But I reasoned that I could at least find people whose common narrative was about traumatic loss. I needed evidence that those exiled in the land of grief were able to survive and even (this fascinated but confounded me) survive *well*.

Survive well? This was going to take a lot of convincing because I was struggling just to keep vertical. Grief assaults both mind and body, and because it does, it becomes an important part of your lifelong medical record. Science has long recognized the dangers of major loss: it disturbs eating patterns (Randall dropped more than thirty pounds in less than two months), upturns sleeping patterns (we had to temporarily resort to medication in order get any rest after weeks of sleep deprivation), compromises circulation and respiratory patterns (for months our hearts palpitated and sometimes skittered to a brief stop altogether; to be safe we underwent EKGs), and it can overwhelm the physical system so that the simplest tasks (walking in a park, climbing stairs, sitting, staring) are exhausting. It can overwhelm the mental system so that you begin to seriously wonder, as I started to, if you have had a stroke. "Now, um, how did I used to put toothpaste on this toothbrush?" and, "Okay, let's see: Keys. Ignition. Keys *in* ignition. Turn. Depress accelerator. Wait. Which little stick is the blinker?"

Randall and I wandered, when we could, throughout Munich's English Gardens trying to stay far from the assailing ooom-pah-pahs of Oktoberfest. Deeper in the park, we sat on its many benches that bore the loving personalized directory plaques: "*Für Mutti, zum 50en Geburtstag,*" "*Helmuth und Brunhilde, Ewige Liebe.*" We sat on them, most of the time feeling unalterably old, limp, and lined in lead, sandblasted down to our dendrites.

One day, I envisioned a similar bench for Parker. Randall and I found our way to the office of the one and only gentleman whose job it is to oversee the installation and maintenance of such benches. Herr Barthlemes was lanky in his worn, beige, corduroy trousers and heavy rubberized walking shoes, his boney shoulders poking from under his sweater like the angles of a metal clothes hanger. As we walked the garden, Randall and I on either side of this man, talking quietly about where to place a bench for our son, Barthlemes wrapped and tucked a frayed, plaid shawl in orange and mustard around his neck.

"Normally," Herr Barthelmes explained, as we walked slowly along the pathway that encircles a big open field in the garden's heart, "we only put the dedication plaques on the backs of these green benches." He pointed to six benches placed along the path we were walking.

"And if we understood correctly," Randall said, "we have to choose a green bench that's already standing in the garden, is that right?"

"Right," the gentleman nodded. I thought then that if he spoke English he might make a good Jimmy Stewart.

"But . . . what if we're thinking of a place other than where these green benches already stand?" I asked. I had thought of something maybe close to water, even next to the small canal-like river that runs through the park.

"It depends on when you want this done, Frau Bradford. You mentioned February 20th? Is this your son's birthday? You want to surprise him?" Barthlemes smiled softly and winked.

Randall and I looked at each other. We all kept strolling.

"Herr Barthlemes, that's our son's birthday, you're right. But it won't be a surprise for him."

The trees were dropping leaves—golden, burnt red, even some bright green ones—as I listened to my husband explain to this tall stranger the story of our boy.

When Randall was done explaining, Herr Barthlemes stopped in his tracks. I looked at him. His face was different from how it had looked two minutes earlier. Melted. His eyes seemed larger.

"*Herr Bradford, das ist ja doch eine ganz andere Geschichte.*"

Mr. Bradford, that's a whole different story.

By February 20th, Herr "Jimmy Stewart" Barthlemes, whom I never again saw and whom I have never thanked in person, had hand-made a brown bench, the *etwas anderes*, or *something different* he had told us he was going to do for our son. He had affixed our inscribed bronze plaque, had had the whole thing weatherproofed, and had installed it in the place he thought, after hearing of Parker's story, was ideal, next to a tributary of Munich's Isar river, where two canals meet and rush under a bridge.

In spite of what we thought would happen in that first brutal year, we did not in fact die in our sleep. And, just as surprising, we did not in fact move back to Paris. We did, though, return there frequently. There were memorials and conferences where we heard our son's name spoken candidly but with the softest center of longing, and where we, too, were invited to speak of him. Friends took us into their homes, shop owners wept when they heard, neighbors embraced us in the street, their eyes wounded like ours.

The first time we flew back to Paris after Parker's accident, we were still unsettled as to whether we would remain in Munich and try to make it some kind of home, or if we would immediately return "home" to Paris for good. I told God I needed to be told in boldfaced, italicized, capitalized letters that we should *not* return to Paris, if Munich was where we, in God's wisdom, should be. I buckled my Air France seat belt and waited for His answer, having no idea He really did the boldfaced-italicized-capitalized signs so well and even, if the situation called for it, blinking neon. But then, He *is* God.

The very instant our plane touched the tarmac at Charles de Gaulle airport, the crew announced that all luggage handlers were on strike. I smirked and rolled my eyes to the heavens. *Some pesky strike? A sign? This is boldface?*

The entire plane was unceremoniously disemboweled of everyone's suitcases right there on the ground as the rain started falling (of course), and we had to carry all our pieces (we were hauling large rolled posters and a dozen framed pictures for the memorial plus seven suitcases) up and down escalators, which were, expressly on that evening (of course), out-of-order. *Quirky escalators? Still, not really enough to . . . Those are some impressive italics, though.*

Our rental car broke down thirty minutes into our drive in bumper-to-bumper traffic in one of the seediest neighborhoods of Paris, so I was flagging down taxis to try to shuttle Claire, Dalton, and Luc all over the city where they were scheduled to stay with three best friends and attend their former schools the next morning. I remember how Randall, his face drawn and grayish and his expression calm but creased with fatigue, was on his cell phone, pleading with the rental car personnel, who were unmoved by our quaint crisis, and who, of course, kept him on hold and then lost his call twice, then told him to call another number, then finally told him he'd have to wait at least an hour for any help to come. This meant leaving Randall sitting alone on a lightless, seamy curbside with our big pile of valuables in the dark. I thought, *He'll be stabbed and robbed. Okay, Father in Heaven, ALL CAPS.*

I left Randall there at his insistence. And I ordered the driver of the taxi I'd hailed to drive me with my children to three corners of town, where I would hand off each child to a different family. I would pay him a flat fee up front, I said, if he'd just get us there safely, and in record time. It was getting late, and by now, the families had already been waiting for us for over two hours longer than planned. Anxious, tired, and reining in the mounting anger I felt toward my beloved Paris, I put a bill in the driver's hand, made sure all the kids and all their bags were snugly in place, and we were off to battle rush-hour traffic from one side of town to, literally, the other. I rested my aching head on the window of the smelly taxi as the driver honked and cursed his way through aggressive traffic. *Boldface. Italics. ALL CAPS. Got it.*

Two hours, several near-accidents, and a taxi driver who disappeared with our prepayment and Luc's overnight bag later, I was seeing neon. Poor, exhausted, and confused spindle-of-a-kid Luc curled into a knot of limbs and tears on Dalton's friend's living room couch and, giving up on ever getting to his own friend's apartment, just slept there, one of Parker's sweatshirts pulled tightly over his head.

As Randall and I finally drifted off to sleep at another friend's home, I was on my side facing away from Randall, teary from exhaustion and a residual anxiety, but more from those danged boldfaced, italicized, capitalized, and now blinking neon signs. (Wait. Has God added sirens, too?) How, in our years here, had I never noticed that Paris had such sharp claws? I was a different person now, I knew it: depleted, skinless, with nothing in me to fight, clawless as a worm. I knew in my bones I no longer had the physical stamina to wrestle with this city. And Lord, how I needed sleep.

Somewhere in those half-sleeping, half-waking hours that immediately followed, all the lights went on in my inner dream cinema. Parker was there.

I wrote in my dream journal:

> He was standing, smiling, and fully in his element in the center of a crescent shape of five people: two figures to his left, two to his right. He wore a light blue and white horizontally stripped rugby shirt with a collar and short sleeves, faded jeans, and sandals. Both his hands were in his pockets and his head was turned to look intently at the person to his left. That person, carrying some stacked books in her arms and dressed conservatively, was talking quietly to him. The setting was campus-like, with a backdrop of brilliant, glimmering green trees, and there was a neoclassical building like a specific one I knew from my own alma mater's campus. Behind this crescent of figures, there were just a few other figures, all in their

late teens or early twenties, crossing behind Parker and going up and down these steps into the neoclassical building.

Again, Parker was calm, but in no way indifferent, in fact, he was nodding lightly and seemed eagerly engaged. It was clear to me that he was learning something from whatever the young woman to his left was explaining. She was teaching him something, this I somehow intuitively understood, as he was new there, and was being introduced to these people, to their conversation, and to their ways.

As well as looking wholesome and healthy, he was radiant, cheerful. There were no multiple and severe head wounds, no swollen eyes, no bruises, no protruding contusion over the left ear, no tubes, no corpselike pastiness. Just Parker among all his friends, as natural as the air. Parker as he'd always been, but visibly serene.

As I marveled at all the beauty and tried to get closer to look at him and perhaps get his attention and interrupt (why was I not able to run to him, to get closer faster?), he turned his head slightly from the young woman still engaging him in conversation at his left. He looked right at me. It was a knowing, intimate glance, and it lasted perhaps five seconds. He looked at me and said nothing, my heart startled, and I understood these ideas: "This is how it is, Mom. This is where I am. I am learning. I am with my people. You have done with me what you did with the other kids tonight: You've handed me into someone else's care to be schooled further."

And then he turned his head back to his new friends—ah, my Parker; your friends always got more of your time than I did, even in death—and the lights dimmed and the picture washed away.

Similarly, each of us in our family was slowly encircled by friends, too. Early on and every month or two, and although I feared what their arrival might elicit, we had old friends or family members walk through the big double doors of our place, cracking open our monastery.

Randall, though initially overwhelmed by pain and loneliness, found support and tenderness at work. Everyone there had been, to one degree or another, touched by Parker's accident. Luc spoke from the first day in class about his brother, which allowed his friends and teachers to do the same. Claire began making friends at school and at church, and though she chose to never once speak of her brother (she was sure speaking would trivialize him or what had happened, and was adamant that no one could ever understand her loss), these strangers rallied and showed her genuine love. And Dalton followed his sister's example. For over two years he never mentioned Parker outside of our walls.

It's a spring afternoon in 2009, nearly two years following Parker's death, and the counselor at our children's school in Munich has invited a short list of students and faculty, whom Dalton has hand-selected, to gather in an empty upper floor room during an extended recess and lunch period. The whole building will be empty during that hour, the counselor's assured us, so that we can count on no disturbances whatsoever. We'll need this time. Dalton's been preparing for many months for this moment.

"Now, all of you've been invited here specifically by Dalton," the counselor begins after we're all settled. There are about a dozen girls and boys sitting to my left and my right in a circle, twelve- and thirteen-year-olds all of them. Dalton's favorite teacher, his English professor, is sitting directly across from me, and Randall is to my immediate right. The four chairs to my left separate me from Dalton.

"He's invited you," the counselor continues, "because he has something he wants to share and he trusts you. What we will discuss today stays here, unless Dalton invites any of you to share this information further. Is that good with you, Dalton?"

He nods.

"Good with everyone else?"

Everyone else nods. I'm focused on the middle of the circle where we've set Parker's djembe, his treasured African drum.

"I wonder," says the counselor, "if you all could just note on this slip of paper I've given you something that you've lost. It can be something intangible or it can be a home or a person, anything. But I want this to be a thing which loss has really hurt you. Maybe it still hurts you. Just write it down and then you can place your paper on top of here."

She points to Parker's drum.

I watch as these kids and their teachers soften, and a spirit of thoughtfulness and sincerity seeps around the circle. I also watch Dalton carefully. He had been sleepless and cramped on the floor of the bathroom all night.

"I'm not sure I can do this, Mom," he'd said as I'd wiped his forehead with a cool washcloth around 3:00 a.m. He was on his side in a quasi fetal position. "What if . . . what if I tell them and . . . "

"And . . . and what?" I asked, running the cloth under cold water again. I squeezed out the excess. I dabbed his face.

"What if I tell them and they just . . . they . . . " He was sweating, holding his stomach.

"They don't do anything? What if they don't care, you mean?" I knew my boy. And I knew this same leaden, justifiable fear. What if I bare my soul to someone and he leans away from, not into, the conversation? What if I expose the enormous hole in my torso and no one sees it, no one feels it?

That's the great fear.

And that is why, for these two full school years, Dalton has made acrobatic contortions at school to avoid any discussion about his family. He's done everything to avoid mentioning his brother. In this new community, everyone asked that thing you always ask when you meet the new student, "So, do you have any brothers or sisters?"

Dalton decided to lie. He had no older brother.

But the deception and the denial were making him ill.

So on a spring day during a noon hour, we're in a schoolroom where the students are writing down and then talking of their various losses: grandparent, aunt, uncle, pet. They write about lost friendships and missed opportunities and forfeited stability because of moving from country to country their whole lives. Some write down a lost possession—their home in another hemisphere, for instance—some write down "lost time."

Not one, however, writes about losing a big brother.

"Thanks, everyone," says the counselor. "Well, you're here today because Dalton has lost something that is extremely valuable to him, more precious than almost anything else in his life." The counselor is no way maudlin, just serious but warm.

"And because Dalton cares so much about this thing he's lost, and because he cares about you, too," she adds, "he wants to share some of that loss with you. Is that good?" She scans the circle. All eyes are fixed, alert. "Okay, Dalton, would you like to share with us?"

I watch my boy—soft, blonde, cautious, eyes like chips of aquamarine—I watch him take a breath. I watch the muscles around his mouth, the place you usually catch the first cracks of breaking apart. I also watch his friend, a small Israeli boy named Itamar, who's sitting at Dalton's elbow, his mop of almost-black hair just brushing into his thick dark lashes, those huge soulful eyes watching Dalton, our Nordic prototype, as he begins to speak slowly, deliberately.

"I want to tell you . . . " Dalton begins as he stretches his fingers out on a gold-brown spiral-bound book he's been holding flat on his lap, "I want to *share with you* someone who is important to me. This," he lifts up the album of Parker to show an enlarged photo of a handsome teenager with a strong chin, a crimson red rugby shirt, and half a grin, "This is my big brother. His name is Parker."

Burning creeps up my face and I look over toward Randall with an impulse to take his hand in mine, but I don't because in the tension of the moment I know the slightest movement could topple things. I wipe my palms discreetly on my pant legs.

The counselor is smiling at Dalton, helping him along. His English teacher is quiet, her eyes large and already rimmed in shine. The boys and girls in the circle, as I quietly look around, are motionless, reverent, even.

"Parker is what I have lost," Dalton adds. He lifts his brows, his mouth is pinching and then shaking a bit, "He passed away in a water accident not so long ago when he was trying to save another student from . . . "

And right then, a sound like a rabbit being injured arises from behind Itamar's dark mop of hair that is now hanging toward his lap, and his delicate shoulders sag under a black and rust-speckled sweatshirt. Dalton stops speaking, and turns toward Itamar. The black-haired boy raises his head. There are already tears dripping down the light olive face, and pain transforms those brown eyes. He's crying openly, like this is his own loss.

Dalton's eyes fill with tears, too, but his eyebrows are raised. These are tears of surprise. But more than that, they're tears of relief and joy, the look you'd see on someone who'd slaved day and night for weeks but still never thought he'd deserve to pass the big final exam, but got—*holy cow!*—the highest score in the class. Surprise, relief, joy. Then Dalton touches Itamar's shoulder, as if comforting *him*, while Itamar continues to wipe the flow of tears with his grubby, oversized sleeve.

"I want you to know about what happened to Parker," Dalton says, "because he's a great brother and he's so important to me."

While the rest of the world outside our building grows more and more quiet (I wonder what's happened with the afternoon recess and all the children's laughter and screaming from moments earlier), Dalton begins narrating with a stronger voice.

He sits straight and tells a bit about the pages of the album, holding each up and turning the book so everyone in the room can see: Parker holding his arms around his two younger brothers at basketball and volleyball championships;

Parker with arms around his family at high school graduation;

Parker hiking with his family;

On family vacations;

Teaching Dalton and Luc to bike or swim;

Hanging out and watching movies with Claire and his brothers;

Going to church;

Eating his favorite food, *ice cream*;

Laughing in the sunshine and goofing around beneath starlight;

Pictures of a real live person, a brother, a friend, an actual human being. A reality.

The students are first speechless, and two girls to my right are wiping under their eyes. Everyone—every last person, I note—is leaning into the conversation, reaching their attention toward this story, asking to hold the book themselves if Dalton doesn't mind. Could they just see—*his name's* Parker, *right?*—if they could see *Parker*. If Dalton could just hand them all his pictures of this real person, this brother named Parker.

At this point, the room on that second floor of the school building is rather quiet except for some whispering and the sound of Itamar blowing his nose as Dalton begins turning pages and narrating his photo album. Students start to chat softly, two and two, as they pass the Parker book around the circle. I keep my eye on Dalton, whose entire posture has changed from closed and shadowed to open and gleaming. He's pointing to the page with a shot of Parker playing a drum solo in his senior class talent show at his school in Paris: "Of everything Parker did," Dalton's smiling now, "basketball, volleyball, swimming, hanging out with all his friends, even eating ice cream . . . I think what he loved the most was drumming. That's why we brought his drum today."

Right then, from directly beneath our feet and as if on cue, someone begins playing a drum set. An explosive, vibrating drum riff that goes and goes and goes. It startles Dalton, the English teacher shoots me a glance, I reach to squeeze Randall's hand, two of the boys look at the floor then all around the walls and then back at each other, perplexed but oblivious. And Itamar holds the tissue at his nose.

I softly shake my head. Randall grins. These kinds of coincidences aren't entirely new to us anymore.

We listen for several more minutes while Dalton tells all he can about his brother, and while some stranger wielding drum sticks tears it up under our feet.

The kids need to return to class, the tin of cookies we've shared is down to crumbs, light is shining through the windows, there are no more tears, and the invisible drummer retreats to whatever mysterious place he'd come from.

But his silent rhythm follows us all the way home and beyond.

Dalton became a new boy thanks, to a great measure, to that one liberating and loving moment.

Before we could prepare ourselves for it, it was October yet again, the beginning of the third cycle. Tubas and trumpets and accordions, pretzels and dirndls and beer steins, the whole oom-pah-pah onslaught. This time around, though, we didn't hunker in our cave. We'd evolved. From exiled citizens of a distant planet called grief, we'd grown into people inhabiting this planet and dressed not in protective astronaut suits, but in a whole new layer of tender, breathing skin.

This was not "healing." It was transformation, and did not simply happen with the passage of time. It was the result of great isometric effort, the synergistic gathering of friends, old and new, and—how else could I say this?—ministrations of Parker himself. We'd worked our way to a place where we could function with somewhat thinner protective armor, even when walking right into Munich's *Weis'n*, the amusement park at the heart of Oktoberfest. The boys even tested a ride or two. We never stopped considering ourselves a family of six—we knew it and we will always know it—but one of us had "gone on" as we trained ourselves to say to strangers who asked, the way another one of us, our Claire, had "gone on to university."

And of course, Ceiling Talk night or morning with Randall was always first about Parker. We continued to cry and feel pain about his physical absence—I had cried daily for nineteen months straight, in fact, and marked on my calendar the first time I made a full twenty-four hours without tears. There were also grief attacks that grabbed us like a hidden undercurrent in an otherwise calm canal, sucking us under, and threatening to keep us in the vortex for too long. But we pulled each other out. Or something or someone else always pulled us out. Maybe Parker pulled us out.

We noted an essential change happening in us both individually and as a family. We noted, to use another analogy, that grief, once a boulder under which we were pinned and scarcely breathing, shrank in size. As it shrank in size, we could pull our crushed torsos out from under it until we could carry it in our arms. Then we could carry it in our hands because we noticed it had shrunk just a bit in weight. Then we could place its heaviness in our pockets for a while. It was there, we felt it all of the time, but our hands and hearts were freer to be of use to those around us.

Perhaps this is where the paradox revealed itself. As my hands were freer to be of use to others (I volunteered at school, sang more, directed some programs, took local and regional positions in our church), the weight was lifted. It was omnipresent for us all, and known to mostly us alone, but we could finger the stone of grief, could touch its rough or slick or cold or comforting contours. And in very rare moments we could take it out of that pocket and share it with another person. Every time we did, the stone seemed momentarily lighter.

Randall and I Ceiling Talked about how we were managing our grief, how grateful we were we'd had our stony monastery, how we were growing from it and from cautiously reentering this world, how we were feeling the heat of light and the sweetness and power of music and deep care for people around us, how amazed we were we'd made it this far, how we'd never have been able to have done it without our faith, our family, our wonderful new friends, each other. The boys were gaining friends and fluency in German, Randall's job was stable, I was feeling more and more settled in a life that, despite my fierce resistance to it on the outset, was now buttressed by service, new and old and local and distant friends, and more blessings and more miracles than I will ever be able to account for. The Norwegian table was back in full service. Dalton and I were running partners. All of us could laugh a lot and without the sickly aftertaste of emptiness.

It had taken two painful years, but we now loved Germany, Bavaria, our jogging route along the Isar River and . . .

Shouldn't we just stay in Munich?

Which question (we know this by now) is the prelude to a phone call.

This time Randall was joining a new company, whose regional headquarters were in Geneva. Could we move there?

"No," Randall said into the receiver, "We can't move right now, it's October. The school year's just begun, the boys are just settling in, it would be unwise . . . right . . . I thought you'd understand. But," he eyed me and I gave him the go-ahead nod from my side of the bed, "I'll move. Or at least . . . I'll commute and come home every weekend or so. Get me a hotel room close to the office. Melissa and the kids will finish out the school year and follow in the summer."

It hardly ruffled me. Little ruffled me, I noticed. True tragedy had set a new watermark on the rim of life, and no other challenge seemed to elicit as much as a pulse hop in me. I think I fluffed my pillow after that

phone call, pulled the covers over my shoulder, and Randall and I probably fell asleep mumbling something about what Geneva would be like in
a year. We were no longer falling asleep in tears. Nor were we awakening
to tears. Life felt livable and even promising, and Parker was always close
at hand.

We lived split by a geographical border that year; Randall in a small,
sterile hotel room during the week, and then from Friday to Sunday night
in our Bavarian home. Between us flew several daily text messages and
phone calls, all helpful when the plot thickened as Randall's job grew
from a regional to an international position and city names were flying as
possible sites for those new international headquarters.

Claire, in the meantime, was stable and thriving in her distant college
dormitory. She got my daily phone call. Dalton and Luc got my constant
presence. Parker got my weekly letter, like this one, when, at the end of
that long year, it was whiplash again:

Dear Parker,

*I am typing this before the taxi comes so you're the last conver-
sation I have in this home that I'm sure you led us to, this place
that has been so important for cultivating hope and peace in our
lives. Dalton, Luc, and I will board a plane like so many planes I
boarded with you over so many years, way back from when you
were a newborn and we moved to Hong Kong, to all those transat-
lantic flights from Norway and France. And now, in the span of a
single day, we will land in a new world, not exactly the world we've
been planning for. It's not going to be Geneva after all. But still, a
promising adventure. We've been wondering out loud, what would
Parker think of this? Would Parker approve? Would he enjoy this
moment, the packing up and heading out to something completely
different? Will he enjoy moving with us to Singapore?*

22

GARDEN-JUNGLE CITY-STATE

Some people, primarily those who know the rest of Asia well, call this city nation "Asia Lite." Some others, Singaporeans, mostly, call it the "Red Dot on the Map," pointing to its 224-square-mile size that packs an increasingly hot economic and cultural punch. Or there are those who call it a "Fine City" for the harsh governmental fining system with its numerous draconian controls. In a circular logical twist, those controls serve to make Singapore both Asia Lite (it's diverse and dense but Listerine clean and arguably one of the safest large cities in the world) *and* an irrefutably formidable Red Dot, a place the whole world is keeping its collective eye on.

The first night our family arrived in what was to become our new home, we wandered through the muggy, teeming streets of Chinatown. It's here where Dalton added his own Singapore descriptor to the list. On his left was a Buddhist temple, a few steps farther, a Hindu temple, even farther, a mosque, and finally, a Christian church. From each of these doorways poured people dressed like extras from either a Chinese, Bollywood, Middle Eastern, or a western movie, and a cascade of languages poured out with them. My cinephile son turned to me and said, "This place is like living on a bunch of overlapped movie sets: choreographed chaos."

Dalton wasn't far off. Singapore is crazily diverse, a dégustation menu of much of Asia with a great deal of the West thrown in for padding. Its population of about five million crammed onto a landmass about the size of Chicago speaks English, Chinese, Malay, and Tamil as officially recognized languages, and then there are all the dialects of the above plus all the Western tongues (French, Dutch, German, Swedish, Italian, etc.) spoken by its million-plus expatriate community. Nearly forty percent of the population is made up of expatriates or foreigners. A high percentage of these foreigners are mostly Indian, Sri Lankan, and Indonesian, who are in Singapore for the heavy construction jobs and domestic labor, which they do for slave pay. It is this workforce as much as any other that drives this city-state into the clouds and the economic stratosphere.

Walk just about any given road and you see turbans next to Red Sox baseball caps, headscarves next to Hermès scarves, Punjabi suits next to Chanel suits, ninja abayas alongside Teenage Mutant Ninja Turtle t-shirts. Besides Chinatown there is Arab Street, Little India, Peranakan corners, Indonesian pockets, a Goethe Institute, and an Alliance Française. There are German, Canadian, French, Swiss, and Dutch schools, not to mention the several international schools offering instruction in Chinese and English.

In our neighborhood off of Bukit Timah Road on the outskirts of center city, there are Chinese-speaking Malaysians, Malay-speaking Indians, Tamil-speaking Indonesians, Filipinos, Germans, Canadians, Koreans, Japanese, Mainland Chinese, Irish, Australians, Kiwis, a Texan or two, and some pretty serious looking guys who look like native Singaporeans (although who can say what that is?) but who don't speak at all. They carry machine guns. They're the guards outside the home of Goh Chok Tong, former prime minister of Singapore, who is reported to have said that with all these cultures converging in one tiny place, Singapore is not a nation, but a "society in transition."

Here's an example of what Singapore's multi-ethnicity looks like. When Luc celebrated his twelfth birthday, his twelve friends were like a mini United Nations with Luc as the only fair-haired, light-skinned kid in the bunch. As we made the guest list and I quizzed him about these friends, Luc never once mentioned that one was African or Thai or Indian, that they looked brown, yellow, or any color at all. He did, however, casually mention dietary restrictions: "You'll know who Ali is, Mom. He's got the biggest eyes and is Muslim, so, you know, he doesn't *do* pork." And when I asked Luc after the party to help me write thank-you notes to each gift-giver, Luc didn't describe them racially. Instead, this gift? It was from the kid who is the fastest in the class, and that one was from the funniest, the other one was from the smartest. And this last gift? It was from the one who could do the loudest arm fart.

So maybe not *exactly* like the United Nations.

After our monastic years spent tucked deep in the pleats of the sturdy Bavarian landscape, arriving in the middle of such a diverse, busy, commerce-ravenous lifestyle was an awakening. A jolt. Asia, particularly the Singaporean brand of Asia, meant noise, speed, drive, looking forward, moving upward.

In a matter of hours from touchdown, Randall was packing for his first of back-to-back trips overseeing what was now his area of responsibility: the whole globe minus the United States. The boys' school with a predominantly international/Asian student body was sprawling and state-of-the-art, like a UFO that had landed on the upper lip of the island across the causeway from Malaysia. Church was not a scrappy, seat-of-the-pants handful of mostly locals mixed with a few anomalous non-locals, as we were used to. Here, it was a burgeoning independent 450-plus member assemblage of expatriates. From that community as well as from the international schools dotting the map gushed what felt to us like a fire hose jet flow of activity: monthly charity bazaars, fund-raising events for Tibet (or Laos or the Philippines), book clubs, local and extra-island excursions, multiethnic dinners, playgroups, architectural and historical visits, cultural outings, yoga classes, Chinese classes, Bahasa classes, calligraphy classes, flower arranging classes, photography classes, and more, all arranged by and for the overwhelmingly robust expatriate community.

"Expatriate community." In our eighteen years living abroad I'd never spoken those words. And I'd never been called an "expat," at least not to my face. But, "Here you go, I'm sure you'll love this," Deepti, our beautiful Singaporean/Indian relocation agent said, as she put a big glossy magazine, *Expat Living,* in my hands. "This will be your guide to Singapore." Enough of us "expats" to make a magazine the size of all of Singapore's phone book? I didn't know what to do with this life.

My inclination to retreat into safety and silence I knew already would serve no one, least of all my boys, who were now quickly becoming young men. But I grappled with basic questions: How would I ever come to share our family story, the one with the absent son, with yet another world of total strangers? How could I enter such fast-moving abundance and not grow superficial? How could I be *me* here? Somewhere, in a letter to Parker (it was natural for me to continue my relationship with my son through personal letters) or in a phone call with Claire or in a prayer to

God or in Ceiling Talk with Randall, I'd vowed not to hold back in fear or self-protection. I would create and find and share joy in this world, however and whatever that would look like.

Joy, in Singapore, starts and ends with food. It began that first night in Chinatown as we sampled exotic fruits and unidentifiable skewers of grilled something-or-other from the local stalls, and we shamelessly ate our way through the many months ahead. Food, its ingredients, its origins, its preparation, its presentation, its authenticity, its variety, its accessibility, its artistry, its pure fun is a gravitational center in Singapore, as much recreation as creation, as much a quasi-religion here as it was in Paris. There was chili crab at East Coast Park, the Thai place, the Cambodian place, the vegan Vietnamese place, and (wouldn't you know it?) the *Bonheur Patisserie*.

The cultural diversity makes for a robust cross-pollination of cuisines that's made easily accessible thanks to something called hawker centers. They are Singapore's original hot dog or Philly cheese steak street vendors, but sell the likes of crispy jelly fish, roasted Peking duck, chicken rice and fish head curry, cuttlefish and cockles, fried carrot cake, oyster omelets, and, if you are up for it, a piping hot vat of pig organ soup.

Being a quasi-vegetarian, I politely opted for things without claws, jaws, fangs, and knuckles. And since Singapore has a dominant Hindu culture, I had no trouble at all finding fragrant, spicy vegetarian food everywhere and anywhere I went. There were vegetarian dives on every corner where we were the only Caucasians and where we had to speak a mix of pantomime and tai chi to communicate with the staff. We learned to order our favorite spicy sauces which were then slopped onto the big waxy green banana leaves from which Dalton and Luc, like every one else, ate with their fingers.

A few months into our residence, after having just eaten some of the best Indian food of my life with my friend, Geri, we two were weaving our way through a subway station. Geri, who after years living in Asia was a self-proclaimed Asiaphile, was converting me, the European-American, to Singapore, to Asia. "So really, what is it that you love here, Geri?" I asked.

A cluster of black-haired schoolgirls in plaid parochial school uniforms shuffled past us in their white athletic shoes, chirping and giggling, hands over their mouths, each of their backpacks many times their combined weight.

"Oh . . . just about everything," she said.

A hunched grandmother hobbled in front of us, grandson's pudgy hand in her sparrow-like grip, her face a study in erosion, shoulder blades protruding under the stretch of her thin floral blouse, legs (thinner probably than my forearm) barely discernable under baggy pink stretch pants. Furry purple house slippers.

"So what do you mean, 'everything?' The buildings? The easy and cheap access to the rest of Asia? The hawker centers? The Esplanade concert hall? The immaculate Botanic Gardens?"

People darted toward approaching trains, heads down, shoulders bearing so many backpacks, most referring to their iPod, iPhone, iPad, their i-what-have-you. A small man, maybe four feet tall and thirty-five kilos (average size here) and wearing an official-looking blue jumpsuit, swept the floors with a natural bristle bamboo-handled broom. I nodded to thank him. He smiled back, flashing more holes in his mouth than teeth. There was a tattoo of an impressive Chinese dragon spitting flames up the side of his neck.

"I love the dark hair. All this wonderful, dark hair." Geri was fading off in thought. "And little things. So many, many little things."

We spent our subway ride discussing, in half-whispers because people hardly talk in subways, the many little things to love about Singapore. There was, right there as we whispered, holding on to our subway poles, the smallness in others that made me restrain myself, bind my feet, and even my whole body. Already feeling overbearing just standing there and breathing, I reined in my volume and gestures so as not to blow anyone over or away. In Europe I knew to be circumspect. Here, I learned to be microscopic.

There were hundreds, thousands of adults smaller than my already-skinny preteen, Luc. There was our little shoe repair man whose open-air shop was no more than a shoe box on a curb, and was one of my regular haunts. He crouched in a thin splotch of shadow, and whacked away at people's shoes while they caught lunch barefoot, I guess, in a neighboring hawker center. He did good, cheap work and was physiologically impossibly, wondrously little. When I paid him, he did a little thing I learned to wait for. I'd hand him my twenty SGD bill with two hands, of course, nodding and looking him right in the eye (handing with one hand and avoiding eye contact when paying is rude and sends bad luck), and he'd reach up to take the bill either with two hands or, if he had a tool in one hand, he took the bill with the free hand, the other hand bent to touch the inside of the elbow of his extended arm. This gesture was repeated every time I exchanged anything with anyone, business or credit cards, a receipt, money, a gift. We extended with two hands, received with two hands (or at least with the one hand touching the inside of the extended arm's elbow), nodded slightly, and looked one another in the eye.

There was another person, a little woman, who wandered through my favorite hawker center, selling individual packets of tissues for one SGD each. When I bought my platter of baby *kai lan* (my favorite leafy green vegetable doused in garlic and oyster sauce) I didn't automatically get napkins. I paid extra from a roving napkin vendor like this woman who had a case of scoliosis that reduced her four-foot frame to three feet, making her smaller than my five-year-old nephew.

In contrast and only a few blocks away, there were the little ladies strolling Orchard, which means Orchard Road, the shopping boulevard which tallies through Singapore's commercial center like a cashier's receipt unrolled to a length of about three kilometers, three dozen interlocked anchor stores, or a year's wages. Shopping, like eating, is Singapore's national sport, played by no one more than this, the mani-pedi crowd, who were, again, remarkably little but made less so by wearing platform heels that weighed as much as they themselves did, doubling both their weight and height in one teetering step. The skirts were little and the shorts littler, leaving little to the imagination. The handbags and false eyelashes, however, were not little. In fact, Dalton once wondered aloud about the caloric expenditure from balancing on such shoes *and* carrying a hardware-encrusted handbag *and* holding up the weight of a patio awning on each eyelid.

And in case I'm misunderstood, these ladies were not for hire. There is legalized prostitution in certain areas of Singapore and there are prostitutes who solicit actively after hours along Orchard Road. But what I'm describing are your typical daytime shoppers.

Some of these women carried parasols against the sun, like I noted Geri always did, and when there was no parasol, there was a book, a placemat, a plucked palm leaf; I'd seen them all. Flawless pale skin is the beauty standard in Asia. Equatorial sun is blistering, tropical rains are bludgeoning, so Asian women are serious about their parasols and umbrellas. When the parasol women laughed, they drew their hands to their faces, covering their open mouths and teeth, in a Geisha-esque gesture of modesty. At first, the hand-over-mouth gesture puzzled me. But before long, I realized I was flapping both hands over my mouth every time I laughed.

Little signs charmed Geri, charmed me, like the one over the public toilet in one shopping center: *Ladies, please do not stand on seat for your performance.* Geri had lived in the countryside of Taiwan, and I had stood in a long acrid line to use a public squatter toilet in Beijing and another in

Xiamen, so we knew that certain habits, no matter how unappetizing and degrading for those with different habits, die hard.

Singapore, with its sparklingly opulent public bathrooms, glamorous mile after mile of shopping malls, shiny subway system, government subsidized taxis, housing and medical care, with its impressive universities and lavish art centers, with its Sentosa Disney-esque island, with its opulent Marina Bay Sands architectural wonder, with its extravagant casino, with its one-of-a-kind nighttime Formula One race and sumptuous award-winning Changi airport, was still in many ways just a small town full of dense culture capsules. One I experienced the week we moved in.

Our moving crew, a team of six Malaysians, barefoot, good humored, serene, and skinny as sticks, was clucking away in Bahasa, a florid, trilling language, one of the many you hear on the streets in town. I asked them what we could buy them for lunch.

"Madame," said the leader, a gentleman with shoulder-length black hair, "It can be anything only if it is halal."

He said the last phrase with his palms pressed together as if in prayer, fingers touching the underside of his chin.

I learned that afternoon that McDonald's (at least Singapore's McDonald's) *does halal*, and that a big sheet of moving-grade cardboard spread wide in a carport can serve both as a midday prayer carpet as well as for a picnic spot.

Singapore offers you intimate culture capsules like that, and then, virtually every month, it wows you with spectacular scenes from its potpourri of so many diverse cultures. The first I ever witnessed was the Hungry Ghost festival, where for weeks people built small makeshift shrines on the streets filled with food and paper facsimiles of material goods (clothing, electrical appliances, cars, and money) to leave out as a gift for deceased ancestors. As was always the case with any subsequent festival, there were loud day-into-night clanking and shrilly singing celebrations at temples all around town. And, of course, feasts. There was Deepavali, where Serangoon Road became the Vegas strip; Taipusam and the famous firewalkers; Chinese New Year, with the huge and dynamic parades down Orchard; the Festival of Holi and its brilliant rainbow of powdered dyes splashed over the streets and people throughout Little India; Moon Cake Festival; the Dragon Boat Festival; Vesak Day, when the Buddhist monks paraded in their elegant saffron colored robes; Thimithi, when men carried sacrificial pots on metal rods fastened into the skin on their face and backs; Hari Raya Haji; Christmas, when Orchard Road erupted in all colors of neon; and New Years, with fireworks over the bay.

While I was attending all of these festivals and getting my bearings on the Red Dot on the Map, Randall was taking the Red Eye all over the map. From Singapore, which was his company's newly established international headquarters, he was flying around the world all month every month. In fact, it wasn't unusual for him to be in five countries and five time zones in five days. The unyielding pattern of sleeping half-reclined in an airplane and taking 2:00 a.m. conference calls wore on him. One night in particular, just returned (again) from fifteen time zones away, he collapsed in a chair in our bedroom and fell asleep sitting up still holding the handle of his suitcase, only to startle and awaken twenty minutes later, frantic that he'd missed a flight or phone call, unsure of what hotel, country, or year he was in.

We discovered the benefits of one of the cheap services typical to Asia: reflexology and massage. Considered fundamental to one's health care, highly reputed reflexology and massage businesses are just about everywhere in Singapore, and I tried to schedule sessions when Randall arrived home from a long trip. Since his weekly transglobal travel not only continued relentlessly, but increased steadily, he was on the road a week or two at a time, and home the infrequent weekend. Now the trips weren't just two or eight or even twelve hours away, but eighteen, twenty, sometimes twenty-four. He gave up running and exercise; he was running on adrenalin and Ambien. He slept through a lot of massages.

At the same time, Dalton and Luc were thriving as perhaps never before in their school and circle of new friends. They were making school trips to Indonesia, Malaysia, Sri Lanka, Thailand, the Philippines, and picking up on Mandarin, both written and spoken, requisite curriculum in their international school.

At the same time, Claire, who was at university in the States, understood but disliked German because of its associations with losing Parker. She selected French as her minor and still spoke to us in Norwegian.

Like Parker, she felt an affinity to things African, and began learning Swahili in preparation for an internship in Tanzania, where she was a warden at a juvenile detention center in Arusha. There, surrounded by a group of abandoned, lost, mistreated, or troubled teenaged boys she could love and inspire, she found unlikely but fast friends.

I, too, had gathered—or was gathered in by—many new friends. There were friends for hiking up and down Singapore's hilly tropical rain forest, friends for yoga, friends for making music, friends for serving in church and traveling to near-lying Asian destinations. There were, to our surprise, friends to mourn with, friends to remember Parker although, of course, no one here knew us; no one had ever known of Parker. There was the one friend who remembered every single 19th of every month, the day of Parker's accident. Or another who digitally designed an up-to-date family photo into which she magically added Parker's eighteen-year-old face. The woman who, on Mother's Day, sent a brief but soothing email, "Hey, thinking of you today. How are you doing?" and the friend who spent months painting Parker's portrait from a photo—one of the last photos ever taken of him while he played a drum solo in his senior class talent show. People were there on every hand, it seemed, enfolding us in love and compassion.

I felt this kind of deep generosity of spirit in what might seem like an unlikely setting, my Chinese class. Danielle, a new friend, and I agreed to take on learning Mandarin in a serious, methodical way, so we found a native Chinese tutor and had classes three times a week.

Chen Xihua was from Nanjing and spoke pure Chinese, the kind that is difficult to find among Singaporeans, given the presence of a dozen or more Chinese dialects (among them Hokkien, Teochew, Cantonese, Hakka, and Hainanese) and the general destandarization of Chinese on the island over generations. Our *laoshi*, or teacher, was professional, but I saw through her professionalism and knew that she was above all a diffident, soft-eyed single mother, a woman with hunger and tenderness in her face, the receptacle of a complex story. She was often a bit too complimentary of us two linguistically ambitious American mothers, the duo she loved to call her Desperate Housewives.

First time I heard her apply that term to me, I hit a never-before-heard tone in Chinese. "I'm *nothing* like *any* of those women!" although I'd never watched the show, so how could I say? It was hearing "desperate" and "housewife" and my name in the same paragraph that brought out the megaphone in me.

This all made Xihua smile and giggle, hands covering her mouth. She told us that the women in that TV show were her trusty guidebook to all things American. *Desperate Housewives* was what she watched every night without fail. She had every season in DVD packages she'd saved up for. How else could she "beef up" (her *Desperate Housewives* expression for that day) on her English?

Xihua was in her forties, of delicate build though she frequently said she was "*tai pang le*" (too fat). She had black shoulder-length hair she often complained about, and silky skin and sympathetic eyes that she said were "*tai xiao le*" (too small). She was embarrassed by them, as she was by most of her appearance , which I quickly learned was standard Asian self-effacement.

One morning she listened patiently as we practiced our Mandarin vocabulary, describing, as Xihua suggested, our upbringings. "When I was a girl," I began, "I had my own bedroom and decorated it in pink and purple." "I shared a bathroom with two sinks with my sister," Danielle said. "We all had piano, cello, violin, and ballet lessons."

Smiling, Chen laoshi gently corrected our verbs and tones. Then I asked her in Mandarin, "Chen laoshi, what about your childhood? Tell us what it was like to grow up in post-Cultural Revolution China."

Xihua put down her pencil and brought her hands together where her ivory-colored fingers interlaced under her chin. She blinked twice. Then she began in quiet Mandarin:

"I grew up in China in the years after Chairman Mao's Cultural Revolution. Many people were starving. They did not have clothes. The winters, especially in the countryside, were terrible. I cannot tell you how terrible it was. People so terrible to each other. Doing terrible things. Fighting for survival. Terrible. We lived in Wuxi City in Jiangsu province. My parents worked hard. Very, very hard. They were simple people, good people, and loved my brother and me. When my brother was three years old and I was two, my mother then got pregnant with a third child, and my parents did not know how they would survive, how mother would continue to work, how they would have food and clothing for all three children. My parents were almost desperate."

Danielle and I eyed each other. Our new vocabulary word.

Xihua adjusted herself in her chair and crossed her thin arms across her torso, each hand cupping the elbows she held tight to her sides. She looked down in her lap, blinked a few times, then looked back up at us.

"One day my mother was walking with us two children after dinner as she always did, and some neighbors, an older couple, saw how cute my brother and I were. My mother made our clothing, even our shoes, and we only had one pair of shoes. Thin shoes. I told you winter was coming, right? It is terribly cold in Wuxi in the winter. The couple asked if they might help my mother when the baby came. My mother gratefully accepted. And when my baby sister was born, this couple offered to take me into their home. They would care for me for as long as my parents needed it."

Here, Xihua was looking back and forth into Danielle's eyes and then into mine, urgent, emphatic.

"For over *two years* I lived with this kind couple. I called them *Niang Niang*, which means aunt, and *A Gong*, which means uncle in local dialect. When I cried especially in the first weeks away from my family,

Niang Niang or A Gong held me through the night and sang to me. Then they fed me and taught me. They gave me clothing and shoes. And for all of this they never took money from my mother. No money, even though they, too, were poor. For over *two years!*"

She quickly wiped her cheeks and shook her head.

"I don't know, maybe that does not seem so wonderful, especially if you have always had plenty of your own, extra that you could share. If you have extra rice, a few vegetables from your own ground, if you have enough cloth to make more clothing, material to sew more shoes."

Xihua looked at us without incrimination. But I felt a cold flat weight on my back, a keen realization of my unfamiliarity with the kinds of hunger and desperation this woman—that so many women like her—had known.

She continued, "These two plain people from the countryside, they were desperate, too. But they sacrificed so that I would survive, so that my entire family would survive. When my parents then learned that we had to move to Chengdu province, which is a place of great hardship, Niang Niang and A Gong wanted to keep me to make sure I was fed and clothed and went to a good school. And so they tried to persuade my parents to let me continue to live with them. But my mother cried. She could not leave me. I cried, I did not want to leave either set of parents."

Both Danielle and I were stone silent. Tears filled our eyes.

"And so we left and went to a poorer, harder life. But I always felt the simple goodness of this couple. Two years! Strangers who helped a little poor girl with homemade shoes!"

Long after Xihua finished telling us that story, after we'd all wiped tears and bowed heads, that story sat in me like glowing coals. It heated my thoughts and spread its warmth over the months and years that followed. When I would think of it, I couldn't help but well up, and once or twice the tears fell, and I would weep like the earth weeps forth an estuary: slowly, broadly, continually draining rivers of sorrow, all our streams of loss, into one bruise-colored body of everyone's collected grief.

23

A GIRL, A BOWL, AND A PYTHON

"Un-dow-laaaah-un-dow-laaaah-un-dow-laaaah-un-dow-laaaah??!! Un-dow-laaaah-un-dow-laaaah-un-dow-laaaah-un-dow-laaaah-un-dow-laaaaaaaaaaaaaaaaaaaah??!!"

Her voice is plaintive, frantic in pitch but mechanical in rhythm, and her spindly arms with brown claw hands scratch at the sticky air between where she and I sit. She bobs on the water in an oversized aluminum mixing bowl, while I sit under the shade of the canopy that tops our eight-man boat, knees tucked primly together, my fingers spread out on them. Those fingers rest no more than a meter from where her fingers grope toward me. I re-adjust a fraction of an inch. But I have nowhere to hide.

And honestly, I have nothing to give her. Not "one dollar," for which she begs, nor Cambodian *riel*, for which she is not, oddly to me, begging. I don't have her native currency either, the Vietnamese *dong*.

The day's heat and mugginess—it is mid-July and this is the middle of Cambodia—and the persistence of her nasal chanting weakens my resistance. I ask Randall, "Didn't we bring *anything*?" He mouths, "Only a fifty."

She's leaning precariously in that bowl, and the waters reach all the way to its upper rim. Again, out of nowhere, that grinding hate I feel toward water. I'm thinking through what I'll drop—handbag and phone—to jump in when she flips over.

The boat driver snaps something at her that silences her for two beats. Then she resumes, a Vietnamese auctioneer in the last seconds of a bid that's going nowhere. This all produces a wilted bill from our tour guide's breast pocket, which his limp hand draws out and his tilted head offers, crossing right in front of my eyes. He crumples the paper, leans toward the boat edge, and her fingers—unwashed for months, probably—grab the wad.

While trying to stuff it in the pocket of her sodden and oversized yellow pajama bottoms, she adjusts something I only now see is wrapped around her left leg and is lying across her lap. It could be a deflated bike tire or a waxy rope. But bike tires and ropes usually don't have grayish-green geometric patterns. And they don't slither.

Without ceremony, the girl whips the python up over her shoulder in order to grab what is the more important object of the moment to her, a very large wooden spoon paddle. With a quick flick of her shoulders, she adjusts the snake like another kid the same age might adjust the hood of a sweatshirt, and plunges the paddle into the water ahead of her.

She's elegant. Feisty. Proficient. Gritty.

And she's outta there. There's another boat approaching.

"Un-dow-laaaah-un-dow-laaaah-un-dow-laaaah-un-dow-laaaah??!! Un-dow-laaaah-un-dow-laaaah-un-dow-laaaaaaaaaaaah??!!"

Surviving the death of your beloved is a radical learning experience. It drags your living heart along a cutting edge that causes the kind of spiritual injury that either destroys inch-wise or teaches endless much. Above all things it teaches, it can teach you something about suffering. Something.

I thought I'd learned something when I was sliced wide out of the insularity of illusion in which I'd lived, that cozy idea that my family and I were somehow safe, that tragedy only happened to other people and always "in another country,"[1] as a fine poet has written. My small corner of agony connected me viscerally, I thought, with the whole map of humanity and history and with some private corners of hell and heaven, too.

Personal pain has been a grim but thorough tutor. But it has not taught me everything or enough.

Another passage, the geographic passage from west to east, luckily, continued the tutorial. One of the blessings, if I can call it that, of living in

Singapore, an oasis of plenty in Southeast Asia, was the immediate access to the surrounding countries where there was exquisite cultural variety and historical wonder, but also frequent extremes of poverty, disease and corruption.

We spent as much time as was possible traveling through parts of Asia, and there visited crowded orphanages and prisons, contaminated inner cities, unlit mud huts, rotted rice paddies, filthy and poorly staffed hospitals, ill-equipped school shacks, cinder block women's shelters, and the floating Vietnamese refugee villages on Tonle Sap lake, where girls in floating bowls begged life-sustaining pittance while serpants hugged their calves. I saw, thanks to Singapore, suffering and bleakness that overstretch powers of description.

Though I know something about suffering, I can only claim to know of one kind. About the countless other forms of pain and loss like those I've just alluded to, I know nothing. It would be offensive for me to suggest that by being a "poverty tourist" I could *know* much at all about poverty. I can no more *know* about the poverty and suffering of refugee life from staring into the face of that girl than I can *know* about the realities of cancer by strolling through a cancer ward. The experience is vicarious and therefore escapable. I stay in my boat. Get back to A/C. Sleep in clean sheets. Eat until I'm full. And catch a flight home. Because the experience of observing extreme poverty is escapable for me, the lessons, however deeply felt in the moment, are too easily unlearned.

So if I cannot *know* about the suffering of these people I have visited unless I enter fully into their lives, what then? Am I truly willing to have their lives? And what good is achieved if we are all impoverished? What, then, *can* I learn from this girl? Better put, what *must* I learn?

Lesson #1: Who is this girl? Her age is hard to tell, but judging from the proportions of everyone else (our boney twelve-year-old Luc out-sizes most adult Cambodians I've seen this week), this girl who looks eight for western standards is probably closer to Luc's age. Still a child.

This means she is the same age as my Indonesian girlfriend's daughter, who for four days went missing in the countryside of central Indonesia. When she finally staggered into the family village, she was dazed, her manner and countenance darkened. Where had she been? Even she couldn't tell anyone. She retold what she remembered: riding her bicycle close to the beach; men in a car asking for help; walking closer to help them; a cloth with a bad smell over her face; then awakening far from where she remembered having last been. Disoriented and petrified by every passing car, she wandered home by following the seacoast, all the while adjusting her clothing, which had been dirtied and, for lack of a better term, rearranged.

The scenario was so typical for a girl in Indonesia that the family thought it useless to cause a fuss by calling the local police. Best to forget it. At least she was one of the ones who came back.

If this story feels too sensational, it's enough for me to suggest that the girl in the bowl stands a very good chance of being abducted, abused, and/or sold into the sex trade which is rampant and prefers poor Vietnamese, Cambodian, and Thai female children. Even our guide, when I asked what the biggest threat to local children was, said, without a pause, "Being sold or abducted into human trafficking."

Malnutrition (including lack of potable water), slim chances to be educated, few suitable job opportunities, or even the inaccessibility of adequate medical care were all secondary, in his estimation, to the burgeoning business of child pornography and forced prostitution for which Bangkok and Phnom Pehn are hot spots. For either of the last two fates, the girl in the bowl would be a sitting target.

She is also a sitting target for virulent strains of viruses. The water in which the girl paddles her bowl is not only her work space, but is where the floating village's sewage is dumped, where clothing and dishes are washed, where fish (a dietary mainstay) are caught, and where the children bathe and swim. Will a girl in an aluminum bowl, if she is not sold or stolen into the grisly world of child prostitution, be correctly diagnosed should she fall ill with such a lethal virus? Will she be taken to a doctor? Has she ever, in her life, even seen a doctor?

Lesson #2: What is this bowl? Most probably, the bowl is vital to this girl's and her family's survival. If I were cynical, I might say the bowl is a means to keep her grandfather in his pack-a-day habit. But it's more than likely she needs that bowl to beg that one dollar, and that one dollar will buy a bag of rice, food for a family for a month. In a country where the average annual income is between $700 and $800, a dollar is a windfall. A bowl, the difference between life and death.

I've seen bowls like this one before. At Pennsylvanian bobbing-for-apple contests. At church parties in Utah where they're filled with Jell-O marshmallow salad. At double baby showers, filled with dozens of fingernail polish party favors. Full of caramel popcorn at a teenager's movie marathon. Filled with fertilized soil to plant window pansies. Puffing over with dough enough for eight loaves of bread for the middle school bake-off.

One man's eight-loaf bake-off entry.

Another's daily bread.

Lesson #3: What is a python? That snake gives her power. Near super-power. The boys were wowed by the snake, amazed at the spectacle, and later, when we passed a mother holding up her child while shoving a live python's head into her child's mouth, our normally talkative two were left speechless. Could there be, for a western audience, a better show of superpowers?

What power did we, in turn, have? Simple: we were white. To be white, our guide explained, is to have power, and to be white *and* to speak English, he added, was to have superpower. I tried to assure him that there are places in America that are very, very poor and where people die, too, of malnutrition, lack of adequate medical care, violence, contaminated water. But he just stared at me, smiling broadly at what he was sure was a joke.

"Prosperity, it seems, speaks English,"[2] writes Russ Rymer, and as I noted the several television antennae and the few satellite dishes perched atop these floating homes—satellite dishes powered by car generators so these Vietnamese can pull in western programs, our guide explained, and many from the United States—I understood clearly Rymer's observation about some eastern cultures that idolize the west: "The arrival of tele-vision, with its glamorized global materialism, its luxury-consumption proselytizing, is . . . irresistible."[2]

Even if she only speaks two English words—"one dollar"—those words are, in the mind of the girl with the python, the only words she needs. They mean *superpower.*

Lesson #4: What is this water between us? Differences aside, there is one watertight similarity between the girl and me: the girl in the bowl and the woman in the boat are all floating in the same water. Humans, both of us. Either one of us can capsize, perish. That's a given. But the wake from the larger vessel has a disproportionate effect on the viability of the smaller one.

I am at relative ease. While she's paddling her guts out.

I somehow feel I bear a responsibility for her welfare. Does she feel that about me, too?

What keeps her in her bowl, then, and me in my boat?

As I described the place of these floating villages, I typed the name of the vast body of water whose tributaries house these communities of refugees. Its name is Tonle Sap.

T-O-N-L-E. S-A-P.

But my fingers—white, clean, soft, and privileged—wrote something else first:

Tonie Spa.

Freud himself couldn't have forced a more incriminating slip.

There is so much more than water that separates me from the girl in the bowl. There is the Khmer Rouge and Pol Pot, his killing fields, the Vietnam War, all subsequent governments, whether American, Vietnamese, or Cambodian. There is more water between us than the whole of Tonle Sap, in fact.

But I know as I watch her paddle away from my boat, metal bowl swirling in the brown water, arms flicking as if dancing, paddle churning like a rudder, and snake sliding noiselessly down her back, "There I go. There goes my sister."

"Un-dow-laaaah-un-dow-laaaah-un-dow-laaaah-un-dow-laaaah??!!"

If she beats the many odds stacked against her and most of the children of her culture and gender, her life might stretch out for a few decades yet. But it will be a life of material scarcity, likely abuse, and probable illness. She will scrape by every day, barely eking out survival for herself and for her family. She will know the kinds of lack and loss that would, I know, drain the very blood from every speck of my being. If she one day has a child, and if that child actually survives to eighteen, and she then loses him to death—loses him, let's say, in a water accident on Tonle Sap—that loss will probably be just one of the litany of losses she will endure. She will suffer a black grief then, I imagine, but that blackness will be felt against her life's general backdrop of charcoal gray, her maternal grief just a few more degrees of saturation.

With each loss, that polished face with its steely determination of youth will grow lines of surrender, will bloom the grooves and drapes of defeat. And she will finish her brief passage of life, at least the passage I'm picturing here, thoroughly intimate with suffering. She will leave this life knowing things about which I would probably have only a cursory, virtual acquaintance. And she will never know, except from her aluminum bowl and across deep water, most things of my life. But we will have loss in common. Loss is the link. Whatever we have, we will all lose it.

It was true. I had become drawn to people with troubles, people in pain—the displaced, the marginalized, the injured, the lonely—my radar seemed to zero in on them. I felt comforted and comfortable in their presence. This is perhaps why, within a short time of living in Singapore, I had discovered a circle of friends among Singapore's tens of thousands of foreign domestic workers or maids. And because I had them often in my home for dinners and conversations, they encircled me and invited me to attend functions organized by the governmental and cultural bodies that oversaw their welfare.

One day in particular, I found myself on the stage of a large auditorium singing at one of these functions. Between presentations from the head of Singapore's Ministry of Manpower, and speeches from the Indonesian embassy (the embassy took in the constant traffic of mistreated, underaged, and escaped maids), I watched intently the women's faces surrounding me. Most of them were giggling and chatting in Bahasa, but some of them were as still as a cloud, floating between two worlds, frightened, remote. Some could have easily been eighteen, the legal age of employment, but some might have been thirteen, too, since every month there seemed to be that uncovered story of some poor family having sent their underage daughter to "work domestic," as they called it, in Hong Kong, Kuala Lumpur, Taipei, or Singapore, and had sent her with falsified papers. The girl's family of origin couldn't afford to keep her at home, was always the story; indeed, they needed her to go away to work to send home money so they could survive. Some of these girls, then, were probably close to Dalton's age. Some just Parker's age when we lost him.

Many were in full orthodox Muslim attire with headscarves, sleeves to their wrists and pants with tunics to the floor. Others were in t-shirts and jeans. Most were in traditional Indonesian kabayas, the skin-tight floor-length batik or bejeweled skirt that makes any movement beyond simply standing almost impossible, and the lace overlay fitted blouse under which a corset is worn, making anything beyond keeping a faint pulse also impossible. *

Invited as the guest vocal artist to this annual gathering for their community, I was fitted for and then gifted with a kabaya. It was vivid lime green lace on top and sparkled under the stage lights. I wore it as I judged their Miss Indonesian Maid contest, which was an honor; except I had to sit to judge, which was a challenge; had to breathe to sing afterwards, which was also a challenge; and I had to (well, I didn't have to, but I wanted to for solidarity) wear my hair in a baroque Indonesian up-do which included a black mass of fake Indonesian hair the size and weight of an American football, which would have been passable had my own hair been black or any shade of brown, even, but I am quite blonde. And with the black football staple-gunned into place on the top of my head, I looked like a chocolate dip Dairy Queen cone whose spiral someone had licked in a frenzy. My makeup, too, was done by a visiting Indonesian theater star, who, with her thick inky eyebrow crayon, iridescent lime green eye shadow, leather-feathery false eyelashes, rouge the color of a salmon steak, and brown lip liner applied liberally, turned me into a stunning transvestite.

Dairy Queen or Queen or whatever, I felt something in common with those dispossessed maids, and I gave the winners of the Miss Indonesian Maid beauty contest a sincere standing ovation. Had fate twitched a different eyebrow, I knew this, any one of them could have been a Hollywood starlet. Instead, they were sleeping, many of them, on mats in a laundry room, working sixteen-hour days, many without a day off, and sending $450 of their monthly $500 to family back home. More than "un-dow-lah", maybe, but still scarcely enough to keep a thatched roof over the heads of those they might never see again, those waiting in villages dotting Indonesia's typoon-shredded shoreline.

Un-dow-lah? Or five-hundred? Like the girl in the metal bowl, I was going to see all these young women—sisters of mine—drift away from me much sooner than I'd thought.

Because somewhere in that same time frame, we were feeling the rumblings that a company restructuring was around the corner. International headquarters would be reduced and eventually closed, and those positions would be dispersed to other corners of the globe. Our Asian phase would probably end very soon. Too soon. As it played itself out, there was no time for a phone call from headquarters, let alone months of Ceiling Talk. We had to move. And we had to move immediately.

I find myself in my kitchen packing up my tableware with an Indonesian moving crew. They babble away in Bahasa.

"Tell me what you are saying," I say to the man with sloping shoulders and no upper teeth. "Teach me Bahasa."

"We saying you have so many plate." The two other men laugh at him. Or maybe at me. Or at my many plate.

"Oh," I apologize, "I have many plate because many friend."

The men all look at me like, *And?*

"Um, friend come, we have party," I explain, looking at the stack of plate.

"In village, have party, friend bring plate," the smallest man with a mole on his eyelid says. "But you no need, Ma'am. You have plate for whole my village."

More laughter, including mine. I probably do have enough plates for his whole village, every last one a wedding gift from so many years ago. So should I tell him whole my village gave me many plate?

But the thing is, today I have more than many plate. I also have many pot. Many knife. Crepe griddle, raclette oven, rice cooker, juicer, blender, bread maker, roaster. Salad spinner. I have nutmeg grater, for heaven's sake.

"In village, have one plate, one wok, one knife. Many children." This man must be fifty, probably has many wife, too, and as a result, those many children.

These men look at me earnestly. Accusatorily? Or is that my own guilt? Good grief, I want to give them *some stuff*. Or at least my pizza stone.

Am I the same gal who had so little stuff when she got married, we fit it all into Randall's 1970 VW? And did we drive that bug from my parents' home across town to his parents' converted basement, where we lived for five years? In that one bedroom space, were we not poor students but broadly happy folks with our adapted lawn furniture, press board shelves, four university degrees, first computer, and firstborn, Parker?

So whence—and as importantly, *why* all this *stuff*?

Stuff. A good Biblical word, believe it or not. When Joseph of Egypt was finally residing in Pharaoh's court where he was decorated as Pharaoh's right-hand man, he revealed his true identity to his brothers, who came begging for food during Canaan's famine. Joseph, moved by the sight of his brothers (and especially by the sight of his baby brother, Benjamin), couldn't restrain himself, and told his brothers who he in reality was, the brother they had sold into slavery and into Egypt. He was the brother they had essentially killed. Now he stood before them, whole, splendid, a heart-stopping surprise, their practical savior.

Pharaoh himself is moved by the reunion, and tells Vice President Joseph to hurry and pack up some beasts, his little ones, and his wives, and head straight to his father, Jacob, who is still living in Canaan, still mourning the loss of his favored son. Joseph is commanded to bring his family to safety (and salvation) in the king's courts of Egypt.

Gorgeously symbolic narrative, all of it. But here's the verse I wanted to point out. In telling Joseph to get to his father, Pharaoh adds, "And regard not your stuff, for the good of all the land of Egypt is yours."[3]

Regard not your stuff. Well, I'll tell you, moving as often as we do makes that one a bit hard. It is a stuff-loaded and stuff-loading sport, where you're forced to take painstaking inventory, measure, weigh, catalogue, photograph oh so much stuff. No wonder I can't sleep, and why my overstuffed brain splits its seams, jolting me out of my slumber with the need to write. Maybe, I think, writing it down will relieve some of the cranial pressure or something. Unburden me of some of this stuffing.

The stuff spills onto my carport, my computer files, my mind. When I try to pray is my mind so overstuffed that I cannot get clearance?

A signal? Space? Overstuffed with things or overthumbtacked with so many competing Post-It Notes on my mental corkboard, how do I expect to pick up on the subtle needs of those around me, or on the more subtle promptings of the spiritual?

I *did* feel it in that serendipitously choreographed moment back in Paris. I *did know it*, even, knew it in my bones when the mover slammed the truck closed, and announced to me and to the heavens, here were my treasures, and I saw that van of ours rounding the corner, saw long arms with long baguettes, heard loud voices calling to me, and countered my moving man with, no, no sir, you are mistaken, you don't know me: *These are my treasures.*

But now I know that I did not—*could not*—know then all that much about what it means to treasure. And I do not think most people know or can know. What I am saying here is the truth, that no one can know the fluffiness of stuff and the weight of treasures, at least there is no way one can fully discern the difference between those two hefts, unless one joins the haunted ranks of those who have lost the heaviest things.

The afternoon after working alongside those moving men in my kitchen, I hole myself up in a far bathroom. In tissue and a handmade quilt I wrap up an oil portrait of our eighteen-year-old Parker. The quilt was made by Lisa, a friend who took Parker's volleyball and basketball jerseys and spun comfort out of them. She is from the haunted ranks, having lost her prized teenage daughter to a ski accident. She knows the true weight of that quilt.

The painting was done by Jennifer, a friend who never knew Parker, just like all the friends I've made since July 2007 and all the people I will meet until the day I die. But this unusually sensitive woman grew to feel something of him by painting his profile. She cropped out his hands from the photo which are otherwise twirling drum sticks or as the French call them, *baguettes.*

That talent show was one week before he was waving other baguettes out a van window in Paris, calling to his mom. And that was one month before he would lose his life trying to save another's.

"This you ship special," I say as I hand my quilted bundle to the crew leader. My eyes don't flinch, as I dare not give away my sacred secret.

"Airplane, not water?" he asks.

"Right. Airplane. No water."

I give him the two black albums of funeral pictures. "And these." I also hand him Parker's personal journals, kept up until July 18, 2007, the day before the accident. "These are also special."

"Special, Ma'am. Fragile?"

"Yes. Yes, fragile."

Jacob's grief made him fragile, but he withstood being thunderstruck by the news that his treasured son was still alive. His words, recorded in Genesis 45:28, ring sweetly to my heart: "*It is enough*, Joseph my son is yet alive."

It is enough. All the trunkloads and truckloads in the world of other stuff will never be enough. And no amount of stuff could fill the hole left by his absence. You don't know how light, how insubstantial stuff is by losing stuff. You find out by losing the treasures. Then all weights are instantaneously recalibrated to take their correct place, which is lighter than the immeasurable weight of absence.

When my friend pulls up to find me standing in the carport, barefoot, pants rolled to shins, hands on hips watching the stuff piled in boxes, she can not know why there are tears filling my eyes. But she conjectures. I love her for her concern.

"Tough to see it all go?"

"Uh, not so much."

"Worried it'll get damaged?"

"Nah."

"Sick of living out of suitcases?"

"Nope. Not yet."

"I know: tired. Right?"

"Oh, not really."

"So . . . ah . . . what you thinking about?"

The leader places a box marked *Air: Fragile* in a far corner, nodding at me. I shake the tears back down their ducts.

"Stuff."

Endnotes

1. Sexton, Anne. "The Truth the Dead Know," in *The Complete Poems of Anne Sexton* (Boston: Houghton Mifflin, 1981), 34.

2. Rymer, Russ. "Vanishing Languages." *National Geographic* magazine, July 2012, http://ngm.nationalgeographic.com/2012/07/vanishing-languages/rymer-text.

3. Genesis 45:20.

24

Finding Home

L uc called it a "Sadder-day" when we broke the news to him and to Dalton that although we'd promised we'd stay in Singapore for many years after moving there from Munich, we instead would be moving in a matter of weeks from now to the other side of the earth.

It was a factor entirely beyond our control, a sudden company-wide restructuring triggered by the premature and untidy departure of a regional leader, not some flimsy whim of ours that had us moving so soon. Still Randall and I felt responsible for the great hurt we saw in our boys' faces. It's that kind of hurt that creeps outward, beginning in the pupils then spreading to the brows, to the upper lip, the chin, then forehead, like a time-warp paralysis. And then the tears rise like a mini-tide along the shoreline of their lower eyelids making the blueness of their irises swimmy and inaccessible. There was arctic silence. Not of anger. Nor of pouting. Just frozen disbelief. Both sons.

Claire, who was now a senior at university and who had just finished her spring semester, swooped into Singapore to help with the move and cheerlead her little brothers through the transition.

"Hey, Dalton, guys, come here, listen to me." Claire pulled them onto the edge of her bed where she was holding court. "Do you remember the move from Paris to Munich?"

Do we remember?

"Do you know how old I was, Dalton?" She looked like a college professor waiting for a college answer. Dalton was as tall as she, now, with hairy legs and a budding beard.

"Sixteen?"

"Sixteen, yep. Just your age. Heading from all my friends and my locker right next to Parker's and into a brand new language and in *the* worst possible circumstances." She was dry-eyed, would rarely allow herself to shed tears, priding herself on being impervious.

"And when we moved from Pennsylvania back to France, Luc, guess what?" Her baby brother was no longer pudgy with a corn-silk bowl cut but wore braces and had dark blonde hair he kept in a crew cut good for the tropics. "You know what age I was?"

"Twelve?" His nose squirmed, the way he had always adjusted his glasses.

"Twelve, Luc. Right. Leaving my friends, heading away from major comfort and ease and to something I knew was going to be lots, lots harder. And it was. At first."

The boys were transfixed. It is a tremendous and grand thing to watch your grown daughter transfix your younger sons.

Dalton said it first, "I know we'll be okay. We'll be okay. We're together, we'll all be okay." And Luc went silent. I should have known hard times awaited him.

We sighed a big sigh and laughed a real laugh and the whole family geared for the big summer.

"Big Summer" meant not only house-hunting and school-hunting and packing and gearing up for beginning a new life in Switzerland, but sending our Claire off on a new life herself. She had submitted papers to serve for a year and a half as a missionary for our church and her assignment letter had arrived in the midst of all this. She would be heading to Rome. And so for the first time since Claire had left Munich for college in American, our whole family was returning at the same time to Europe. We would be next-door neighbors, only a thin border separating us—a much softer version of what we'd long since learned to do with Parker.

A woman had asked me two months after Parker died (meaning just six weeks, maybe, after we had withdrawn into our German monastery), whether our simultaneous move from Paris to Munich as well as from wholeness to bereavement, was making our grief over the loss of our son "more complicated."

"More complicated?" I asked, thinking she meant *messy* (which grief always is) or *complex* (which burying your child cannot but feel like) or *far reaching* (which it was since it surpassed anything and everything we had felt in our lives) or *tragic* (which the loss of promising life in a violent twist of irony surely is and will always be).

"Yes, complicated," she said. "After all, you know, you had to leave *Paris.*"

I listened, head steady. I didn't understand what she meant.

"I mean, you are so sad," she continued, "because . . . I'm thinking . . . because you miss the monuments, right? The cafés? Cobblestones?"

One of my eyebrows lifted.

"All the bridges, you know, and those romantic gardens." Her voice had a singing quality to it. "You miss *Paris.* Is that the problem?"

Was *that* the problem?

I didn't respond intelligibly, I don't think. In my state of mind at the time I probably lacked the emotional distance and energy to walk this well-meaning but mistaken commentator on grief through the difference between the loss of lifestyle and loss of life. Between the passage of place and passage of life. How would she ever understand that my longing for my child was obliterating, suffocating? That it sucked the oxygen out of the universe? That I was having quite a time feeling much of anything but a protracted, cramping gasp?

That I had not mourned for an instant the loss of Paris the city? Not her dead monuments. Nor her dead cobblestones. Nor her gloriously grand but dead façades.

That what I did miss, and painfully, were living faces?

I missed Renée and Lala and Ophélie and Claudine. I missed Valérie and Anastasie and Mary and Anne and Marie-Anne. Chris, Craig, Cathy, Sandy. Michel and Martine, Phillipe and Lauren, Annicke and Isabelle. Church family, like our bishop. School family, like Mr. Hubbard. Work family. Neighborhood family. What Paris held for me that Munich did not, was not the historic Arc de Triomphe, but people who held our history. I missed eyes behind which registered the acknowledgment that history would never be right again, and that it had been bombed straight through. Eyes that *knew.*

You're lucky if you aren't left to search for understanding only in the eyes of strangers. During that first year, we were lucky. Family and friends made visits to us in Munich. With those visits, we had face-to-face contact with people who *knew.* Every so often we had *community*, a gorgeous word that says, literally, "*Come.* Come be one."

We had friends who came to us, and with them they brought story after story of Parker.

"And then he just ran, like *bounded*, you know how he could just *bound?*" Christina, one of Parker's closest friends from Paris, lit up as she spoke. Two other high school girl friends who'd also come to visit us in Munich nodded along with me, half-smiling, all four of us sitting together late at night on the floor of our Munich apartment. "Yeah, he's just *bounding* to me, like *galloping* right across the Place Victor Hugo, and he's waving his arms in the air like this, yelling to me, then he grabs me, he's panting like this, and tells me," Christina coughs on a laugh damp with tears, "he'd forgotten to hug me goodbye."

She fell silent for a moment. Megan and Sarah dropped their eyes. I heard myself swallow.

"Just wanted to make sure he'd said bye to his friend," she added, trailing off.

Silence hovered between all four of us. "Oh, man, I just *love* that guy."

"Then you remember that championship volleyball game?" Megan said, "He had his drum, you know that little, uh, that small steel drum he called, what was it? He called it his 'baby' I think."

Christina and Sarah's "yeahs" tumbled over each other.

"I bought it for him," I said, "It was . . . so, *too* cheap," I closed my eyes. "I'm so sad, so mad! So sorry, I didn't get him a really good—"

"Hey, Mrs. Bradford, it was perfect. Don't regret it," Sarah's eyes fired up.

"Uh-huh," Christina pulled at a little strand in the carpet, "It was perfect for all those games. It *was*. You shouldn't . . ."

Megan and Sarah looked at Christina, who brushed her bangs from her forehead.

Then Sarah reached out to two spots on the floor on either side of her legs and patted them, her palms flat. Patted them softly then louder, Parker-like, post-basketball-victory beat. The rhythm filled a silence impossible to fill with words.

We talked or were speechless like that until 2:00 a.m.

What was this, all this storytelling? And all this silence? Sitting in our pajamas, cross-legged in the near-dark, on the floor of that Munich hallway, Parker's Mom and three of his best high school girl friends, all of us talking so eagerly and easily only about one thing. What was all this talking? Was it brooding? Dwelling? Wallowing?

Or was it what it was? Storytelling. Telling his story. Telling history.

Telling history requires knowing and caring passionately about things, which, though visibly absent, undergird the present. By telling history, we identify and give identity *to* all those things no longer seen, drawing them into this world of words and speaking into the current of current events. Bringing them, if not literally back to life, at least into it.

But there are absences for which no language is fitting. There is at times nothing more apt for great absence than resounding silence. Resounding silence, however, is not retreating silence. It's not the silence of disengagement, fear, preoccupation or judgment. It's not driven by self-protection, but flows from the pure awe felt at another's pain. Resounding silence can be one of the most fluent languages of compassion.

Author Anna Quindlin writes about speaking or falling silent in the face of loss:

> *Maybe we do not speak of it because death will mark all of us, sooner or later. Or maybe it is unspoken because grief is only the first part of it. After a time it becomes something less sharp but larger, too, a more enduring thing we call loss.*
>
> *Perhaps that is why this is the least explored passage: because it has no end. The world loves closure, loves a thing that can, as they say, be gotten through. This is why it comes as a great surprise to find that loss is forever, that two decades after the event there are those occasions when something in you cries out at the continual presence of absence. . . . I write my obituaries carefully and think about how little the facts suffice, not only to describe the dead but to tell what they will mean to the living all the rest of our lives. We are defined by whom we have lost.[1]*

When Jennifer and Olivier, friends from Paris, took the train down to visit us in Munich, Jennifer walked across the threshold of our home, set down her bags on the wooden floor of our entryway, and before we could even turn to get her a drink from the kitchen, she froze midstride. Eyes suddenly wide, searching, glazed with tears, she said, "*He is not here. I feel it. He is gone.*"

With that, we all stood still.

Silence.

Community.

What telling history means, I now understand, is not just talking for talking's sake, "patching grief with proverbs,"[2] as Shakespeare knows one should not because it kills community. Nor is it charting methodically through some timeline in order to make a graph so as to pinpoint key events or scientific equations behind tragedy. Grief is no time for sterile intellectuality because, when things are raw, it is the heart, not the brain, that says, "Come be one."

Telling history means summoning community. Come, be one, it says, and when you're one, you're one both in word and in silence. It is the needful practice of narrating and listening, of gathering the debris of something broken and reordering it, blank spaces and all.

No doubt Toni Morrison says this all better than I. In *Beloved*, and in the words of Sixo, who here is describing his friend and lover to Paul D, is a passage maybe you've already run across somewhere else. It has long captured for me the essence of communing, of entering into one another's hearts, or here, minds:

> *She is a friend of my mind. She gather me, man. The pieces I am, she gather them back to me in all the right order. It's good, you know, when you got a woman who is a friend of your mind.*[3]

All along that broken and patched route have been friends willing to enter into the story, forming our community. They've searched with us for pieces, picking up some here some there, fumbling with them, fingering the cutting edges. They have spoken carefully of the one who is absent, referencing and even reverencing him by name. Together, sitting cross-legged in the hallway after midnight, we have held up a few fragments of what was, peering at them in the shared light, breathing in unison as one shard shines, heaving as we turn it around, feeling the shape, bearing the weight.

We have also clutched that weight in hands hanging bluntly at our sides as if we've just dropped our baggage. We have stood there, all of us, frozen and wordless in our entryway.

Samuel Clemens, aka Mark Twain, knew well the landscape of loss. He buried his only son Langdon at nineteen months, his daughter Jean to a sudden fit of epilepsy, and his lively, lovely Susy. Twain then buried his beloved wife, Olivia. The great social commentator and humorist grew from a familiarity with life's rutted landscape.

He also knew the mountainous landscape of Switzerland, so it's no surprise he came to mind as I prepared to leave Singapore, where people had come to acknowledge Parker both as absent and as present. In *Innocents Abroad*, Twain catalogues his first extended trip roaming from home. In *Tramps Abroad*, he canvases central Europe, including his journey through Switzerland, mentioning Geneva specifically. I read him while I was there looking for a house.

I read him while I anticipated taking a side trip from Geneva to Paris. The American School of Paris was having its graduation and, as had been the case for five years, Randall and I were to present a special award in Parker's name.

While house hunting in Geneva and anticipating that short but significant side trip to Paris and while reading Mark Twain, I couldn't help but think about what it means to not have a fixed home address, when global roaming spans not just a footnote or even a chapter or two of one's life, but the entire sequel-after-sequel series. I was asking myself all sorts of questions about what it has meant to find a house all these times, compared with what it has meant to find a *home*.

This was all on my mind the morning before I had to catch that noon flight from Geneva to Paris where I would meet Randall for the Saturday afternoon ceremony. But first, the owner of the house we hoped to rent in a village outside of Geneva wanted to meet me. I believe (in fact, this was confirmed by our agent) that I needed to be vetted. Good enough. This is how integration starts.

The owner of the house, a gentleman to whom I will refer as Monsieur P., had a sincere glint in his eyes, which I could see even from where our real estate agent and I sat on the other side of a quiet outdoor café table in the cool protection of the shade of a rim of trees. He wore a buttoned-down cotton shirt with hardly a wrinkle, held crisp with his upright posture.

After asking general questions about professions, education, and our former places of residence, Monsieur P. mentioned that he and his wife were parents of five grown sons.

"*Cinq fils?! C'est la vraie richesse, Monsieur,*" I told him, since five grown sons does indeed feel like great wealth to me.

He agreed, and then discreetly asked about our family.

"*Madame Bradford,*" he asked, "*vos enfants, ils parlent aussi le Français?*"

"*Oui, oui,*" I told him. Our children also speak French. All four of them, I said.

I watched his carefully folded hands and what looked like pianist's fingertips, knowing that in perhaps some other culture, he'd dive headlong into asking the particulars of each child. But he was Swiss. Restrained. Discreet. Which helped me quickly direct him into a conversation about Gregorian chants, a point of common interest. His enthusiasm charming, his smiling eyes widening as I talked of music and the *soirées musicales* we planned to hold in his home, which we'd like to be our home.

And it seems that music, as much as French, was our shared language.

"*Madame Bradford,*" Monsieur P. asked as we walked away from our half-empty glasses of mineral water and into the sunlight of the parking lot so I could hurry to the airport, "*Vous avez parlé de vos trois enfants—deux fils, une fille. Et l'autre enfant?*"

It's true, I'd answered his questions about three children: *deux fils*—the two boys—who will move with us to Switzerland and, we hope, into his home. And I'd been able to tell him of *notre fille unique*—our only daughter—who will leave in August for her year and a half of volunteer church service in Rome, Italy.

Yes, I had told him about those three children.

"*Et l'autre enfant?*" He repeated the question as we reached the car. "*L'aîné? Un fils, non?*"

I turned to him, considering his question, "And the other child? The firstborn? A son, right?"

I squinted into the sun, which caused my eyes to water, naturally.

Naturally.

I cupped my hands like a visor over my eyes, shielding myself with a shadow.

"*Ah, Monsieur. Il a déjà quitté notre maison.*"

Which was not an outright lie. That son had, in fact, already left our house.

I did in that instant what I had learned so well over nearly five years to do. I acted casual, flippant even, making a flipping gesture with my hand, oddly enough. Like swatting *l'autre enfant* into the past. Out of the picture. Gone from our house. With one relaxed flick of my wrist.

All to protect polite Monsieur P., of course. I wished to protect him from the startle that experience tells me he would get the moment I were to speak the bare truth, and he would then have no words, realizing he had trodden unwittingly, innocently onto difficult and disturbing and sacred ground.

All to protect Parker, too. I knew I must protect him from the other possibility of having his shortened life shortened all the more into a sentence fragment, delivered with those averted eyes and hands waving or clutched at the chest, and that familiar verbal sprint back into the comfortable coolness of the quotidian: "So, do your other kids like music?" Or soccer? Or moving so much? Or the weather?

That lunge from the blazing heat of truth's sunlight back into the safe shade of life-as-we-all-wish-it-could-be-and-*should*-be.

So I feigned lateness for my flight, put on sunglasses, and ducked into the car.

And as I drove off, I put my hand to my neck, aching in my throat to tell this kind gentleman, this father with five living sons, all about my eldest son.

At the other end of the flight to Paris awaited an experience far removed from house hunting and the stern irony of hiding a son who had supposedly "*quitté notre maison.*" The same son who had not at all left and never would leave *our home.*

When the assistant headmaster of the American School of Paris asks the parents of Parker Bradford to come to the stage while he announces the background of the Parker Bradford Spirit Award and this year's recipient, I look out into many faces I know among the hundreds seated at the graduation ceremony. I had seen some of those same faces at the 2011 graduation ceremony. And others the year before. Others the year before that. And still others in 2008, the first year this honor was granted.

These faces I know are the faces of those who also know Parker. Wherever I go, I am always drawn to those particular faces. Because when "home" is a flexible term that reinvents itself every three or four years, it presents a special challenge of having to retell your whole story, pain and wonders and all, to total strangers. No one can blame them if they cannot fill in the blanks of the plot. They have no idea that there *are* blanks in the first place.

But most of this year's faculty members—Parker's history teacher, music teacher, French and Spanish teacher, his coaches, counselors, mentors—not only know our story but know very well the big blank that is left in place of this big missing boy. These people are characters in our story, have actually been writing that story with us all along, and were there in June of 2007 when Parker was their student, a senior like all the seniors sitting in this year's ceremony, looking awkward but solemn in their blue caps and gowns, tugging so surreptitiously on that one reddened ear lobe. Positively itching to just *get on with life.*

Most of those faculty members would never guess this, but their eyes that look into mine and wince or search or glisten, bring me home. Their words—especially the word "Parker," spoken with the kind of familiarity a favorite pair of jeans has when you can pull them on in one movement, those words bring me home. Their silence, too, when a memory of my son snags their heart, it brings me home. Their laughter at shared memories of things Parker did, his booming voice down the main hall, his three-pointer at the buzzer, his impersonations of their colleagues, also brings me home. Their willingness to ask how Parker is *now*, what our experiences are that continue our relationship with him into the present tense, into the here and on to the future. This is home.

When, the morning after this year's ASP high school graduation and the presentation of the Parker Bradford Spirit Award, I stand again and also by invitation to offer the invocation at our church meeting in the overcrowded chapel in Rue St. Merri a couple of blocks from Notre Dame, I sense home. There, I see in those many faces people who knew and loved our son, who have written into their lives the ongoing narrative of our family. And I am brought to tears, brought home.

When Randall blesses the bread for the sacrament, kneeling in the same spot and saying the same beautiful French words Parker used to recite, I sense home.

And when the widow in the row behind me, the one Parker used to visit monthly with his dad by riding on the back of a cream and brown Vespa, when she leans forward and whispers over my shoulder, "*Je me souviens . . .*" "I remember . . . how Parker always blessed the bread, too," that feels like home.

"So then, uh . . . where *is* your home? *Exactly?*"

We get that question a lot. But we never know how to answer it adequately. Maybe that is because the question itself is inadequate or altogether the wrong question to ask in the first place. Home means something more than a *where*. It is not a structure, not an address, not a city, not even a country. I am beginning to wonder if home is even a place at all.

Home, perhaps, is a disposition of the soul, an acknowledgment that I share with another soul a certain intimate narrative. That narrative, that story, twists and curls and splutters and flows; it folds back on itself defying conventional chronology, suggesting timelessness while weaving the strands of our most consuming questions and even exploring those questions for which we have no language yet.

Home, then, might be the nexus of many individual narratives, not a fixed port, but a portal through which lives have passed and are passing, seeking definition and connectivity. Home, for me at least, has come to mean that sense of intertwining, one of unity and comfort, a state of being where you no longer need to tug at the seams and hemline of your spirit to feel at ease. It's when you feel something deep and native within you expand, enlarge, illumine.

Truth itself, I feel, is a part of home. My religious beliefs, for instance, inform my ideas of home. And, when I was a freshly returned missionary, I felt such an overpowering sense of *home* with Randall it was uncanny and undeniable. So I just *had* to marry him. It wasn't that being with him was like being "at home." It was that he himself *was home*.

Which helps me understand why, when he composed those books about leaving home and roaming abroad, Mark Twain wrote a trusted companion right into his narrative. The character named "Harris" is a figure based on Reverend Joseph Twichell, Twain's friend of over forty years. In the figure of Harris, Twain literally—and literarily—took "home" with him on the road.

And it was to Twichell, who had christened all four of Twain's children, that Twain turned during those black years when he lost three of them.

Twain's words to Twichell:

> *Do I want you to write to me? Indeed I do. . . . The others break my heart but you will not. You have something divine in you that is not in other men. You have the touch that heals, not lacerates. And you know the secret places of our hearts. You know our life—the outside of it—as the others do—and the inside of it—which they do not.*

Finally, it was the Reverend Twichell, who had married Twain to his wife, Olivia, who received this note from the author when his adored Livy died:

> *I am a man without a country. Wherever Livy was, that was my country.*[4]

Countryless. Homeless. Exiled. Expatriate. Nomad. Pilgrim.
Human.
Divine.
Home.
I am only just beginning to understand those words.

But no matter where I might find myself, home, quietly yet quite remarkably, always seems to find me.

ENDNOTES

1. Quindlen, Anna. "Public & Private; Life After Death," *New York Times*, May 4, 1994.

2. Shakespeare, William. *Much Ado About Nothing,* ed. G. Blakemore Evans. (Boston: Houghton Mifflin Company, 1997), 5.2.17. References are to act, scene, and line.

3. Toni Morrison. *Beloved.* (Canada: Vintage Books, 2004).

4. Twain, Mark. *The Complete Letters of Mark Twain.* (Middlesex, UK: Echo Library, 2007).

25

ZWISCHENLAND

Zwischen: (Ger.) among, amongst, inside, betwixt, twixt, between

The Swiss village of Prangins, where we live, lies halfway between Geneva and Randall's office in another village, Tolochenaz. Tolochenaz lies halfway between Geneva and Lausanne. Dalton's and Luc's school, *l'École Internationale de Genève*, lies halfway between Geneva and Prangins. Geneva lies halfway between two flanking rims of France and roughly midway between the Alps and the French mountain range, the Jura. The country itself, famous for its political neutrality, lies in the heart of politically charged western Europe, surrounded by France, Germany, Liechtenstein, Austria, and Italy, the way an island is surrounded by the ocean. We are by any measurement among, inside, and between.

L'École Internationale de Genève is a bilingual school, which puts it betwixt English and French. Our little Sunday School at church, a group of about thirty-five children, speaks French, English, and German with some Urdu thrown in to keep us all awake. Switzerland herself is split linguistically among German (74%), French (21%), Italian (4%), and Romansh (1%). The country is also nearly evenly split with regards to official religious affiliation: half Protestant (the German-speaking regions) and half Catholic (the French and Italian-speaking regions). When new friends from the international community here ask what language our family speaks at home (a typical top-of-the-list question in these circles, as it helps others group you), we say we speak primarily English, but that also depends on who walks through the door, as it might swing to French, German, or Norwegian, and just two days ago a local acquaintance who grew up as an expatriate in China walked over the threshold. Things swung to Mandarin. We are betwixt and twixt.

Upon arrival at the Zurich International airport, you're confronted in a concrete way with the sense of Switzerland being an in-between place, a hybrid of sorts, a meeting place not only of languages and customs, but of old and new. As you board the super sterile, glass-walled, modern train within the airport itself, you are suddenly face-to-face with a hologram projected on the walls of the tunnel: "*Willkommen in der Schweiz,*" "Welcome to Switzerland," "*Bienvenue en Suisse,*" "*Benvenuti en Svizzera.*" Against a muted soundtrack of mooing and yodeling and alphorns, and waving from this hologram of an alpine panorama, is a cheery girl with braids and an apron. Waving at you from only inches away, Heidi seems to have been beamed down into this century along with her cows, their udders and cast iron bells swinging in synch. There, in an ultramodern time capsule, you zip into Switzerland, squashed between high tech and Heidi.

Each time I find myself in that train, I'm that much more convinced that however beloved it is in Switzerland, and however representative of Switzerland it might seem to outsiders looking in on Switzerland, Johanna Spyri's children's novel of an orphan living with her grandfather deep in an alpine setting is really no more than a mere stereotype.

The French Swiss would be quick to say that Heidi has little to do with *their* Switzerland. And the French Swiss would be quick to say that Geneva is not representative of the rest of their region. Once, in one of my first conversations with a local acquaintance, I made the mistake of commenting on this or that about living "in Geneva." (I figured that fifteen minutes from town was close enough for me to form an opinion.) My friend said with emphasis, "You do *not* live in Geneva. You live in the Vaud canton. And besides," she winked, "both of your great-grandparents and *their* great-grandparents have to be Genevans for you to talk about knowing *Geneva*-Geneva."

There is that *Geneva*-Geneva, I've learned. It is composed of old families, old names, age-old traditions. And then there is the international

Geneva, composed of two ancillary expatriates bodies: the government-Geneva (centered on the United Nations, World Trade Organization, World Health Organization, The Red Cross, *the Conseil Européen pour la Recherche Nucléaire*, or the European Organization for Nuclear Research also known as CERN, numerous embassies, and just as many NGOs); and the corporate-Geneva, found in the headquarters for an abundance of multinational companies.

The population of Switzerland is made up of a substantial portion of people with foreign passports; and that concentration of foreign nationals is perhaps more concentrated in and around Geneva than in any other major Swiss city. This creates a unique culture of distinct and almost self-governing factions, a place where Geneva-Genevans (locals) and government- or corporate-Genevans exist, having seemingly little to do with one another.

What does that coexistence look like? And how does multi-national-ism play itself out in my life right now, where I am today?

It was a simple outing arranged by Lauren, mother to Oliver, a school buddy of Luc's. Like other generous and commanding women who, throughout all these years of living internationally, have swept me into their wise friendship, Lauren became in an instant my on-site guide to All Things Swiss. Witty and as energetic as her wild head of bronzy curls she affectionately calls "Hagrid," this native London East Ender wove her own global path as a single woman, then planted herself—along with a Swiss husband and two multicultural kids—in the heart of bucolic Switzerland.

As if coached by Johanne or Bente from Norway or Rita from Versailles, Lauren didn't waste a minute pulling me into her current of friends. Seven of us would all meet in the city at the main train station and walk to a local "dive" for a "cheap" lunch, neither of which actually exists in Geneva, a city consistently numbered among the world's most expensive.

"Cheap," Lauren had nevertheless insisted, "and my Singaporean friend says all her Chinese friends here claim it's authentic."

As I hopped off the train, I quickly spotted Lauren and her curls and trotted right for the cluster of women I was to meet for the first time. We couldn't know it in that moment, but they would soon become part of my new circle of friends. We hadn't walked but two minutes when a young Asian-looking tourist pulling a suitcase stopped us. She was frightened and confused, having been confronted by customs officials during her train ride. The men in uniform had questioned her in rapid-fire French (which she did not speak), while shoving indecipherable forms into her hand. She was now nearly in tears.

I could see from her clothing and gait that she was probably from mainland China, a place where getting stopped by uniformed officials wielding government papers could mean going to high court. Or prison. "*Ni hao,*" I stepped over, saying hello. Her face brightened and she wiped her eyes. We began speaking in Mandarin.

The next half hour was spent switching from Mandarin (with this frightened, transiting tourist from Beijing), to French (with the stiff, Swiss customs authorities, who had intimidated her on the train), to English (with Lauren, who was gracious enough to give me moral back-up), and to German (by cell phone with the tourist's friend awaiting her in Zurich at the end of the final leg of her European train trip). Everything was clarified, this poor but greatly relieved Beijing woman and I hugged, and she went safely on her way, dragging her suitcase and calling out, "*Xie xie, xie xie, thank you, xie xie!*"

Minutes later over fried rice, dim sum, and kai lan, and where the servers and cooks spoke a mix of French and Mandarin, I was introduced to a Pakistani married to a Brit-Hungarian; a Brit married to an American diplomat; a South African who'd raised her three boys here over ten years; a Swede (with whom I spoke Norwegian) who, over twenty-five years, had lived in fourteen different locations stretching from Peoria to Dubai; an American married to an American who had come here for two years and stayed for twenty-five; and then there was Lauren, mother of two, married to a Geneva-Genevan.

Not one of these women, even the one married to a deeply-rooted local, felt her first language or even her children's first language was French. None spoke primarily French at home. And not one felt integrated into Geneva-Geneva.

"It just doesn't happen," one woman leaned over her plate, pointing with her chopsticks. "It is impenetrable. You are forever a foreigner here."

"And you can master French, sure, but they still see you as an outsider, not as one of them," said another. "Somehow, you're seen as a bit of a mongrel," and she laughed at herself.

"Your best attack," said one woman who'd been in Geneva the longest, "is to plant yourself in the international-Geneva. You're an Internationalist." She speared her dim sum to make her point.

"That's it," the Swede piped up. "I tried going back to Sweden. But my life experience is so unlike most of the Swedes around me, I have a hard time connecting with them. I tell you, it's a strange situation to be in."

I nodded. I knew exactly what she was talking about.

"And where do you retire?" asked one of the women, who carries three passports. "That's the question we have to start asking ourselves at this point. After all these years of being on the move and reinventing ourselves over and over again, where do we land?"

I wondered and I listened, picking at my spring roll. So who am I? I spoke Chinese to the waiters and the nervous tourist. But heaven knows I'm not Chinese. I spoke German on the phone with the tourist's friend, the German of my conception and of my studies and of my missionary service and of Herr Barthlemes, the Munich benchmaker. And I wondered: could I claim to be German or Austrian enough to make those places my permanent home? I spoke Norwegian with this new Swedish friend on the other side of the table, spoke it as naturally as if I were back with Johanne or Bente or with tante Britt at barnepark, and it felt at once cozy and bittersweet, making my heart warm and my hands cold. But could we retire in Norway? French I spoke with the customs agents and the train conductor and all the folks in the street. Yet I'm warned that French is no insurance that I'll ever fully penetrate this new terrain.

In many ways, the qualities of where we are living right now, this place I'm calling Zwischenland, mirror the woman I feel I have evolved into being at this midpoint in life. A hybrid. An island. Or better, a merging of disparate influences, languages, traditions. A bit of Singapore, Munich, Vienna, Paris, Versailles, Oslo, Hong Kong, New York. And always a touch of Utah. An adult who has always paid American taxes, but who owns no home there. Or anywhere. Perhaps a perpetual nomad. Perhaps a permanent outsider, only really "at home" in the middle of a larger bunch of outsiders from multicultural Geneva eating Chinese with a half-dozen nationalities ringing round the table and fiddling with chopsticks like they fiddle with our one common tongue, English.

All of this causes me to watch closely and analyze the nomads who come down our narrow road, quiet as if the cobblestones were quilted. The tiny road is, I've learned, a literal crossroads on a nomad's hike system.

We happen to live just a few steps from a château once owned and inhabited by Voltaire. The philosopher and poet, when threatened by the then-extant French government and royalty for his radical political ideas (ideas which eventually spawned a revolution, as you know), fled to here. He was just far enough away in philosophy to save his head, yet still close enough in fashion to keep his powdered wig.

People who hike—and Switzerland breeds them—make a detour for the château. And then they keep walking down our narrow little street lined by renovated homes from the eighteenth and nineteenth centuries. They come along here because of the one small bright yellow sign with the black profile of a person bearing a walking stick. This designates our road as part of a wandering (or hiking) trail on the Swiss government's maps system. And it's here these hikers come to a crossroads.

I was standing there on my cobblestoned sidewalk one morning as we were busy moving into this home, was casually taking in my pretty little street, hands on hips in front of the truck while directing the moving crew. A group of five impressively equipped wanderers wandered toward me. They had two German Shepherds, which slurped noisily in the ancient water trough that faces our front entrance. Between the dogs' slurping, I noticed the adults spoke Swiss German, so I spoke to them in High German. One man responded.

"Hello, you look like you're looking for something," I offered to the man with olive green army-grade hiking boots.

"Yes. We are. Which way to Rue St. Jacques?"

The dogs were nearly dunking themselves front legs and all in the trough. The woman with a yellow tank top and a chestnut braid down to her waistline yanked at their collars.

"Rue St. Jacques? Um, sorry, I'm pretty new here myself. Never heard of it."

I turned to the movers and asked in French if they knew the road.

"Only one I know," said the moving team leader Monsieur Tin Tin, as he called himself, "is in the middle of Geneva."

"Yes," said the head of the hikers. "That's the one."

"You're walking to the middle of Geneva?" I asked, laughing a little. It's a twenty-five-minute drive. But on foot? And with dogs?

"Yes. We are walking. Of course." And he lifted up his walking sticks. As if they would do some magic or something.

The woman with the braid, who had taken a swig from the fountain and wiped her mouth with the back of her hand, echoed, "Yes. Walking."

I smiled and shrugged at the moving crew, feeling conspicuously sedentary. More wuss than Swiss.

"And from Geneva?" a moving crew member asked jokingly, as if they could possibly go any farther. "Where are you heading from there?"

"Back up to Basel. Then Zurich. Then, uh, all the way down to Lugano."

I now saw they had calves of stone. And I wondered about the magic in those walking sticks.

"So . . . you're walking across . . . "

"*Ja. Das ganze Land.*" The dogs shook off forty liters of water from their fur. Then they sat at attention, staring blankly at me.

And then all five wanderers gave a jaunty stamp-stamp of their boots, shrugged up their enormous backpacks, waved Swissly, and walked off down the pathway. Heading across, yes, *the whole country.*

If they can walk a whole country, can I live around the whole world?

Zwischen. I cannot help but experience our entire new life as a Zwischenland, a place and state of being both halfway between other locations—and an in-between state of being, a crossroads, as symbolized, I like to think, by the Swiss flag itself: a bold red background and the strict juncture of two white lines, a perfectly unequivocal cross. Planted solidly at the crux of life and of things, Randall and I have two children who have "gone on," as I have learned to say but never without a burning stitch in my heart, and two still with us. Twenty years of nomadic life are behind us. And who but God knows what lies ahead?

This is a state called limbo. Or a place to become centered. It is also a place to take inventory, to reflect, and to anticipate. Finding myself back in French-speaking territory, all our rich French experiences have been brought up close in my consciousness. That's not always easy. I had such a moment recently when I revisited Paris in my heart and mind.

Luc, now twelve, was then five. He had attended those two years of bilingual preschool across from our apartment in Rue du Colonel Combes. The next day, however, for first grade, he was joining Dalton at the l'École Active Bilingue in Parc Monceau. Dalton had already gone there two years and was fully saturated in French.

At dinner the evening before his first day of this French immersion school, I'd noticed how pasty Luc looked, a bit too calm in the pupils behind his red Harry Potter glasses.

Fork-fiddling with his food. Unable to drink much.

Sip-sip. Long breath in. Sip-sip. Longer breath out.

Head titled. Like he had the weight of the world on one bony shoulder.

I went into his room that night to nuzzle up to his freshly bathed body and stroke his slick bangs.

"How're things, Luc?"

It was dark where I knelt next to him in that bottom bunk, so all I could make out was the general lumpiness of a checkered cotton duvet.

"Hm?" a voice came from under lots of feathers.

"You there? You alright?"

(Muffled breathing sound.)

I burrowed and found a forehead. I smoothed my long fingers across it.

"Sick, sweetie? Fever?"

"Nah-uh."

"Air will help, honey," and I drew back the comforter to see his profile. Nose like a ski jump. Pronounced pout. Delicate neck. "Okay, there you go. So . . . hon . . . you nervous?"

"Uh-huh."

"For . . . ?"

Well, of course I knew full well that he was nervous, and I knew what for. Although he was functional in French, could recite Victor Hugo poetry and sing French ditties at the top of his lungs, although he had a girlfriend Jasmine with whom he managed quite well *en Français*, up 'til then he'd been in a cozy environment with multiple nationalities, everyone buffering everyone else's language acquisition. He hadn't yet been in a classroom where everyone else was French and where all the instruction—reading, math, history, *graphisme*—was exclusively in French. Where he might not be able to figure things out, where he might be mortified, and where he might, oh maybe, wet his pants.

In terror. In front of everyone.

What he was having was a typical fit of language panic, and I recognized well the signs. I knew the signs. I knew the feeling.

"Well . . . " he shifted in bed, turning toward me. We were nearly touching noses. "What if someone says something to me tomorrow?"

"Okay . . . "

"A *lot* of something."

"Right . . . "

"A *big* sentence, Mom."

"I know. *Big.*"

"All in French. In front of the class. And I don't understand all of it. What if there's just this one word . . . and I don't . . . get it?"

I pulled out my wise woman hat and tugged it down tight over my anxiety.

"Well, Luc, know what? You just say this one thing . . . "

I took his polished cheeks in my hands and looked (like a wise woman) into his eyes.

"You listening?"

"Yuh . . . "

"You say these words nice and loud: *Je. Suis. Desolé. Mais. Je. Ne. Comprends. Pas.*"

(Which, roughly, is "Zhe swee dezolay, may zhe nuh comprohn pah."
Very roughly. And it means, "Sorry, but I don't get it." Also roughly.)

Luc looked right through me, right through my irises.

"But I know how to say that already."

"I know, I know. But you have to have it right here," I pointed to my
temple, "ready to pull out of this little brain pocket. It will protect you.
Like a shield."

"Really?"

"Yup. Easy, right?" (I felt so incredibly reassured by myself.) "So, Luc,
let's do it together?"

We cleared our throats and entered on the pitch:

"Je suis desolé, mais je ne comprends pas."

Mom and son, nose-to-nose, in the dark.

"Again, Luc."

"Je suis desolé, mais je ne comprends pas."

Chanting our fear away.

"Again, louder."

"Je suis desolé, mais je ne comprends pas!"

With a rhumba beat:

"Je suis desolé, cha! Mais je ne comprends pa, cha!"

Chanting and rhumba-ing our fear right out the door of the universe.

"Je suis desolé, mais je ne comprends pas! Woo-hoo!! Now give me a
big kiss!"

He froze stiff, "NO WAY am I saying *THAT!*"

Luc, two years later, spoke such fluidly effortless French, I was sick-
ened to leave Paris for fear of his losing that gift. But we headed off to
Munich. Where he had to learn German. But he did so quickly. And just
as he was growing confident in that language, we had to leave there.

To launch into Mandarin in Singapore. Only to return two years later
to Frenchland.

The morning after the moving van and cross-country hikers cleared
out, I took a village walk. Luc wanted to go along on his *trontinette*,
which in the United States, I think, is a Razor scooter. At twelve, he was
searching for independence and responsibility. And at this point I was
anticipating school starting in a few days with a plunge back into French.
So I was plotting these little simple errands to ease him back into inter-
acting daily in French. It was a benign stealth maneuver I always had
on my mind. So I gave him a wad of Swiss francs and told him to whizz
across the square to the *épicerie* (corner grocer) and pick up some things
to bring home.

"And please see if they have a chunk of Parmesan cheese," I told him as I rehearsed with him, just in case, things he would say to the grocer. "I'm making bruschetta, for dinner. We'll put slices of Parmesan on top."

A half hour later we went home.

No, actually, *I ran home*, my handbag strap thumping on my sternum, trailing Luc as he raced past on the trotinette, head down, face unrecognizably grim, strange gasping sounds coming from his mouth.

"Luc? Luc, Luc! Open up for me!"

There were sobbing and punching sounds coming from behind his bedroom door.

"Luc?! What on earth happened?! Listen, open up right this minute, son."

Punch. Grunt. Muffled ugh, ugh, ugh.

"Luc? *Luc??!*"

The door flew open, then Luc dove head first back onto his red bean bag chair.

After some time and some therapy-lite, I discovered the problem. It seems he'd asked correctly for *du fromage Parmesan*. But when the store clerk asked if he wanted it *râpé* (pronounced "rappay," and means "grated"), Luc didn't know what that word meant because he'd forgotten correct Parmesan terminology over five years. So he'd understood *râpé* to mean "wrapped." Which makes perfect sense. Obviously.

So did the boy want his cheese wrapped?

Oui, oui, Monsieur.

But when the grocer then directed Luc to little plastic pouches of pre-grated Parmesan (instead of a chunk), Luc told him, *non, non, non, Monsieur*, he wanted a big piece, *un gros morceau*, as Luc showed with his hands just like he and I had practiced.

But the grocer could go ahead and râpé it, Luc said, thinking he was telling the grocer to wrap it.

Which led, as you might imagine, to a back and forth between the grocer and the twelve-year-old scooter boy, which grew into a lively community debate as another waiting customer suggested the boy on the scooter wanted sliced, and another said no, that one would never râpé Parmesan beforehand, then another added that you really shouldn't wrap *un Parmesan râpé*.

I could envision the scene. My Luc, pinned in the middle, his skinny arms stiff at his sides, his mind whirring for words, the adults trying to help but getting nowhere, no one understanding what it is the boy with flushed cheeks wants, Luc just wanting to manage one simple hunk of cheese to prove his manhood and make his mom proud. And make his favorite dish.

Outnumbered. Outlanguaged.

So he fished out of a brain pocket in his temple the best retort he could muster:

"*Je suis desolé . . . mais je ne comprends pas.*"

Which got him two pouches of râpé cheese. For which he paid, hands sweaty and shaking.

Then he took off, embarrassment drizzling down his limbs, trotting as absolutely quickly as his trotinette was capable of going.

Your common case of language panic.

Oh, boy. How I have been there. And so, so, *so* many innumerable times.

Later, I tried minimizing the ordeal, handled it with kidding and kid gloves, and after some time, some hours, brought the old Luc back to life.

We decided that evening to make pesto instead of bruschetta, which just happens to require Parmesan râpé. While we tooled away in the kitchen, I told Luc he was pretty lucky the grocer hadn't pulled out a pen and paper to try writing the words out.

"Now *that* might have been really disturbing, dontcha think, Luc?" I winced into my pile of crushed garlic. "I mean really, what kind of cheese is *that? R-Â-P-É?*"

Then I told my youngest boy, the one born in France, the one whose name is French, this last child I raise on the road with all its bumps and potholes and language barriers, I told him story after story after painful and mortifying story of my own history of language panic.

Those stories began when I was just a year older than Luc and lived in Salzburg at thirteen. I had a "boyfriend" named Horst, who, thankfully, found my inability to conjugate most German verbs correctly part of my charm. Ladies at the local Bäckerei helped me along, as did random folks on the street should I be obligated to stop and speak to a native to find my way back home. I had just handfuls of phrases to work with, mostly phrases from prayer, since my parents, beginning in our youth, had prayed in German. A method of retaining their own German, I figure, but also a way to infuse us with the sound and feeling of the tongue, to melt it into our gray matter, and to convince us subliminally (was this the point?) that God Himself was German.

My preteen, who's got the mistaken impression that his mom just somehow sprouted the languages she speaks out of thin air, seemed to love knowing how often and thoroughly she'd been humiliated by language, and how often a given humiliation occured in front of a big, glaring, native audience. How often she ran out of places, maybe wetting her pants on the way, punching things, weeping.

Some of these moments were merely embarrassing. Others, indecent. Others, insulting. Still others, full-on dangerous. As you might expect, many happened in grocery stores, much like Luc's Parmesan crucible. But others (and this is where language panic reaches a whole new pitch) happened in doctors' offices. Or in a formal dinner at an embassy. Or in front of hundreds on the concert stage. Or on the telephone with the electrician. When I had a serious car accident. While standing ankle deep in gushing water as my basement flooded. While my child writhed in pain on an emergency room floor. During childbirth. And, most incriminating and unintentionally off-color of all—so off-color I can't even bring myself to write it—hunting for closet hardware (knobs, to be precise) in a bright little aisle of the Versailles IKEA.

"Luc, honey," I told him as we served up our pesto, laughing now, "I've had so many experiences like yours today, I swear I could write a book!"

"But . . . " he said, "I thought you already have."

26

In Medias Res

As I finish writing this book, our family is preparing for our first Swiss Christmas. A Swissmas, Dalton calls it. Leaning on our big pine table as I work on my laptop, I can't help but be taken back to that first "abroad" Christmas spent in a scolding winter outside of Oslo. That's when we found this burly plank of hand-selected, hand-carved pine, our langbord. That's when its story and our global story began. This Christmas—like that Christmas and all the Christmases in-between—will revolve around the wooden comfort of this Norwegian farm table; or better said, it will be centered on the people we gather around the table's edge.

All those who will come to our table this year will be new to us. All but strangers at first, some of us will become friends, some close friends. And some friendships will evolve into permanent fixtures in our small cosmos as we move ahead in this country, and maybe—possibly, almost certainly one day—*from* this country. Their elbows will rest on the table's striated surface with its eye-like knots staring up at us. Their hands will pat its beveled edge, they'll rub their DNA into its fibers the way our new friends in Norway did. And those in France. And in Germany. And so on, and so on.

If the atmosphere lends itself to such communion, friends will hear parts or swaths of the story contained in this book, the story about where we've been and how where we've been has made us who we are. If they keep leaning into that conversation, leaning into the tabletop with its watchful knot-eyes, they'll hear the heart of the story, the one that splits all the other stories wide, the story of our eldest son. At that point, during that telling, we'll share what it means to be human, and we'll see that humanness in one another's faces, in our silence, in that slight shifting in the chair or in the eyes, in that silver rim of tears, in the awkward but rare shrug, more often in the silent, drooping head. This will be that open moment, that point when everything is reduced, distilled, clarified, and expanded, the moment when we can become fused with one another's ongoingness. It's when we have that sense of being bonded. Culturally? Spiritually? Organically, at least, grafted into the great, endless table, the table for endlessly telling tales. For tales without end.

Tales are what draw us human beings together, and at Christmas, this tale is an ancient, numinous one, the story of a child's birth. We'll recite that well-known text, reenact it, share variations of it in poetry, in song. What we won't do, though, because it would snuff out the whole festive atmosphere in one poof, will be to mention that newly born child's imminent death. No, we will not speak of the death that is innate in the story of that birth—the inborn death—because if we did, it would remind us that in every birth story, no matter how numinous, luminous or even voluminous, is rooted the bigger, undifferentiating death story, the story of all of our own deaths. *That* no one wants to speak of, especially when the wassail's steaming and the fire log's glowing and the tree lights are twinkling. Not then.

The first Christmas after we buried our Parker, I was burning with outrage, longing, evisceration, amazement, revelation, and, through it all, a steady robin's egg blue subterranean stream of gratitude. But I had no energy to express any of it. I had no energy, in fact, to do much of anything that year. No energy for a single, thumb-sized decoration. No energy to face the boxes of baubles and mementos Parker had helped me pack away only twelve months earlier. Certainly no energy for gathering, not even my wits. I couldn't for the life of me—or for the death of my son—generate enough energy to face Christmas at all.

As I considered the birth of the Christ child, the heralded grandeur, the coming of the King with glory roundabout and shepherds sore afraid and young innocent wide-eyed Mary cradling him, her splendid firstborn, I wanted to wail at the top of my lungs, "But you will *lose* him, Mary! You. Will. *Lose*. Him!!"

But I had no energy for wailing.

So, for the first time in over fifteen years, we packed carry-ons and flew from our home abroad, which this time was in the Bavarian Alps, to the Rocky Mountains. We would spend Christmas stateside with family. This also meant we were brought for the first time since the funeral to the place where we had buried our boy, a cemetery called Evergreen.

One night when we could no longer bear being in the company of others, Randall and I drove to Parker's grave. The moon was aloft and smoky, shivering in the nothingness of a monochrome winter night. Our snow tires chewed and gnawed along the ice-encrusted roads, our headlights bobbed listlessly from gray headstone to gray headstone among which we weren't searching for Parker's, since there was no headstone here yet for him.

When Randall and I stood at Parker's unmarked grave that winter night I didn't have an avalanche of feelings. I had but one: that though to me Parker's grave represented the end of the world, to the rest of the world it was really not much more than a trifling snag in an otherwise busy highway. The world had slowed down a bit, yes, but the world had also driven right over it—driven over it like you drive over a speed bump—letting it disappear in the rearview mirror.

And was there supposed to be a supernatural zap here as I stood at his plot, I wondered? Because I felt zero. No sense whatsoever of being close to my son, no illuminating comfort, no gauzy rapture, no hint of his warmth butterflying nearby, no surreptitious communiqués from beyond. Just stinging subzero winter, stiff fingers, and a snow-covered expanse with its dozens of iron gray stones.

I'd wrapped my arms around my midriff, which was underneath an oversized brown synthetic coat that hung to mid-thigh. My body beneath was a walking vessel of emptiness, on the surface only paper thin, blown glass, but inside a blazing lantern of white-hot torture, plugged in at marrow depth. There it was, that smoldering outrage again. Not at God. Not at Randall. Not at Parker, nor at myself, nor at those who'd long since walked away from our sorrow, critiquing it. My outrage was directed at *life itself*, at having to *live it*, live it onward, live it stripped to the bone, live it stripped in shreds and belly-crawling on shards of ice.

Outrage at life. At life doing what life does: it goes on.

From nowhere, my knees buckled and I collapsed onto them, one at a time, catching my fall with my bare palms splayed on wind-hardened snow, while I let my coat fall wide open. And then I silently, slowly, stretched myself facedown on the silver cold ice scab that lay over the six feet of frozen earth which kept me from my child's body. I let that snow burn my cheekbone, let it singe and scrape as I lay there with my arms stretched wide to hold the size of the pain, and to touch the edge of the dimensions, as I imagined them, of the casket we'd had to select, and I ground that side of my face and then my forehead and then the other side deep, deep into the freeze.

Randall's hand reached toward me, and I felt it press warmly on my lower back. His voice came as a muffled, sobbed prayer. Heart flat against the heart of our son's grave, I lay there. I lay until my breathing slowed, lay until my front and legs and whatever was not covered by my brown coat grew drenched, lay until I could feel the bite sink into my skin. I lay. I could not, I would not move.

Let me be here with him. Let me be here. Let me be.

Randall lay his hand over one of mine, thawing it with sad heat. At some point and under the eyes of a following moon, we stumbled through the gravestones and across a featureless crust of snow to where we climbed back into the car. We drove home in silence.

That is part of our story I've never shared with anyone sitting at our table. I've never spoken it out loud, as a matter of fact, because I know, even when writing it, that it is too stark, startling, too sharply intimate. And it stirs up things I've trained myself over time to store in a quiet space that gets little light and no air. But I share it here because I believe that the more personal and even intimate the story, the more universal and even global it becomes. And this is, after all, a book about a global mom.

Being a "Global Mom" goes far beyond being a globe-trotting lady with kids, although I suspect that's pretty much what's awaited from a memoir wearing this particular title. True, facing and then falling in love with many cultures is a chief part of being what we call "global." It's a multi-colored part of it, a demanding, invigorating, humiliating, and sometimes, as I've shown, a downright hilarious part of it. It's enlightening, too, straight-up titillating at times, and I hope that goes as much for reading it as it does for living it. Because, really, who doesn't want even a brief voyeuristic glimpse of a bigger world with its other-worldly faces, a view of this whole lush planet? And if, okay, we can't visit the entire earth, well then we'll settle for at least a few parts of it, and if it can't be the literal visit, then please, we'll take the literary one.

Still, there's this crucial thing that I can't possibly underscore enough. Of all the borders I've crossed, of all the addresses I've inhabited and of all the lands I've been privileged to call my home, there's but one terrain that's defined me more than any other: that is the land of loss. The very soil that no soul wants to visit. The one topography no parent ever wants to feel underfoot. The haunted land of loss has taught me more than any foreign land ever could. Unlike other geographies one might know for a year or two or even for decades, the landscape of loss becomes a kind of permanent overlay to whatever and wherever follows. As much as I "know" France or Germany, and as much as I feel at times quite Austrian or deeply Norwegian or even a little bit Singaporean or Swiss, no matter where I go or what language I speak, I am always and primarily a mother who buried her firstborn child.

Does everyone around my table know that truth about me? No, not everyone. What they do find out, though, if they're willing to sit with me and talk long enough, is another truth that is, I feel, a counter-weight to being bereaved, and that is that the story we're writing with our brief lives can never be told in its entirety, neither its length nor its fragility nor its density. By that I mean that we're all born into the middle of a perpetual narrative, and our simple strand of personal story does not begin when our life does. In view of that, whenever we leave this place—be that at eighteen or at eighty—we are always, inevitably leaving in the middle of our story. That singular tale is interwoven in multiples of others, so our leaving will inevitably be in the middle of others' tales. Our stories go on. We go on. We are always in the middle of the Great, Infinite Story.

Which brings me back to this table I'm sitting at. I was mistaken when I wrote that when we brought it home, *that* was when our family's "global" story really began. "Global Mom," whoever she is, was spawned long before our table's arrival, though it's hard to say where, exactly. Did her story begin with the decision to leave the predictable (New Jersey town home) for the less predictable (Nordic island)? Or did it begin before that, when she and Randall, a year into marriage, taught German to American university students in Austria? Did it start when, three times, she was a teenager studying in Salzburg then Vienna, trying on the feeling of that identity by collecting phrases in the crazy hybrid of local dialects, gluing them into her nature the way other people might scrapbook or collect stamps? Or did the story start when her father and mother studied music in Munich and conceived her, the legend goes, after seeing an especially stimulating opera performance? Or when her father served as a Mormon missionary in post–World War II Germany, is that where it all started? Or was it when Randall's father served as a Mormon missionary in pre–World War II Germany? Or was it a whole century earlier than all that, when Haakon and Julia Aamodt converted to The Church of Jesus Christ of Latter-day Saints and left the farm in Østfold, Norway, wrapped a few belongings in handspun cloth and packed it all in a couple of leather satchels then sailed and covered-wagoned and trudged westward until the trail petered out in a vast dry basin called Deseret? Did it begin well before that, even, in a hard-to-categorize but nevertheless spontaneously-multiplying coil of some sort of Internationalist DNA? Can anyone mark the beginning of this global story? Of any story?

Likewise, this table began long before the craftsman fell the tree, cured it, carved it, and sanded its knot-marked spine. Measure its physical dimensions, yes. Pinpoint the day it assumed its place in our home, easy. But we can't trace its beginnings unless we claim it derived from the tree of life itself. It is generational, and by nature so are we, linked by some undying whirlygig of chromosomes if not by the ties of spirit, and if we are all that, then there will be no true end to us. There cannot ever be an end to this story or to any of our stories.

And so, taking all of this into consideration, although I was cramped with outrage as I stood at my son's grave because my life was going onward while his was over, fixed forever in length—eighteen years and five months to the day, like the farm table, chopped off bluntly at exactly three meters—that feeling came from an innocent human misconception. A fully justifiable one, to be sure. But a misconception, nonetheless. The little boy from Blakstad barnepark, the one from the Versailles Club du Basket, the drummer from the Pont des Arts, the same one all his French buddies called "Par Cœur" or "by heart"—*he continues*. His nature, like his story, is eternal and can do nothing *but* continue.

How? I'm a writer, so this is easy for me to answer: He is an "epistle" himself. He is "written in our hearts," to borrow from the Bible, written, I might add, "not on tables of stone, but in fleshy tables of the heart."[1]

Heartwood. That's what Peter, our Norwegian carpenter, called this pine. It is the substance of this table of ours, the dense and richly colored timber that comes only from the deepest tissues of a tree. The evergreen itself is a vigorous specimen, more flourishing and enduring than many others of the forest. I like to think as I sit and write on it and as I gather others around it, as I listen to new languages that mark the opening of yet another part of this world to my family and to me, as I finger the table's imperfections—everyday scratches and scars, watermarks, burned spots—and as I slide my fingers along the faint pulse of its grain, I like to think that this big plank of ours is listening, too, and that it knows it is a token of the one who is absent. It is the constant thing, the ever-presence of the one who is, owing to his absence and his endless stories, also always with us wherever we are on this globe.

ENDNOTE

1. 2 COR. 3:2–3

A note to my readers:

All of the events, locations, and characters in this book are true as I experienced and remember them. In nearly all instances, the persons are exactly those to whom I refer by name. In six cases, however, and in order to protect someone's identity, I consolidated two or three characters into a composite personage and changed the name.

BIBLIOGRAPHY

Hill, Hamlin. *Mark Twain: God's Fool*. Chicago: University of Chicago Press, 2010.

Hoffman, Eva. *Lost in Translation: A Life in a New Language*. New York: Random House, 2011.

Morrison, Toni. *Beloved*. Canada: Vintage Books, 2004.

Shakespeare, William. *Much Ado About Nothing*. Edited by G. Blakemore Evans. The Riverside Shakespeare. Boston: Houghton Mifflin Company, 1997.

Sandemose, Aksel. *En Flyktning Krysser Sitt Spor (A Refugee Crosses His Tracks)*. Oslo, Norway: Den norske bokklubben, 1972.

Sexton, Anne. "The Truth the Dead Know," in *The Complete Poems of Anne Sexton*, 34. Boston: Houghton Mifflin, 1981.

Rymer, Russ. "Vanishing Languages." *National Geographic* magazine, July 2012, http://ngm.nationalgeographic.com/2012/07/vanishing-languages/rymer-text.

Twain, Mark. *The Complete Letters of Mark Twain*. Middlesex, UK: Echo Library, 2007.

ABOUT THE AUTHOR

Melissa Dalton-Bradford is a writer, independent scholar, world citizen, and mother. She holds a BA in German and an MA in Comparative Literature, both from Brigham Young University. She speaks, reads, and writes fluent German, French, and Norwegian, is conversant in Mandarin, and has taught language, humanities, and writing on the university level.

Bradford has performed professionally as a soprano soloist and actress in the United States, Scandinavia, Central Europe, and South East Asia. Parents of four children, she and her husband have built their family in Vienna, Hong Kong, Oslo, Paris, Munich, Singapore, and Geneva, Switzerland.

About the Publisher

Welcome to a place where mothers are celebrated, not compared. Where heart is at the center of our families, and family at the center of our homes. Where boo boos are still kissed, cake beaters are still licked, and mistakes are still okay. Welcome to a place where books—and family—are beautiful. Familius: a book publisher dedicated to helping families be happy.

Familius was founded in 2012 with the intent to align the founders' love of publishing and family with the digital publishing renaissance which occurred simultaneously with the Great Recession. The founders believe that the traditional family is the basic unit of society, and that a society is only as strong as the families that create it.

Familius' mission is to help families be happy. We invite you to participate with us in strengthening your family by being part of the Familius family. Go to www.familius.com to subscribe and receive information about our books, articles, and videos.

Website: www.familius.com
Facebook: www.facebook.com/paterfamilius
Twitter: @familiustalk, @paterfamilius1
Pinterest: www.pinterest.com/familius

CPSIA information can be obtained at www.ICGtesting.com
Printed in the USA
BVOW08s1635090114

341349BV00002B/2/P